The POLITICO'S
BOOK *of the* DEAD

The POLITICO'S
BOOK *of the* DEAD

Edited by IAIN DALE

POLITICO'S

Contents

Introduction

The reputation of politicians has rarely been lower. This unique collection of more than one hundred political obituaries is intended to demonstrate that although there have been a few bad apples, most politicians actually go into politics with the intention of doing some good. They don't always succeed, but that's true in any walk of life. Just like the rest of us, politicians have human failings, but because of their job these failings are put under the magnifying glass to a sometimes terrifying extent by today's scandal-driven media.

The characters in this book are not shy and retiring. They are not perfect examples of rectitude and probity. But they all have one thing in common – colour. They made a difference, and in some ways that's what counts most.

The majority of the obituaries relate to politicians who have died in the last twenty years, but we have included some characters from the early and middle parts of the twentieth century both to entertain and provide an insight into the different kind of characters who inhabited our political halls of fame in those times. They are by no means all household names but are no less interesting because of that.

In the headings to the obituaries I have used the name by which most people have known the political figure concerned. For example. Alexander Murray was better known as the Master of Elibank, so I have used this name in his heading. Where a person was raised to the peerage I have used their previous name, unless they were better known as a peer, in which case I have used their baronial title.

The reader should be aware that the majority of the obituaries appeared in newspapers shortly after their subject's death. But a number have been specially commissioned by us for this book. There is therefore an inevitable difference in writing style.

The obituaries are featured in chronological order by date of death and within the book are three specially commissioned obituaries of much loved characters from political fiction – Harry Perkins from *A Very British Coup* and Jim Hacker and Sir Humphrey Appleby from the outstanding political comedy of the 1980s, *Yes Minister*.

In particular my thanks go to the doyen of political journalists Andrew Roth, who has contributed a large number of the obituaries. I am also grateful to Duncan Brack, the editor of the *Dictionary of Liberal Biography* (Politico's, 1999), and Greg Rosen, the editor of the *Dictionary of Labour Biography* (Politico's, 2001), for their cooperation in the compilation of this book.

Finally, my thanks go to those who have contributed the obituaries you are about to read. They are, in alphabetical order, John Barnes, Lewis Baston, Vernon Bogdanor, Duncan Brack, Matt Carter, Jane Bonham Carter, Peter Clark, Tam Dalyell, Matthew d'Ancona, Colin Dingwall, Roy Douglas, Paul Farrelly, Nigel Fountain, Jonathan Fryer, Mark Garnett, Jennifer Gerber, Peter Golds, Geoffrey Goodman, Richard Grayson, Alan Haworth, Antony Jay, Kevin Jefferys, Graham Jones, Andrew Kean, Peter Kilfoyle, Richard Kirby, David Lammy, Julia Langdon, Helen Liddell, Jonathan Lynn, Andy McSmith, Michael Meadowcroft, Chris Mullin, Pash Nandhra, Ian Packer, Edward Pearce, Bill Rodgers, Greg Rosen, Matthew Seward, Dick Taverne and Aidan Thomson.

Iain Dale
London, July 2003

Dadabhai Naoroji

born 4 September 1825, *died* 2 July 1917

When four black Labour MPs were elected to the House of Commons at the 1987 general election, much was made of the political breakthrough this represented for Britain's ethnic minority communities. But the first non-white to win a Parliamentary seat had achieved his victory, as a Liberal, nearly a hundred years earlier.

Dadabhai Naoroji was born at Khadka, near Bombay, on 4 September 1825, the son of a Parsee priest. At the age of 11 he was married to Gulbai, then aged seven, herself the daughter of a priest. Together they had a son, who died in 1893, and two daughters. Naoroji was educated at the Elphinstone School and College in India where he stayed on to teach, becoming the first Indian professor of mathematics and natural philosophy. He took part in social and political debate as a proponent of reform, opened a newspaper, *Rast Goftar*, in 1851 and was a founder member of the Bombay Association in 1852. He first came to England in 1855 as a partner in the first Indian firm established there, but went on to become Professor of Gujerati and a life governor at University College, London. He developed his interest in reform and was prominent in campaigns to open up the Indian Civil Service to Indians, which he helped achieve in 1870.

On return to India he continued with the political life, serving as Prime Minister of Baroda in 1873–74, but he did not enjoy this role. He went on to become a member of the Corporation and Municipal Council of Bombay between 1875–76 and again from 1881–85 and was a member of the Legislative Council of Bombay from 1885–87. He served as President of the Indian National Congress in 1886, 1893 and 1906.

Naoroji came back to England and was chosen to fight Holborn for the Liberals at the general election of 1886. After he lost, he put himself forward as candidate for Central Finsbury, fighting and winning a divisive selection battle in the constituency. Commenting on the outcome, the Conservative Prime Minister, the Marquess of Salisbury, remarked that he 'doubted that a British constituency would elect a black man'. Naoroji gained sympathy as a result and at the general election of 1892 defeated the sitting Tory member, F. T. Penton, by 2,961 votes to 2,956 – a majority of just five, but how sweet that victory must have tasted in the aftermath of Salisbury's arrogant, racist, assertion. On a brief return visit to India in 1893, he received an ecstatic welcome and was fêted as the first non-European to be elected to the House of Commons. However, in 1895, he lost the seat by a margin of 805 votes to a new Conservative candidate in the Tory landslide. He never got back in to Parliament. Falling out with the Liberal Party, he stood as an Independent Liberal in North Lambeth in 1906, but did not split the vote significantly enough to prevent the official Liberal from winning. He came third, behind the Conservative but ahead of an Independent Tory.

Naoroji espoused many then-unfashionable radical causes, including the equality of women, and was at the heart of many campaigns on behalf of India. He was President of the London Indian Society for many years and moved an enquiry into Indian affairs in the House of Commons in 1894. He was the first Indian member of a Royal Commission, serving on an inquiry into Indian expenditure between 1895–1900, signing a minority report. In 1894 he was a member of an Inter-Parliamentary conference at the Hague.

In 1907 he retired to India. His wife died in 1910. In 1916 he was awarded an honorary LLD degree by the University of Bombay. He died in Bombay on 2 July 1917.

Pash Nandhra

Master of Elibank

born 12 April 1870, *died* 13 September 1920

The great achievements of the Edwardian Liberal governments are usually ascribed to the party's dynamic combination of social reform with traditional Radicalism. But, just as importantly, the party had, by 1914, developed into a disciplined parliamentary force and a superb, well-funded electioneering machine. In his role as Chief Whip, Elibank made a vital contribution to this process, though his name is now remembered, if at all, mainly for his involvement in some of the shadier aspects of pre-First World War politics, particularly the Marconi affair.

Alexander William Charles Oliphant Murray was born at Folkestone on 12 April 1870, the eldest son and heir of the tenth Lord Elibank – hence for most of his political life he was known as the Master of Elibank, the traditional style for the heir to a Scottish peerage. His family were modest Borders landowners and, before taking over the family estates, Elibank seemed destined for an army career, proceeding to Sandhurst from Cheltenham College. However, while recuperating from a minor accident, he decided he would be better fitted to public life. Unlike his father, Elibank held Gladstonian Radical views and the Liberals welcomed him as a rare and valuable recruit from the Scottish elite. He served as Assistant Private Secretary at the Colonial Office in 1895 and then unsuccessfully contested a series of elections at Edinburgh West in May 1895, Peebles & Selkirk in the general election of that year and York in February 1900, before being returned for Midlothian at the 1900 general election. He exchanged this seat for Peebles & Selkirk in 1906, returning to Midlothian in January 1910 and holding the constituency until he became a peer in August 1912.

Elibank's talents as an electioneer and organiser won early recognition and he served as Scottish Whip in December 1905–09, with the rank of Comptroller of His Majesty's Household, before briefly becoming Under-

Secretary of State for India. In February 1910 he achieved his ambition to be appointed Chief Whip and Patronage Secretary to the Treasury. Elibank faced a critical situation. The Liberals had just won the January 1910 election, but were dependent on Irish Nationalist and Labour votes in the Commons. Moreover, the Cabinet was badly divided and at odds with its allies over how to end the House of Lords' veto. Elibank won grudging admiration from most parts of the political spectrum for his skill in quelling discontent among Liberal MPs, building links with the Irish and inspiring an exhausted party machine. He also correctly advised Asquith that the Liberals would not lose ground in a second election in December 1910, despite the stale electoral register. This accurate forecast allowed the Liberals to retain power and go on to defeat the Lords. Elibank naturally received a good deal of credit for this outcome.

However, he also faced increasing criticism for the lengthy honours lists submitted in 1910–12. It was widely, and accurately, alleged that many peerages and baronetcies had been bestowed in return for donations to party funds. Elibank was merely following the practice of all chief whips since the late 1880s, but the expense of two elections in a year, and a revamped party machine costing £100,000 a year to run, encouraged him to push the system to its limits. Moreover, his love of intrigue, taste for wealthy and slightly raffish company and smooth manner (he was dubbed 'Oilybanks' by the Tory journalist Leo Maxse) increased the distrust in which he was held by some in all parties. It was ill health, though, that cut short his career. In March 1912 he had to take a complete break from politics and in July he accepted the advice of his doctor and family to retire. On 6 August he resigned as Chief Whip and from the Commons, taking a peerage as Lord Murray of Elibank. He became a director of S. Pearson and Son, a contracting and oil firm headed by the Liberal businessman, Lord Cowdray. Elibank's father had passed the family estates on to him and he was in dire need of money to restore their viability.

However, before he left office, Elibank made the disastrous error of purchasing shares, on his own and the party's behalf, in the American Marconi Company. His friends and fellow ministers, Lloyd George and

Rufus Isaacs, also bought shares in this firm. They soon found themselves accused of corruption, as the company was closely linked to the British Marconi Company, which had just been awarded a government contract, and of lying to the Commons about their share dealings. Elibank avoided all comment by going to Bogota on business in January 1913, but in May the bankruptcy of his stockbroker revealed that he had bought £9,000 of Marconi shares for the party and concealed the transaction from his successor as chief whip. This proved the most sensational aspect of the affair and Liberal speakers for some time found themselves heckled by Tory cries of 'Bogota'. When Elibank returned to England in 1914, he was censured by a Lords select committee for a 'grave error' and 'most unwise reticence'.

Elibank remained a useful intermediary for Liberal politicians and he played a rather shadowy role in the negotiations for a settlement of the Irish Home Rule crisis in July 1914 and to reconcile Asquith and Lloyd George in 1917 and 1918. His health, though, precluded a more active role and a short stint as Director General of Recruiting at Munitions in 1915–16 was not a success. For most of the war he flitted between Paris and London on business, though rumours of his financial transactions and relations with the press continued to excite interest in political circles. He died at his Scottish home on 13 September 1920.

Elibank married Hilda Wolfe Murray, the daughter of a neighbouring Peeblesshire landowner, in 1894. They had no children.

Ian Packer

Sir Alexander Sprot

born 24 April 1853, *died* 8 February 1929

December 28th 1918 was the day in which the votes were counted for the 1918 'Khaki' general election. The poll had been two weeks earlier, but there had been a delay in the count for the service votes to be returned. There was no doubt that the coalition government headed by David Lloyd George would be returned, as in most constituencies candidates who were supporters of the coalition were in receipt of the 'coupon', a joint letter signed by Lloyd George and the Conservative leader, Bonar Law.

On that day President Woodrow Wilson had received the Freedom of the City of London and on the High Table at the Guildhall sat the Rt Hon Herbert Asquith KC, former Prime Minster and leader of the non-Lloyd George Liberals and candidate, as he had been at every election since 1886, for Fife Eastern. Rumours were flying around during this lunch about election results and by the time the Asquiths left many knew that he had been defeated. Asquith himself learned his fate after reaching his home at Cavendish Square and his wife Margot had telephoned the Liberal Headquarters. Asquith had lost his parliamentary seat of 32 years by 2002 votes to Colonel Sir Alexander Sprot.

Alexander Sprot had been born in 1853 and was educated at Harrow and Trinity College, Cambridge, where he was a forward in the first Varsity Rugby Match. After university he joined the army and served with distinction in both the Afghan and Boer Wars, being twice mentioned in dispatches. He enlisted for the First World War and was again mentioned in dispatches whilst being awarded the Mons Star. The army ran deep in his family for after his marriage in 1879, he had seven daughters, five of whom married army officers (one was awarded the VC and another was knighted for his army service).

His communal life was also important, as was an interest in politics. He contested Montrose Burghs in 1906, polling just 30 per cent of the vote. In both 1910 elections he fought Fife Eastern, losing to Asquith by substantial margins each time. However, he secured some favourable comments from the press, who said that 'he charmed agricultural workers at meetings.' He retained his interest in Fife during the war and, according to *The Times* commenced 'the long process of nursing the constituency'. When the post-war election came, the boundaries were slightly changed and the agricultural workers were joined by many voters from fishing towns and villages. Colonel Sprot was not given the 'coupon' which in the event did not matter.

Asquith for his part subsequently wrote to a correspondent 'now that it is over, I never did like East Fife'. His views may have been affected by whispers of 'Asquith almost lost us the war, don't let him lose the peace' which were apparently prevalent. He subsequently won a by-election at Paisley, which he was to hold until his final defeat in 1924 by a Labour candidate. In Fife Liberals are reputed to have said 'We would rather have been beaten by Sprot than anyone else.'

Colonel Sprot commenced a Parliamentary career that was described in the *The Times* as 'useful rather than conspicuous'. He regularly spoke and asked questions on agriculture, the army, Fife (very regularly) and Scotland. In short he appeared to be a model constituency MP. However in 1922 he lost the seat to a new Liberal candidate by 2,800 votes. Nothing if not tenacious, he stood again in 1923 and once more lost.

Later that year he took up residence in his father's former home in Garnkirk, Lanarkshire, and was adopted as Unionist Candidate for Lanarkshire Northern, where he was fighting a Labour candidate. In 1924 he resumed his parliamentary career having defeated the retiring Labour MP by 2032 votes in a straight fight.

His career continued in a somewhat similar vein as to before. However, in this Parliament he was greatly affected by the General Strike in a seat that had a substantial mining community and considerable local opposition arose following his unswerving loyalty to Stanley Baldwin. He did not speak at all in the debates on the mines dispute of 1926, but did speak on the Mining Bill, firstly to support the provision of pit head baths and secondly on dividends. He also made a number of interventions during the passage of the Roman Catholic Relief Bill, in particular raising the issue of religious processions and the wearing of vestments, indicating amore than slight touch of Orange!

In February 1929, when he was 75, he collapsed in Parliament and was certified dead on arrival at hospital. He was buried in Fife with pipers and the local hunt in attendance along with friends and family.

Colonel Sprot was a man who believed in absolute loyalty to his country and party. Had he lived to fight the 1929 election, his constituents would themselves have had strong views on the latter point, and he almost certainly would have been defeated for the second time after a single term.

Peter Golds

Horatio Bottomley

born 23 March 1860, **died** 26 May 1933

Horatio Bottomley was a Liberal MP in the Edwardian heyday of the party, but owes his place in history to his record as the greatest confidence trickster of his age. As he was to say: 'I hold the unique distinction of having gone through every court in the country – except the divorce court', and he was spared that only by the forbearance of his long-suffering wife.

Horatio William Bottomley was born in Bethnal Green on 23 March 1860, the only son of William King Bottomley, a tailor's foreman, and his wife, Elizabeth, the sister of George Holyoake – though Bottomley claimed in later life that he was really the son of Charles Bradlaugh, a neighbour. He lost both parents before he was five, and was placed by his uncle in an orphanage. He ran away at the age of 14, finding employment successively as an errand boy, solicitor's clerk and shorthand court reporter. Bradlaugh introduced him to the world of books, and he worked for a time on the *Secularist* and *Freethinker*, papers produced jointly by Bradlaugh and Holyoake. He married Eliza Norton in 1880.

He entered the printing business and started a string of local papers, all of which failed. In 1893 he was charged with conspiracy to defraud (related to kickbacks from overpriced property transactions), defended himself, and walked away scot-free; the judge was so impressed that he urged Bottomley to read law. Instead he turned to Australian gold-mining, and in ten years floated almost 50 companies, only to liquidate and wind them up after having creamed off much of the shareholders' money. It was estimated that he made a personal fortune of £3 million out of a total capital of about £20 million. The money went on a racing stable, gambling, theatrical adventures, newspapers, lawsuits, mistresses, a country house in Sussex, a flat in Pall Mall and a villa in France.

Between 1901 and 1905, 67 bankruptcy proceedings and writs were filed against him. A brilliant speaker, his skill and wit in defending himself in court drew large crowds and generally baffled leading counsel. He was also a journalist of genuine ability, and founded *John Bull* in 1906. The paper was an early version of today's tabloids; it was vulgar, cheeky, populist, and appeared under the slogan 'politics without party – criticism without cant'.

In 1906 Bottomley was elected as Liberal MP for South Hackney, after a previous unsuccessful attempt in Hornsey. He was re-elected in both the 1910 elections. His campaign director, Tommy Cox, organised men to deface rivals' posters and march out of Conservative meetings wearing steel-capped boots, drowning out the speeches. A string of Bottomley's racehorses trotted down Hackney High Street wearing saddlecloths reading 'Vote for my owner'. By 1911, however, his financial situation was so desperate that he presented a petition for bankruptcy, with liabilities of almost a quarter of a million pounds; in 1912, he resigned from the Commons. Many of his assets were in his wife's name, however, and he continued to make large sums, this time through organising lotteries and sweepstakes.

When war broke out in 1914, Bottomley assured friends that he would break with his 'sordid past'. His innumerable patriotic speeches (for each of which he charged at least £50) contributed to the recruiting drive and gained him national popularity. This possibly went to his head; he started to sell government Victory Bonds through *John Bull*, charging £1 against the official price of £5. The subscriptions, of almost a million pounds, were never used to buy the real bonds; Bottomley paid off his creditors and started yet more loss-making ventures. In 1918 he was re-elected for South Hackney, this time as an Independent, with a huge majority.

But his financial affairs were increasingly coming under suspicion, particularly when he made the mistake of suing a former colleague for libel over allegations over the Victory Bonds. The court case revealed embarrassing details, and the Director of Public Prosecutions brought an action against him for fraudulent conversion of bonds. In May 1922 he was found guilty on 23 counts out of 24, and sentenced to seven years' penal servitude; after his appeal was rejected in August, he was expelled from the House of Commons.

He was released after five years for good behaviour and, supported by his favourite mistress, Peggy Primrose, attempted a comeback as a speaker and journalist. But his attempts failed, and his health was not up to it; he collapsed during a lecture at the Windmill Theatre, London, in 1932, and died on 26 May 1933. His wife had died in 1930; they had one daughter. His *Daily Mail* obituary claimed, reasonably enough, that he could have been a success at anything he wanted: journalism, law, business. He is remembered instead for his reply to a prison visitor who found him one day sewing mail bags. 'Ah, Bottomley,' inquired the visitor, 'sewing?' 'No,' came the response, 'reaping'.

Duncan Brack

Margot Asquith

Countess of Oxford and Asquith

born 2 February 1864, *died* 28 July 1945

Emma Alice Margaret Tennant later became Mrs Asquith, and eventually the first Countess of Oxford and Asquith, but she was universally known as 'Margot'. Margot was married to an immense personality, yet was also a great personality in her own right, who appears to have exerted significant influence over the career of her husband.

Unlike H. H. Asquith, Margot started life with a silver spoon firmly in her mouth. She was born in Peeblesshire on 2 February 1864, the sixth daughter and eleventh child of Sir Charles Tennant, a wealthy ironmaster and later a Liberal MP.

Margot was a woman of many parts. Educated privately, then briefly at a finishing school and eventually at Dresden, she became an avid reader of serious literature, for which she had a remarkable memory. In her youth she showed considerable interest in the welfare of people less fortunate than herself, joining with her sister in establishing a crèche at Wapping, in London's East End, and later making frequent visits to a factory in nearby Whitechapel, an area notorious for sweated labour.

Soon she became associated with many of the most remarkable men of her time. Gladstone commemorated her with a piece of doggerel. The celebrated classicist Benjamin Jowett, Master of Balliol, was a close friend, and perhaps it was from Jowett that she acquired an enthusiasm for Plato. Soon she became one of the 'souls' – a cross-party group of intellectuals which included A. J. Balfour, the Marquess of Hartington, Lord Rosebery, John Morley and Archbishop Randall Davidson.

She had very strong likes, and perhaps even stronger dislikes, for people who came into her circle of acquaintances. As her step-daughter Lady Violet Bonham Carter noted, Margot's political concern was with men rather than with measures. When she died, *The Times* would reflect that she was 'not a wholly endearing personality. but of her scintillating endowment of mind there could never be any question'.

In May 1894, she became the second wife of Herbert Henry Asquith, Home Secretary in the Liberal government, and future Prime Minister. She was a mixed blessing to her husband. She was utterly loyal to him, and brought sufficient wealth to make it possible for a man with much talent to attain the highest political office. Both spouses were able to introduce the other into circles with which they had hitherto been unfamiliar. But her tactlessness, and her disposition to see public matters in personal terms, were less helpful. Perhaps the most important example of her dislikes – or intuitions? – was signalled in July 1916. Lord Kitchener, Secretary for War, had recently died. As Prime Minister of the wartime coalition, Asquith eventually picked on Lloyd George as the successor. That night, Margot noted in her diary: 'We are out, it is only a matter of time when we shall have to leave Downing Street.'

Was that a premonition of the inevitable, or a self-serving prophecy? Asquith's position was in some ways a very lonely one, and his wife, who had such pronounced views, was one of the few people in whom he could confide. Later in 1916, a difficult question arose concerning the conduct of the war, with Asquith and Lloyd George inclining to different sides. Until almost the last minute, a compromise appeared likely; but Asquith suddenly backed off. Within a short time, Lloyd George was Prime Minister in his place. Was Margot's influence of crucial importance in bringing about the Asquith-Lloyd George split which would prove so disastrous to both men, and to the Liberal Party?

Margot was capable of astonishing indiscretions. Her scribbled top-of-the-head letters may be found in various political papers. When Bonar Law brought about the destruction of Lloyd George's coalition government in 1922, Margot sent a gushing and congratulatory letter to the new Conservative Prime Minister, assuring him of her husband's 'generosity in the future, and indicating that the Asquiths would rather be out 'for ever' than encompass a return of the coalition. Whether this correctly represented Asquith's view or not, it is unthinkable that he would have approved the transmission of such a letter, which might easily prove a high political embarrassment.

Margot was the author of several books, including an autobiography (1922) and a novel, *Octavia*, and late in life was an occasional broadcaster. She had five children, only two of whom survived infancy. She died on 28 July 1945, a few weeks before the end of the Second World War.

Roy Douglas

Hilaire Belloc

born 20 July 1870, *died* 16 July 1953

Hilaire Belloc died in 1953 and is remembered, with his un-English name, as an eccentric Catholic writer, a defender of the indefensible and a champion of the Church Militant. He was a prolific writer, author of over a hundred books – verse, comic and serious, novels, travel accounts, essays on social, political issues, and partisan histories of England and the Reformation. His name was so closely associated with that of G.K. Chesterton that George Bernard Shaw invented the pantomime beast, the Chesterbelloc.

But for a decade Belloc was a serious and active politician, elected as a Member of Parliament in the Liberal landslide election of 1906. Moreover he had strong Liberal political roots through his mother, Elizabeth (Bessie), the daughter of Joseph Parkes, Radical Birmingham solicitor who had acted as a backroom intermediary between Radicals and Whigs in the 1830s. Bessie was brought up in a world of free-thinking Victorian Radicalism but rebelled and became a Catholic, received into the Church at the hands of Cardinal Manning.

Bessie travelled to France with an artist girlfriend and met a French artist, Louis Belloc. They married in London in 1867 and Hilaire was born at St-Cloud just before the Prussian siege of Paris. The family escaped to London, but Belloc's childhood was spent on both sides of the Channel. He went to the Catholic Oratory School in Birmingham, excelling in the classics, English and mathematics. Between school and university he tried out a number of careers – journalist, Sussex farmer and artilleryman in the French army. He went up to Balliol College, Oxford, at the age of 22, older than most of his contemporaries. He held his own in oratory with contemporaries such as the future Lord Chancellors John Simon and F. E. Smith, became President of the Union and obtained a first class degree in History.

After graduation Belloc travelled and published his first volumes of verse. He married a Californian girl, started a family and bought a house in his favourite English county of Sussex. He was also seen as a serious Liberal thinker and contributed, with J. L. Hammond and others, to *Essays in Liberalism*. His Liberalism was based on a romantic Catholic aversion to industrialisation, a Liberalism owing more to Cobbett than Cobden. He was adopted as Liberal candidate for the working-class constituency of Salford South, then held marginally by the Conservatives. Belloc was sound on Free Trade and Irish Home Rule, but only tactically allied to popular non-Conformist Liberalism on educational and temperance issues.

In the general election campaign, the Conservative candidate appealed to a Lancashire working-class Protestantism. Belloc faced the issue squarely. 'If you reject me on account of my religion,' he declared, 'I shall thank God that he has spared me the indignity of being your representative.'

Elected by a small majority, Belloc became a rumbustious parliamentary speaker. But his Radicalism was idiosyncratic and his Catholic convictions did not always chime in with the Party's non-Conformist conscience. He also took a salaried job, as literary editor of the strongly Conservative *Morning Post*. As time went on, his hostility to organised Puritanism and to the Suffragette movement alienated him from mainstream Liberalism. However, he stood again in the January 1910 general election, winning by a reduced majority. But he was becoming disillusioned by what he saw as 'the party game'. During 1910 he told the Salford Liberals that he would stand for the next election only as an Independent. Not surprisingly they would not accept that condition. In his last speech in the House of Commons, Belloc gave vent to his disillusion for politics: 'Even the most modest pen in the humblest newspaper is as good as a vote in what has ceased to be a free deliberative assembly'.

His pen had already exposed the corruptions, as he saw them, in parliamentary politics in two hastily written political novels, *Mr Clutterbuck's Election* (1908) and *A Change in the Cabinet* (1909). More memorable was his comic – or caustic – political verse:

The accursed Power which stands on Privilege
(And goes with Women, and Champagne, and Bridge)
Broke – and Democracy resumed her reign:
(Which goes with Bridge, and Women, and Champagne).

Belloc continued for the next few years to be interested in political ideas. With Chesterton they developed the idea of Distributism, whereby property was spread widely, not in a socialist way, but creating 'a society of highly divided properties bound together by free co-operative organisations.' The prevailing machinery of political action was not helpful. Indeed in *The Servile State* (1912) Belloc argued that the state was incapable of being instrumental in achieving social justice. Extended state powers would erode individual liberties. Although these views might seem to belong to the Right, Belloc's friends continued to be on the Left of British politics. He spoke at Fabian gatherings and his influence can be seen in Guild Socialism and in the ideas of George Orwell.

His comic verses – comic yet with a serious undertone of satire – had a wider impact. Some apparently cynical apothegms have become proverbial:

Pale Ebenezer thought it wrong to fight,
But roaring Bill (who killed him) thought it right
or

Whatever happens, we have got
The Maxim Gun, and they have not.

The First World War gave Belloc an opportunity to indulge his interests in military history, and he commented regularly for *Land and Water*, a weekly journal devoted to the progress of the war. Over-optimism damaged his credibility. The war turned completely sour for him personally after the death in action of his eldest son.

Peace brought few consolations. His wife had died just before the war. After the war Belloc seemed a broken man. Though he continued to be a prolific writer for 20 years, his militant Catholicism seemed to be defined by what he disliked – Protestants, Germans, capitalists, Jews, Bolshevism. He took solace in family and friends, and especially younger friends, but he withdrew more and more. His last ten years were dogged by illness and introversion. His last book was published in 1942. In his old age he read only his own books (and, of course, he had plenty to choose from) and the works of P. G. Wodehouse. Younger admirers, such as Malcolm Muggeridge and Evelyn Waugh, called on the house in Sussex and found a heavily-built sad old man.

Compared with his literary contemporaries, George Bernard Shaw, G. K. Chesterton or H. G. Wells, his posthumous reputation has not held up. As a politician and political theorist he is forgotten. There have been several sympathetic biographers but he has not lived up to the memory he pithily hoped for:

When I am dead, I hope it may be said:
'His sins were scarlet, but his books were read.'

Peter Clark

Sir Frank Mason Macfarlane

born 23 October 1889, *died* 12 August 1953

Polling day for the 1945 election was 5th July but to enable the return of the service voters ballots from overseas, the votes were not counted and the result declared until 26th July.

On the morning of the count, most newspapers anticipated that Churchill would be returned to office. Beaverbrook's *Express* confidently predicting an overall majority of 60. Churchill himself had not been able to vote as he had not been included in the electoral roll for Downing

Street, Chequers or Chartwell. According to his memoirs Churchill had his doubts and as soon as the results started to emerge during the morning it was clear that the Conservative Party was heading for a devastating defeat. The first cabinet casualty was Harold Macmillan in Stockton. He was followed by the First Lord of the Admiralty, Brendan Bracken, who lost the Paddington North constituency by 6,544 votes to a very distinguished soldier, Sir Frank Mason Macfarlane.

Sir Frank had been born in October 1889 and was educated at Rugby. Joining the army he fought with distinction in the Boer War, and in the First World War was awarded the Miltary Cross with two bars. He then served in the Imperial Defence College and was appointed to posts of ever-increasing importance. On the way he showed some surprising traits – whilst serving in India he took up 'pig sticking' as a hobby. He also directed a play performed by and for service personnel.

As the situation in Europe worsened, he became Military Attaché to Budapest, Berne, Vienna, Berlin and Copenhagen and following the outbreak of war, he led the British Expeditionary Force to Gibraltar and then became Head of the British Military Mission to Moscow. He remained in Moscow until 1942 and was described as the best ever Director of Military Intelligence. In 1942 he was appointed Governor of Gibraltar, a key appointment with regard to the Mediterranean, and stayed in post until 1944 when he became Chief of Allied Control Command in Italy. The honours followed, with his receiving the CB in 1939, the DSO in 1940 and the KCB in 1943.

He resigned his commission, citing health reasons, and joined the Labour Party, returning from Gibraltar to become Parliamentary Candidate for Paddington North.

Paddington North had, since 1929, been the political base of Churchill's most loyal supporter, Brendan Bracken – one of the earliest of political spin doctors. He was PPS to Churchill when he rejoined the Government in 1940 and in 1941 was appointed Minister of Information. Following the break-up of the war-time coalition in May 1945, Churchill appointed him First Lord of the Admiralty, which he held for just two months until his defeat in July. It was the only cabinet position he was to ever hold. A talented journalist, Bracken was a director of Eyre and Spottiswoode and Chairman of the *Financial Times*.

The 1945 election, fought in a glorious summer, was a campaign of outside meetings and limited paper. Newsprint was still rationed and national papers were limited and many local papers had been suspended during the war. There was no television, but radio assumed great importance.

It does appear strange how so few commentators noticed the groundswell that was to engulf Churchill, or chose to ignore evidence that was before their eyes. In Paddington (which in those days returned two Members of Parliament), there was clear evidence of hostility to Bracken and Vice Admiral Taylor, the 69 year old MP for Paddington South. A milk bottle was thrown at Bracken at a meeting in St Saviour's School and whereas a huge crowd was present when Churchill appeared to speak on behalf of Bracken and Taylor, correspondents wrote to the local paper expressing surprise at the level of heckling.

Sir Frank left hospital in June, after being injured in a plane crash, and returned to England and commenced his campaign with the comment that 'My chassis is to a certain extent dilapidated, but my engine is running very well.' He was unable to stand to speak at meetings and a picture of him exists showing him addressing a meeting, wearing a lounge suit (Vice Admiral Taylor was photographed in his uniform) sitting on a table. In the days before the election he spoke almost every night, in both Paddington constituencies and also St Marylebone.

The excitement of his victory, early in the morning of 26th July was recorded by Richard Clements, then aged 17 and a future editor of *Tribune:* 'The crowds were immense. We were jubilant and marched around singing and cheering.'

Sir Frank joined the throng of new Labour MPs at the beginning of the Parliament and signed the register alongside John Freeman. However, he was never to speak or ask a single question in the Commons.

His health deteriorated and it became clear that he would be unable to continue as an MP. He resigned from Parliament in the autumn of 1946 and a by-election took place. The Labour candidate was Major William Field who had turned the super safe Conservative seat of Hampstead into a marginal. Bracken having fought and won a by-election in Bournemouth was succeeded by Laurence Turner. Field was returned in November 1946, at the same time as he became leader of Hammersmith Council. Turner and Field both fought the 1950 election with Turner going on to succeed Quintin Hogg as MP for Oxford.

Paddington was to see a bewildering number of MPs, without either seat changing hands. In 1950 Vice Admiral Taylor stood down in Paddington South and was replaced by the author, Somerset de Chair, who only served until 1951 when he stood down in favour of Richard Allen.

For the 1951 election Field, who had by this time stood down as leader of Hammersmith Council, was opposed by Julian Ridsdale (later MP for Harwich). Then in 1953, the unfortunate Field had his personal moment of madness. He was arrested for importuning in a public lavatory. After being found guilty and fined he left Parliament and public life completely, even removing his address from *Who's Who*. He was to live into his 90s until 2002. Another by-election ensued and was won by Ben Parkin for Labour. His Conservative opponent was John Eden, who was to enter Parliament in 1954, succeeding Brendan Bracken in Bournemouth, who had accepted a Peerage.

Sir Frank Mason Macfarlane retired to his home in Berkshire where he died in August 1953. His all-round experience should have warranted a biography. Had he remained and played an active part in Parliament he would have had much to say, although the colourful political history in Paddington would have been somewhat less.

Peter Golds

Oliver Baldwin

Viscount Corvedale and 2nd Earl Baldwin of Bewdley

born 1 March 1899, *died* 10 August 1958

Baldwin is not a name one immediately associates with the Labour Party. Rather it conjures up images of the Conservative Prime Minister Stanley Baldwin, who engineered much of inter-war Britain's era of Conservative dominance. However, Oliver Ridsdale Baldwin's career does more than justify his own place in twentieth-century political history, for he successfully emerged from his father's shadow with a completely different political outlook and ethos.

His career is perhaps more extraordinary, given that his upbringing and education should have led him in the political footsteps of his famous father, rather than creating the self-proclaimed socialist and Labour MP. Moreover, Baldwin was not only a politician, but also an author, soldier, journalist, playwright and colonial governor. Each achievement was the result of Baldwin's adaptability and a reflection of his diverse character.

Baldwin was born on 1 March 1899, the elder son of Stanley and Lucy Baldwin, of Astley Hall, Worcestershire. At this time his father was the owner of a great iron and steel business, entering Parliament in 1908. Oliver was educated privately at St Aubyn's School, Rottingdean. This was followed by four years at Eton, up until July 1915, which he described in his autobiography, *The Questing Beast* (1932), as 'the most useless and unhappy years of my life up until then.' Many have attributed this dislike for education to his nonconformist roots, which he inherited from both sides of his family.

Having joined the cadets in May 1916, Baldwin had the opportunity to demonstrate his physical courage, for in 1917 he was commissioned in the Irish Guards and in May 1918 saw action in France. He spent the early months of 1920 in Algeria and Morocco and wrote about this time of his life in the publication, *Six Prisons and Two Revolutions*. In Armenia, Baldwin witnessed the invasion of the Bolshevik army and was briefly imprisoned, demonstrating an early rebellious streak that was to emerge consistently throughout his life. These foreign experiences further isolated him from Conservative politics, partly owing to his disillusionment with Lord Curzon's foreign policy and his increasing association with the Armenian radicals. Nonetheless, soldiering would remain one of his great loves, and during the Second World War he became a Major in the Intelligence Corps, serving in Egypt, Palestine, Syria, Eritrea and Algeria from 1940 to 1943.

However, it was in the early 1920s that Baldwin began to articulate his own set of political beliefs. At the time this was attributed partly to his having met in 1922 John Boyle, Baldwin's lifelong partner with whom he set up home in London. Others simply pointed to Baldwin's contentious streak, as immediately after his father became PM in 1923 he declared himself a socialist and promptly left the family home. This contrast between the Conservative father and Socialist son aided rumours that their relationship was often strained and formal. However, such differences did not affect the natural affection they held for each other, exhibited in their correspondence in Cambridge.

Joining the SDF, in 1922 Baldwin thence progressed to Labour politics. He stood unsuccessfully for Parliament at Dudley in 1924 before winning the seat in 1929. However, moving to Chatham in 1931 and Paisley in 1935, he was twice defeated. It was not until 1945 that he returned to the Commons, as Labour MP for Paisley, carrying the courtesy title Viscount Corvedale. Never a minister, he was, however, briefly a PPS: to Jack Lawson in 1946 and to Fred Bellenger in 1947, successively Attlee's Secretaries of State for War.

It was Oliver Baldwin's association with Oswald Mosley and his New Party that caused the most political controversy. His relationship with Mosley was close and in February 1931 Baldwin resigned the Labour whip, joined the New Party and even contributed to the drafting of the party manifestos, though he resigned from the New Party the following day and rejoined the Labour Party. Thus he never endorsed or associated himself with any of Mosley's fascist tendencies. However, this episode reflects not only Baldwin's wilfulness, but also his haphazard political judgement. Baldwin himself often felt his political career was something of a failure, feeling that his theoretical principles and high ideals were not reflected in the reality of Labour politics. On the death of his father in December 1947, Oliver automatically succeeded to the earldom and was forced to resign his Commons seat and adjust to life in the Lords. Despite all this, his brief career in the Commons forged many of Baldwin's closest friendships, including those with Labour stalwarts such as James Maxton, Ben Tillet, Seymour Cocks and Arthur Greenwood.

In 1948 the Labour Government appointed the new 2nd Earl Baldwin as Governor of the Leeward Islands. His open hostility to the actions of the British Government in sending out missions of inquiry and inspection attracted criticism. His outspoken views and eccentric behaviour nearly cost him his position, and on being recalled by the Colonial Secretary, Arthur Creech-Jones, for 'consultation' Baldwin talked openly to the press of his expectations of a 'carpeting'. He was, however, a popular governor and V. C. Bird, one of the main local Labour leaders, publicly backed Baldwin's continuation as Governor. Hence, after apologising and retracting some of his previous statements, Baldwin was returned to the islands, continuing in post until 1950. This incident gave the Conservatives a degree of political capital, but Baldwin was genuinely concerned about the condition of the islands, some of the poorest in the West Indies.

This concern for those less fortunate than himself was demonstrated throughout his various careers. As a politician, soldier, playwright, journalist and author he displayed generosity, loyalty and a belief in the principles that had guided him as a young man. His propensity for causing controversy was legendary, but he was not a deliberate trouble-maker. Rather, he simply said what he thought, and this was often the cause of some discussion amongst more reserved politicians.

Earl Baldwin of Bewdley died in a London hospital on 10 August 1958; he was 59. Very little has been written on any part of the career of this fascinating man and principled politician. He was somewhat of a black sheep, isolated in equal measure by society's view of homosexuality and by his own ability to shock and amuse. However, his diverse and colourful life, and his sortie into Labour politics, are testament to a man who did not always accept the status quo and broke away from the conservative future that had seemed his destiny.

Jennifer Gerber

Sir Henry 'Chips' Channon

born 7 March 1897, *died* 7 October 1958

Although he sat as a Member of Parliament for some 23 years, Sir Henry Channon is not now remembered for his political achievements. Nor indeed did he have any to be remembered by. 'Chips' (as he was universally known) rarely spoke in Parliament and, having risen briefly to the lowest government rank of Parliamentary Private Secretary, he resigned the position in order to avoid moving to what he considered the 'boredom' of the Board of Education.

Instead, 'Chips' Channon has acquired a footnote in history as the author of a splendidly frank and indiscreet diary recording the many events and people with whom he came into contact both politically and socially. This document, which seems to have been written with at least half (and probably more) an eye to being read by posterity, was discovered and published after Channon's death in 1958 – but only after having been heavily edited, and not just to address the problem of volume. As the diary's editor, Robert Rhodes James, himself acknowledged, certain material was omitted in order not to upset or offend people who were still alive to read the diaries or, more pertinently, to avoid any potential harm to the nascent political career of Chips' son, the future Cabinet Minister Paul Channon. The latter consideration meant effectively expunging all references to Chips' bisexuality and his relationship with long-term partner Peter Coats, given both the law and the general public attitude to such matters at the time of the diary's publication in the 1960s.

Henry Channon was born on 7 March 1897 in Chicago, son of local businessman Henry Channon II and his wife Vesta. Little is known of his early years, other than that he was schooled in Chicago and briefly in Paris. Nor is it known precisely when or why he acquired the nickname of Chips (one theory was it resulted from his sharing a flat with a man called 'Fish').

Channon returned to Paris with the American Red Cross in October 1917 and, whilst there, became an Honorary Attaché to the American Embassy. Some of this period is captured in his earliest surviving diary, for the year 1918, which provides an early glimpse of the delight in society and friendships which were to strongly mark Chips' later life. There then followed a four-year diary gap, covering the period in which Channon (having been summoned home from Paris by his parents) studied as an undergraduate at Oxford. It is not clear whether those years went unrecorded or whether the relevant diaries were deliberately destroyed. However, the nature of their likely contents are hinted at by an unnamed Oxford contemporary who, when told of this gap in the sequence, uttered a relieved 'Thank God!'

On completion of his studies, Chips moved to London and began to establish himself on the capital's social circuit. According to Rhodes James, the diaries for that period are a procession of dinners, balls and country house parties. A particular focus is a close friendship with the former Foreign Secretary, Lord Curzon, and his wife with whom, in a display typical of future behaviour, Chips remained close friends even after Curzon's fall from office and favour. From then on, Chips was a constant fixture in society, both as host and guest, as a result gaining access and insights to many of the important people of the age. This included the then Prince of Wales (later Edward VIII), whose friendship with Channon gave the latter an inside opportunity to record the events leading up to his abdication in 1936.

Chips' political life began, almost accidentally, following his marriage to Lady Honor Guinness (of the brewing family) in 1933. To the extent that he had had any career plans or ambitions, Chips had planned to be a writer. Indeed, he had already published three well-received books – a novel, *Joan Kennedy*, in 1929; a description of Chicago life, *Paradise City*, in 1930; and a history of *The Ludwigs of Bavaria* in 1933. Following the marriage, however, Chips was asked to take on the family parliamentary seat of Southend-on-Sea, held at that time by Lady Iveagh, who had herself succeeded her husband on his elevation to the House of Lords. As recorded in his diaries, Chips' selection process consisted largely of presenting himself at the local Conservative Hall, whereupon the 100 people present broke into a chorus of 'For he's a jolly good fellow' and informed him that he had been adopted unanimously.

Once elected, in 1935, Chips took slowly to the Parliamentary life and did not make his maiden speech until early the following year. He seemed principally to enjoy the Commons not for its political life but rather as another source of social intercourse, and as such to prefer the Lobby to the Chamber. However, he did in 1938 push himself forward as a candidate for PPS to the up-and-coming Rab Butler, who had just been appointed a junior minister at the Foreign Office. Appointment to this post allowed him an inside view of the negotiations and manoeuvrings which led first to Munich, then to war and finally to the installation of Winston Churchill as Prime Minister. However, Chips' appetite seemed principally to have been for excitement and intrigue, rather than for power, and when Butler was transferred in 1941 to the Board of Education Chips chose not to go with him, fearing the prospect of dealing with 'school-mistresses and children in provincial towns'.

From then onwards, Chips returned to the familiarity of his social circles and friendships, whilst remaining an active advocate for and representative of his constituents. An attempt to 'sacrifice' himself to the

House of Lords in order to make his safe seat available to others came to nothing, although he did receive a knighthood in the 1957 New Year Honours list. On his death in 1958, Chips was buried in the churchyard at his country house at Kelvedon in Essex where, fittingly, he had previously arranged for his diaries – his true achievement and legacy – to be buried for protection during the war.

Andrew Kean

Clement Davies

born 19 February 1884, **died** 23 March 1962

Edward Clement Davies was born on 19 February 1884 at Llanfyllin, Montgomeryshire, the youngest of the seven children of Moses Davies, an auctioneer, and Elizabeth Margaret Jones. He was educated at the local primary school, won a scholarship to Llanfyllin County School in 1897 and proceeded to Trinity College, Cambridge, where he became senior foundation scholar and graduated with first class honours in both parts of the law tripos. He won a glittering array of prizes.

He earned his living as a law lecturer at the University College of Wales, Aberystwyth, from 1908–09 and was called to the bar by Lincoln's Inn. He joined the North Wales circuit in 1909 and the Northern circuit in 1910. In the same year he migrated to London, soon establishing a successful and lucrative legal practice, displaying a rapid mastery of his briefs and publishing respected works on agricultural law and the law of auctions.

In 1914, at the outbreak of war, he was appointed adviser within the Office of the Procurator-General on enemy activities in neutral countries and on the high seas. He was later made responsible for trading with the enemy, a position within the Board of Trade. In 1918–19 he served as Secretary to the President of the Probate, Divorce and Admiralty Division, and subsequently as Secretary to the Master of the Rolls until 1923. He was one of the junior counsel to the Treasury, 1919–25, and took silk in 1926. He served as Chairman of the Montgomeryshire quarter sessions from 1935 until his death in 1962.

From his boyhood Clement Davies had been fascinated by political life. He was approached as a possible Liberal candidate as early as 1910, but did not consent to stand for Parliament until 1927 when he was chosen as the Liberal candidate for his native Montgomeryshire. Seen initially as an avid radical and a stalwart supporter of David Lloyd George, Davies was returned to Parliament in May 1929 by a majority of just over 2,000 votes. In August 1930 he accepted a lucrative position as legal director to Lever Brothers, which seemed to spell the end of his political career. But, at the eleventh hour, the company resolved to permit Davies to continue in Parliament.

In the general election of October 1931, after some complex political manoeuvres within Montgomeryshire, he was returned unopposed as one of the Liberal National followers of Sir John Simon, and again in November 1935. As a backbencher, he served as a tireless member of a number of committees. From 1937–38 he chaired an influential governmental inquiry into the incidence of tuberculosis in Wales, probing the standards of public health care and housing in all the Welsh counties. He consistently argued for the appointment of a Secretary of State for Wales.

At the outbreak of the Second World War he chaired an action committee which pressed for a more effective conduct of the war effort, and he is credited with persuading Lloyd George to speak in the House of Commons in May 1940 in favour of Neville Chamberlain's resignation. Lord Boothby, a first-hand observer of these events, was to describe Davies as 'one of the architects – some may judge the principal architect' of the coalition government led by Churchill.

In 1941 he resigned his position with Unilever, and in August 1942 rejoined the mainstream Liberal Party and spoke extensively throughout Britain. Re-elected with a majority of a little over 3,000 votes in the general election of 1945, Davies was now one of only 12 Liberal MPs. He was made Chairman of the party by his somewhat reluctant fellow members in succession to the defeated Sir Archibald Sinclair. Throughout his tenure of this position until 1956, he faced an appallingly difficult political task.

At the 1945 Liberal Summer School he warned party members against the 'Tory spider', ever ready to trap Liberal supporters, and he consistently and doggedly distanced himself and his party from doctrinaire socialism. Consequently he faced no Tory opponent in Montgomeryshire in the general elections of 1951 and 1955. Yet his party faced manifold financial and organisational problems, and constantly lost members to both Conservatives and Labour. Even Lady Megan Lloyd George, whom Davies appointed as his Deputy Leader in January 1949, seemed ever more likely to 'move left'. When Churchill offered him a Cabinet post as Minister of Education in October 1951, Davies refused, thus preserving the integrity of his party as an independent political force.

During subsequent years, until Jo Grimond succeeded him in September 1956, he spared no effort to revive and reunite his feud-racked, often ailing party, which he at least kept intact at a most critical time in its history. He was highly popular within Montgomeryshire and earned the respect of members of all parties within the Commons. Rightly described as 'a radical evangelist' by temperament rather than a party boss, he disliked rigid party organisation and conventions. He spoke widely throughout England and Wales, most notably to university audiences, and never wavered in his heartfelt devotion to worthy causes such as social justice and reform, collective security, freedom of the individual, and world government.

He found his role as President of the Parliamentary Association for World Government in his latter years especially gratifying. This work led to his nomination (albeit unsuccessfully) for the Nobel Peace Prize in 1955, a move advanced by over 100 parliamentarians.

In 1913 Davies married Jano Elizabeth Davies, adopted daughter of Dr Morgan Davies, a London-Welsh surgeon. An accomplished public speaker and astute politician in her own right, Jano gave unstinting support to her husband's public work. Of the four children of the marriage, three died at 24 years of age.

Clement Davies died at a London clinic on 23 March 1962, still an MP, shortly after the sensational Liberal victory at Orpington. His seat was held at the ensuing by-election by Emlyn Hooson. In 1960 he had announced his intention to retire from the Commons at the next general election, and, had he survived, would probably have accepted a peerage in 1964.

His biography, *Clement Davies: Liberal Leader*, by Alun Wyburn Powell was published in 2003.

Graham Jones

(Henry) Percival Pott

born 29 March 1908, *died* 17 January 1964

Percival Pott's apparent qualification for inclusion in this volume is his highly unusual name but if you scratch the surface he enjoyed a varied career in public life, of a sort almost unheard of today.

He was born in March 1908, was educated at Oundle, and farmed originally in Northamptonshire. After wartime RAF service, he settled and resumed farming in Hampshire. With a moustache and a pipe, he looked the model of the 1940's squadron leader he had been promoted to.

A distinguished ancestor was the famous surgeon Sir John Percivall Pott (1714–1788), after whom Pott's Disease and Pott's Fracture are known. To this day there is a Percival Pott Club, open to surgeons at St Bartholomew's Hospital.

Return to civilian life brought marriage to Mary Vera Larkworthy in 1946, and election three years later to Hampshire County Council. He represented his home ward of Bramshott, even after his subsequent election to Parliament.

He became a member of the local NFU Executive Committee, a director of two water companies, and was appointed to the Hampshire Magistrates Bench (juvenile court panel).

He also found the time to act as temporary Bursar at Gordonstoun School, and was involved in the scouts and voluntary youth club activities.

The education link was reenforced with almost continuous membership of the County Education Committee, and various Education subcommittees, on which he was still serving at the time of his death. Seniority on the Council brought membership of the Finance and Civil Defence Committees.

His background and interests clearly appealed to the Devizes Conservative Association, who in May 1953 selected him to succeed Christopher Hollis, and defend a majority of 1577. Pott's farming background was crucial in a rural seat, where the Labour candidate Wilfred Cave lived, had fought every general election since 1945, and farmed 2000 acres.

Pott conducted his May 1955 general election campaign straight from the textbook, in support of the new Prime Minister, Anthony Eden. He summarised his philosophy in his election address: 'As Conservatives we believe that it is the family, and not Whitehall, that is the hinge of national endeavour and national strength.'

The Conservative campaign slogan was 'United for Peace and Progress',which Pott neatly adapted to:

Peace
Opportunity
Tolerance
Teamwork

He offered himself as a member of the Church of England, who apart from the war, had always been a farmer, with his experiences broadened by travel within Europe, and to USA, India, Ceylon and Burma.

He was rewarded with a 0.7 per cent swing and a majority of 2,075, in a straight fight with Labour – no Liberals in rural areas then! Typically, he was in no rush to make a maiden speech, and when he did so after 11 months, it was inevitably on agriculture. Unlike present-day convention, he did not pay tribute to his predecessor or praise the qualities of his constituency. He did advocate loans to farmers backed by public funds, a suggestion the Minister, winding up, promised to consider. Pott also called for a long-term policy for agriculture, but recognised this was as an elusive quarry as the 'abominable snowman'.

Although relatively silent in Parliament, he was not politically inactive. He chaired the Conservative Party's Local Government Committee and was President of the Wessex Area Young Conservatives, attending every one of their council meetings and many of their weekend schools.

The 1959 election campaign, with the Chancellor of the Exchequer visiting Devizes, produced a further 2 per cent swing and a 3,838 majority over Wilfred Cave who stood for a fifth and final time. An independent Liberal polled 2,707 votes.

Percival Pott's photo shows him looking older and thinner than four years earlier, and more than his 51 years. He campaigned fully in support of the Government's record, particularly on Suez – right to go in and right to stop. Again he adapted his name to neatly sum up his approach:

Peace   Prosperity
Opportunity   Ownership
Trade   Tradition
Tolerance   Teamwork

Other interventions in the Commons were usually on education or local government matters, where he was always logical and businesslike. In his final speech in April 1961, on the adjournment, Pott raised the issue of a factory closure in his constituency, and the problems that would arise for those moving into the area when a new factory opened, and the cost of housing was prohibitive.

There was one final intervention in 1962, when Pott aggressively defended the interests of the City of London against an attempt by Islington Council to take over City land at below market value.

Following a serious illness in 1961, and given his double workload in Hampshire and Wiltshire, Pott decided not to seek re-election at Devizes and wrote to his constituency chairman in March 1963 citing 'the increasingly heavy burden of Parliamentary duties'.

At the Association Annual Meeting ten days later there was much regret at his decision and he was praised by the President for his programme of visits, and the amount of publicity he had achieved. There was a genuine sense of sadness that he would not be available to defend his seat.

Within a year of this announcement Percival Pott was found dead at his London flat in January 1964. Two memorial services were held the following month at St Mary's Marlborough, with another a day later at St Margaret's, Westminster. The man who delivered the address was none other than Peter Thomas, the minister who had replied to the adjournment debate three years earlier.

It had been a career of quiet public work by a man who had literally given his life to the service of others.

Peter Golds

David Logan

born 22 November 1871, *died* 25 February 1964

In 1885 the City of Liverpool, which had since 1868 returned three Members of Parliament on a block basis, was divided into nine single member constituencies. In the election of that year eight of these new constituencies returned Conservative MPs. The odd one out was Liverpool Scotland which returned Thomas Power O'Connor as an Irish

Nationalist. In the same election O'Connor was also returned, as a Nationalist, for Galway City (which he had won in 1880) but elected to represent Liverpool, Scotland – where he remained the Member of Parliament until his death aged 81, in 1929.

O'Connor was a journalist who began his working career on the *Daily Telegraph*, and went on to become a prolific author and founder of newspapers, including the *Star*. His constituency was a true melting pot, which contained a massive Irish population One section of Vauxhall Ward had four Roman Catholic parishes before 1855. By the time of his death, O'Connor was a Privy Counsellor and much loved figure.

Liverpool, Scotland was about to set the record, unlikely ever to be broken, for having just two Members of Parliament in 79 years!

Liverpool politics was extremely complex, cutting across class, race and religion. The city council included members elected from the Protestant Party, and, as it seems difficult to believe today, Labour has only ever held an overall majority on the City Council for 19 years (1955–61, 1963–67 and 1983–92). In Parliamentary terms Conservatives and Unionists usually swept the board. Issues of orange and green were often underneath many aspects of city life, with Catholic and Orange religious parades and even the two great football teams appealing to either Catholics or Protestants. Steve Norris, for example, remembers being a supporter of the Catholic Blues (Everton) as a youngster during the 1950s. During the 1950s a Protestant Party councillor served as Lord Mayor of the city.

Yet when O'Connor died, Labour secured the constituency, and made a gain, without a contest. David Logan was the Chairman of the Scotland Labour Party, and an Alderman of Liverpool City Council. A former member of the Nationalist Party, he had joined Labour after the Government of Ireland Act. He was a life-long resident of the Scotland Road, the area which gave its name to the constituency.

He was by profession a pawnbroker and was the founder of the Approved Society of Pawnbrokers Assistants, (which was to make him one of the most interesting trade unionists in the Commons). In December 1929 David Logan was also 58 years old.

His appearance in Parliament was swift: he was selected as Labour Candidate and when nominations closed on Saturday 14th December, he was declared elected unopposed. He contested the next two elections, but was again unopposed in 1945 – the last MP in England to be returned without a contest in a general election. He fought his last election in 1959, aged 87.

Logan was deeply religious, but had an empathy with his constituents, regardless of their religion. Numerous stories were told of his kindness to people at a time when the pawn shop was almost an extension of social services. This was particularly necessary when after 1950 the boundaries of the Scotland constituency were included to include the Netherfield and St Domingo Wards – strongholds of the Protestant Party.

His maiden speech took place in January 1930 during the second reading of a Blasphemy Bill, introduced by Ernest Thurtle, Labour MP for Shoreditch. Logan was an opponent of the measure, claiming to speak for 98 per cent of the Catholic population of his constituency. It was in this speech that he said 'to me, God means everything'. It was significant that he was prepared to oppose members of his own party so early in his Parliamentary career.

Logan was also a believer in what may now be regarded as old fashioned concepts of home and the family. He himself was a strong family man with six children (his *Times* obituary incorrectly states that he and his wife were childless).

He tenaciously held on to his seat throughout the 1950s, opposing age limits for both Justices of the Peace and Members of Parliament.

His last speech in the Commons was in January 1959, on the subject of home in a debate on education.

Even in old age, he was dedicated constituency member. For example, in 1949 the city council was clearing slums and attempting to repair bomb damage. The solution, as in so many places, was to build huge estates on the outskirts and decant the population to these estates. The result was new homes, but often disjointed families as ties of generations were broken. In Liverpool's Vauxhall Ward, the city council proposed to move almost the entire northern part of the ward, known as 'Over the Bridge' Local people, many of whom were connected with the docks and mostly of Irish descent, fought this, wishing to remain in an area that had been home for generations. Logan supported them and the council listened to him, and this particular community stayed together.

Logan fought the 1959 election in his 88th year, but his parliamentary activities decreased. He did not speak at all during the Parliament and tabled a handful of questions. His supporters were saddened when in 1963 the satirical TV programme *That Was The Week, That Was* broadcast a sketch of inactive MPs including both Logan and Sir Winston Churchill (who was three years younger than Logan).

David Logan passed away in February 1964 of respiratory problems in his home City.

The by-election for his successor was held in June 1964, the last of the 1959 Parliament and the Labour candidate secured an exceptional (for those days) swing of over 10 per cent. Liverpool was changing: it was the era of the Beatles, the Mersey sound, the ascendancy of Liverpool Football Club and perhaps most of all politically, of Harold Wilson whose constituency bordered the city and whose constituents included many who had been rehoused as a result of the slum clearances. Times were more secular and religious barriers were breaking down. In the October general election Merseyside recorded the biggest swing to Labour in the country and the Conservatives lost four of their six seats.

What would David Logan have made of the fact that in his city within two decades of his death the once mighty Conservative Party would have been effectively wiped out as a political force?

Peter Golds

Megan Lloyd George

born 22 April 1902, *died* 14 May 1966

Megan Lloyd George was born at Criccieth, Caernarfonshire, on 22 April 1902, the third daughter and fifth child of David Lloyd George and his wife Margaret. Until the age of four she could speak only Welsh. She was educated privately, in part by Frances Stevenson, who became her father's mistress and in 1943 his second wife, and later at Garratt's Hall, Banstead, and in Paris.

Her natural brilliance was sparked by her unique upbringing; from the age of eight until 20 she spent much of her time at Number 11, and subsequently Number 10, Downing Street. She savoured political life at the hub of events, and, following the death of the eldest daughter Mair in 1907, occupied centre stage in her father's affections. She accompanied him to the Paris Peace Conference in 1919, meeting a glittering array of world statesmen, diplomats and military figures, and to a succession of post-war international conferences. She was at her father's side on his triumphal tour of Canada and the USA in 1923. She spent a whole year (1924–25) as the guest of Lord Reading, Viceroy of India (Rufus Isaacs).

She was widely regarded by the mid-1920s as her father's natural political heir. In 1928, after some underhand tactics in which both Lloyd George and Dame Margaret were much implicated, Megan secured the Liberal nomination for Anglesey. On 30 May 1929, she was elected to the Commons, the first-ever woman MP from Wales and the only Liberal lady to enjoy a relatively safe seat.

She soon made her own distinctive mark in the House as an independent-minded, highly individualistic MP with strong radical, even Labourite leanings. Her eloquent maiden speech in 1930, witnessed by her adoring father, discussed the problems of rural housing. She subsequently spoke to great effect on agriculture, unemployment and Welsh affairs. In the autumn of 1931 she was one of the tiny group of four Lloyd George family MPs who, unlike the rest of the Liberal Party, opposed the formation of Ramsay MacDonald's National Government.

She secured re-election to the Commons as an Independent Liberal in the general elections of 1931 and 1935. Although flirting ever more closely with the Labour Party, she remained true to her father's brand of Liberalism. She supported his ambitious 'New Deal' programme in 1935, accompanied him on his visit to Hitler in 1936, and opposed the policy of appeasement, urging him to press for Chamberlain's resignation in May 1940.

During the Second World War Lloyd George served on an array of consultative committees and became a keen advocate of women's issues. She was a member of the 1944 Speaker's Conference on Electoral Reform and a leading light on the Woman Power Committee devoted to women's rights and the employment of women in wartime. She was also an unrelenting champion of Welsh causes, helping to press, unsuccessfully, for the appointment of a Secretary of State for Wales in 1943, and for a 'Welsh Day' debate in the Commons.

In 1945 her majority sharply reduced in Anglesey. She was one of only 12 Liberal MPs re-elected to Parliament and was the only national figure among them. When Clement Davies became Chairman of the 'motley group', Lloyd George, who saw herself as 'a minority radical in a minority party', looked increasingly askance at what she perceived as Davies' inclination to veer towards the Tories. 'Small, vital, with unlimited energy', she formed a close bond of friendship with Attlee and Herbert Morrison and, crucially, Labour's General Secretary Morgan Phillips, and was widely considered 'one of us' by Labour MPs.

In January 1949, in an attempt to improve party unity, Clement Davies made her Deputy Leader. But she caused renewed dissension in her party's ranks, culminating in November 1950 with the revolt of four Liberal MPs, including herself, against the party leadership – though this rebellion eventually petered out.

Lloyd George faced Tory opponents on Anglesey in the general elections of 1950 and 1951. In the former contest she was re-elected by a majority of 1,929 votes, but in the latter she was defeated by Cledwyn Hughes (Labour), standing in his third successive general election in the county. A tenure of 22 years thus came to an end. In November 1952 she declined to stand again as the Liberal candidate for Anglesey and at about the same time stood down as Vice-President of the Liberal Party.

A number of prominent radicals including Lloyd George and Dingle Foot had been considering the possibility of joining the Labour Party en masse, naively hoping to have some restraining influence on the Bevanites within the party. Lloyd George scuppered that plan by announcing her defection in April 1955 and she was subsequently to contribute substantially to the Labour election campaign later the same year. The death of Sir Rhys Hopkin Morris caused a fiercely contested by-election in the Carmarthenshire division in February 1957, and Lloyd George returned to the Commons as a Labour MP by a majority of more than 3,000 votes.

During her years in the political wilderness she served as the charismatic and indefatigable president of the tenacious 'Parliament for Wales' campaign of the early 1950s. She appeared on the platform at its inaugural conference at Llandrindod in July 1950, subsequently speaking at meetings and conferences throughout Wales, and serving as one of the deputation which in April 1956 presented a petition of more than 250,000 signatures, ironically to her brother Gwilym, at the time Conservative Home Secretary and Minister for Welsh Affairs under Anthony Eden.

The personal popularity which Megan Lloyd George had undoubtedly enjoyed in Anglesey soon became evident in Carmarthenshire, where she developed a substantial popular following, gradually increasing her majority to more than 9,000 votes by 1966. Within the Commons she spoke generally on Welsh affairs or on agriculture, but neither Hugh Gaitskell nor Harold Wilson ever invited her to speak from the opposition front bench, and, when Labour returned to power in 1964, she remained a backbencher.

By this time, she was already suffering from cancer, an illness which prevented her from campaigning at all in the 1966 general election. On 14 May 1966 she died at Brynawelon, her Criccieth home, within days of receiving the CH, ironically from Harold Wilson, whom she disliked intensely. She was buried at Criccieth in the Lloyd George family vault. She remained unmarried.

Throughout her life, as both a Liberal and a Labour MP, she remained true to the passionate radicalism which was the hallmark of her father's political career. She was addressed in 1949 as 'a true daughter of the Welsh Wizard: she witches friend and foe alike'. Megan was, moreover, a Welsh radical who never failed to advocate policies beneficial to her native Wales, and who served as a member of the Criccieth Urban District Council for several years. An unfailingly eloquent orator, she was equally at home in the Commons, on the hustings, in a packed Royal Albert Hall or on the radio. Whether, had she survived, she would ever have been rewarded with a post in government, however, is debatable.

J. Graham Jones

G. P. Gooch

born 23 October 1873, **died** 31 August 1968

George Peabody Gooch was born during Gladstone's first government and died during Harold Wilson's second. In the early 1920s Harold Laski described him as 'the most learned man in England today'. For nearly 70 years he was publishing major historical works. But he devoted much time to humanitarian work and was Liberal Member of Parliament for Bath from 1906 to 1910.

Gooch was born in London in London in October 1873. His father was born in 1811 and was a partner in a City banking firm founded by

George Peabody, the American businessman and philanthropist: hence the name. His mother was the daughter of a Norfolk rector. From an early age Gooch was an avid reader. He went to Eton College but was not happy there and switched to a day school in London. From there he went on to Trinity College, Cambridge, to study history, falling under the influence of Lord Acton. He perfected his German and French with spells in Berlin and Paris. Gooch's first book was on English democratic ideas in the seventeenth century, published in 1898.

He failed to obtain a Fellowship at Trinity College, and settled in London. Private income enabled him to research, study and write. A social conscience politicised him. In the years before he was elected to Parliament he regularly taught – for no fee – adults in the East End of London, at clubs, churches and institutions such as Toynbee Hall. A committed Anglican, he worked with the London City Mission on the alleviation of alcoholism.

Humanitarian work turned Gooch into a social Radical. The Boer War turned him into an anti-Imperialist. His opposition to the war brought him into contact with leading soul-mates in the Liberal Party – Henry Campbell-Bannerman, James Bryce, John Morley. He wrote for the newspaper *Echo* owned by his Eton contemporary, Frederick Lawrence (later Pethick-Lawrence), and got to know a number of similarly minded younger men. In 1901 he contributed an essay on imperialism to a volume, *The Heart of the Empire*. Other essays by other young radicals – most of whom achieved later great distinction – discussed issues of social reform, temperance, housing and child welfare.

When confronted by a political issue Gooch would read intensively (and at great speed), consult those who had a greater personal acquaintance with the subject and apply strongly-held moral beliefs. Gooch's maintained that in all communities there was a consensus of moral interests based on mutuality and toleration.

After the 'Khaki' general election of 1900, he determined to get into Parliament himself. The opportunity came in 1903 when he was selected as the Liberal candidate for the two-member Bath constituency that had generally been Conservative. The other Liberal candidate was Donald Maclean, father of the 1951 defector to the Soviet Union. At the general election of 1906 the two Liberals were elected, joining a huge Liberal majority.

By the time he was an MP Gooch was married to Else Schott, a Saxon art student whom he had met on his early postgraduate trip to Germany. Gooch's private income always allowed a comfortable life that included a large house in west central London, an ever-expanding library and ample servants. Two sons were born while Gooch was a MP.

In Parliament Gooch was immediately appointed Parliamentary Private Secretary to the Chief Secretary for Ireland, James Bryce, another historian. Both had worked together on promoting human rights in the Ottoman Empire. Office inhibited Gooch's freedom of speech on Irish matters, but he spoke regularly on foreign affairs and was active in committees promoting the interests of imperial subjects, especially in India, Egypt and South Africa. Some of these brought Gooch in close touch with a range of influential MPs, Liberal and Labour. On domestic matters he spoke on education, temperance and old age pensions.

Gooch was a supporter of Lloyd George's 'People's Budget' of 1909 but disliked his tone of personal vituperation. In the January 1910 election Gooch narrowly lost, and Bath reverted to being represented by two Conservative MPs. He stood again for Bath in the December 1910 election, but without success.

In the constitutional crisis of 1911 the Prime Minister, H. H. Asquith, was poised to create a massive number of peers if the House of Lords continued to vote against Liberal measures. On Asquith's list of potential peers was the name of G. P. Gooch.

Loss of a parliamentary seat was compensated by being appointed co-edited of *The Contemporary Review,* a journal that examined current political issues in a way that was authoritative without being academic, accessible without being shallow. He was to continue to be co-editor or editor for half a century.

In 1913 Gooch became Liberal candidate at a by-election at Reading, following the promotion of Sir Rufus Isaacs to the House of Lords as Lord Chief Justice. But Gooch's temperance did not go down well with the brewery workers in a constituency that had been held only narrowly by Isaacs in the elections of 1910. Gooch lost on a 92 per cent poll, high for a by-election: and that was the end of Gooch's formal political life.

But Gooch retained an interest in politics for the rest of his life. His main historical contribution was to the study of diplomatic history. He was co-editor with H. V. W. Temperley of a collection of documents tracing the origins of the First World War. He also wrote extensively on the modern history of Europe. Perhaps his most extraordinary work was *History and Historians of the Nineteenth Century*, published in 1913 before his fortieth birthday. In this he lightly displays a phenomenal familiarity with history writing in many languages. His broad-minded appreciation of ancient, medieval and modern history is unprecedented and unlikely ever to be equalled. All the more amazing is the fact that it was written when he was busy in public life.

He continued to be involved in humanitarian activity, extending it in the 1930s and 1940s to work for refugees from Europe. Though he never held a permanent university post he was in demand for temporary academic attachments in Europe and in the United States. His productivity never flagged and he was producing major works in his eighties.

In old age he wrote his memoirs, *Under Six Reigns*. This is an urbane account of his political life, but lacking both revelations and passion. Gooch's Liberalism never wavered. He abstained from voting if there was no Liberal candidate. He became a Companion of Honour in 1940 and received the Order of Merit in 1963. A personal warmth and a serenity of outlook offset the infirmities of old age until he died in August 1968 shortly before his ninety-fifth birthday.

Peter Clark

Violet Bonham Carter

Baroness Asquith of Yarnbury

born 15 April 1887, *died* 19 February 1969

Violet Bonham Carter was born in Hampstead on 15 April 1887 as Helen Violet Asquith, the daughter of Herbert Henry Asquith and his first wife Helen Melland. In 1891 Violet's mother died of typhoid fever, and in 1894 Asquith married Margot Tennant. At the time of Violet's birth, Asquith had just entered the House of Commons. His ascent was rapid: in 1892 he became Home Secretary in Gladstone's last administration, in 1905 Chancellor of the Exchequer and in 1908 Prime Minister. Violet's lifetime covered the zenith and the nadir of the Liberal Party and she occupied a ringside seat.

Educated at home, and 'finished' in Dresden and Paris, she was, despite this lack of a formal education, a woman of formidable intellect. She was a passionate Liberal, and her father's 'champion redoubtable' (Winston Churchill's characterisation): she worshipped him and he depended upon her. After his fall from power she became his standard bearer, discovering her own considerable gifts as an orator as she fought his Paisley campaigns. She continued after Asquith's death to be his most resolute defender, and the voice of Asquithian Liberalism.

She was president of the Women's Liberal Federation twice: 1923–25 and 1939–45. In 1945 she became President of the Liberal Party Organisation, the first woman to do so. She stood for Wells in 1945, and for Colne Valley in 1951; she was unsuccessful in both campaigns. In 1964 she was belatedly made a life peer and entered the House of Lords as Baroness Asquith of Yarnbury. Although by then 77, she made an immediate impact.

Bonham Carter's interests ranged wide. She was a fervent believer in the League of Nations, and was a member of the League of Nations Union until 1941. Alongside her father, the other dominant political figure in her life was Winston Churchill, whom she first met when she was 18. Despite occasional differences of opinion, pursued vigorously on both sides, they remained devoted friends throughout their lives. She was an early and active supporter of Churchill's anti-appeasement campaign, being passionately anti-Nazi. In 1933 she vigorously attacked Franz von Papen for the deal he brokered with Adolf Hitler which led to the Nazi leader's appointment as Chancellor. After the war she embraced the European ideal, and in 1947 became vice-chairman of the United Europe Movement. She was an annual member of the Königswinter Conference, her fluency in German as well as her character ensuring active participation.

She was a governor of the BBC from 1941–46, a role she relished. Subsequently she was a frequent broadcaster on both radio and television. She was also a member of the Royal Commission on the Press (1947–49), a governor of the Old Vic from 1945, and a trustee of the Glyndebourne Arts Trust from 1955. In 1953 she was appointed DBE.

She was a great orator; her first reported speech was in 1909 when she was 22, and she continued until her death 60 years later to speak up for the creed she believed to be the only embodiment of political morality, Liberalism. In 1963 she became the first woman to give the Romanes lecture at Oxford. She spoke on 'the impact of personality on politics' – a subject of which she had such first-hand knowledge. In 1915 she married Maurice Bonham Carter, her father's principal private secretary, and they had two daughters and two sons. She died in London on 19 February 1969.

During her lifetime Bonham Carter only wrote one book: *Winston Churchill as I Knew Him* chronicled their relationship and shared experiences, and was published in 1965. Since her death two volumes of her letters and diaries have been published: *Lantern Slides, The Diaries and Letters of Violet Bonham Carter 1904–14* (Mark Bonham Carter and Mark Pottle, eds., 1995) and *Champion Redoubtable, The Diaries and Letters of Violet Bonham Carter 1914–45* (Mark Pottle, ed., 1998).

Jane Bonham Carter

Sir Archibald Sinclair

Viscount Thurso

born 22 October 1980, *died* 15 June 1970

Archibald Sinclair was the Liberal leader from 1935 to 1945. He was a leading figure in British politics in that period, first as an outspoken critic of appeasement, and then as a minister during the war. For Liberals, his importance lay in his belief in the possibility of a Liberal revival, which was crucial in helping the party to survive the challenges of the 1930s and 1940s.

Archibald Henry Macdonald Sinclair, fourth Baronet and first Viscount Thurso of Ulbster, was born in London on 22 October 1890. Educated at Eton, he attended Sandhurst, and became a regular soldier in 1910 with the 2nd Life Guards. Serving with distinction on the Western Front throughout the First World War, he was Winston Churchill's second-in-command with the 6th Royal Scots Fusiliers from January to May 1916, and ended the war as a major in the Guards Machine-Gun Regiment. In 1919–21, he was Churchill's personal military secretary at the War Office, and was then his private secretary at the Colonial Office until 1922. At the 1922 general election, Sinclair successfully stood as a pro-Lloyd George 'National Liberal' in Caithness & Sutherland. In each election until 1945 (when he lost the seat), and in 1950, he stood as a Liberal.

Sinclair soon became a prominent figure on the opposition benches, assisting Lloyd George with revisions of Liberal policy from the mid-1920s. He was a founder member of the Land Committee, and chaired its Scottish equivalent, which wrote the Liberal 'Tartan Book' proposing Scottish devolution. In November 1930, he became Liberal Chief Whip in the House of Commons, making the maintenance of party discipline and unity his highest priority. In 1931 he took part (with Lloyd George, Samuel and Lothian) in talks with the Labour leadership over various areas of shared interest. This meant that he was an obvious choice as one of the Liberal ministers in the National Government from August 1931, when he ceased to be Chief Whip.

Sinclair served as Secretary of State for Scotland from August 1931 to September 1932, with cabinet rank from November 1931. The main battle for the Liberals in the National Government was for free trade, and after agreeing to differ with their Labour and Conservative colleagues over minor tariffs in January 1932, the Liberals eventually resigned from the Government in September 1932, when extensive tariffs were introduced under the Ottawa Agreements. Samuel had replaced Lloyd George as Liberal Leader after the 1931 general election and, when Samuel lost his seat in the November 1935 election, Sinclair replaced him.

From then until 1939, Sinclair's leadership was marked by two themes. Firstly, he was a resolute proponent of Liberal independence, vigorously pushing the Liberal viewpoint in Parliament and throughout the country, persistently believing that the Liberal Party was about to make an electoral breakthrough. Secondly, Sinclair opposed appeasement, wanting instead to pursue a policy of 'collective security'. This involved developing the League of Nations' ability to remedy just grievances, while at the same time rearming so that League members could resist aggression. He accepted that Germany and the other expansionist powers had legitimate complaints, but he wanted them dealt with from a position of strength and through international negotiations, rather than by the Government's piecemeal concessions to the dictators. Sinclair cooperated with members of all parties in support of the League, including Churchill and Attlee, through the 'Arms and the Covenant' movement. However, their message was often at odds with what most British people wanted to hear, and Sinclair and the other anti-appeasers were constantly denounced as 'warmongers'.

When war broke out in September 1939, Sinclair was invited to join the government by Neville Chamberlain, but he demurred. However, when a broad coalition government was constructed under Churchill in

May 1940, Sinclair accepted the post of Secretary of State for Air, holding the post until the coalition broke up in May 1945. Sinclair did not gain a War Cabinet seat, but Churchill agreed to consult him on general issues and principles. Sinclair's influence within the Government was questionable and even at the Air Ministry he was weakened by Churchill taking a prominent role in decision-making himself, but Sinclair was important in supporting Arthur 'Bomber' Harris's strategic bombing of Germany. Sinclair believed that it was an effective way of destroying Germany's war effort and morale and maintained that targets were industrial rather than residential.

Party campaigns were effectively suspended on the outbreak of war, and Sinclair strongly believed that military victory was the main priority. This meant, for example, that he did not campaign vigorously for the Beveridge Report, which had provoked much enthusiasm within the Liberal Party and the country, but was put aside until after the war by the coalition government. After pressure from party members he did commit the Party to contest the post-war general election as an independent entity, but he personally favoured the continuation of coalition long after the war. With the war in Europe won, the general election took place in July 1945, and the Liberals did poorly, winning only 12 seats. Sinclair himself lost his seat, and was replaced as leader by Clement Davies. The change was intended to be temporary following a rash promise by Sinclair's Conservative opponent to resign his seat in Sinclair's favour if he won. Needless to say, the promise went unfulfilled.

Sinclair again stood unsuccessfully for Parliament in 1950 and after the 1951 election there were rumours that Churchill wished to bring him into his cabinet. When Sinclair became Viscount Thurso in 1952, it was intended that he would lead the Liberals in the House of Lords, but a stroke prevented him from taking an active part there until 1954. Outside Liberal politics, Sinclair was Lord Lieutenant of Caithness (1919–64); Lord Rector of Glasgow University (1938–45); President of the Air League of the British Empire (1956–58); and a member of the Political Honours Scrutiny Committee (1954–61).

A second stroke, in 1959, meant that he was severely debilitated in his last years, and he died on 15 June 1970 at his home in Twickenham. Sinclair had become fourth Baronet of Ulbster in 1912, a Companion of the Order of St Michael and St George in 1922, and a Knight of the Order of the Thistle in 1941. He married Marigold Forbes (died 1975) in 1918; they had two sons (Robin and Angus) and two daughters (Catherine and Elizabeth). Sinclair wrote no books or memoirs, although a number of his speeches were published as pamphlets. There is one short biography: Gerard J. De Groot, *Liberal Crusader: The Life of Sir Archibald Sinclair* (1992).

Richard Grayson

Tom Driberg

Lord Bradwell

born 22 May 1905, **died** 12 August 1976

Thomas Edward Neil Driberg never held ministerial office, blaming 'deeply prejudiced puritans' such as Attlee and Wilson for barring him because of his homosexuality. He was however a leading figure of the Labour left in the 1940s and '50s, he held the chairmanship of the party in 1957–58 and prior to entering parliament he was a well-known journalist for the *Daily Express*.

He also has the reputation of being one of the more colourful and outrageous Labour MPs, mainly due to his frank autobiography *Ruling Passions*, which was published posthumously in 1977. In it he described the three main passions of his life: promiscuous homosexual sex, left-wing politics and religion (he was a High Churchman and liturgist).

Born in Crowborough, Sussex on 22 May 1905 to elderly parents, he was the youngest of three brothers, though being the youngest by 15 years, he was very much a solitary child. His father, John James Steet Driberg, a retired Indian civil servant, was already 65 when he was born and his mother, Amy Mary Irving Bell, later told him he was meant to be a girl to keep her company in old age.

He was educated at the Grange School in Crowborough and then Lancing, where his contemporaries included author Evelyn Waugh and John Trevalyan, later the chairman of the British Board of Film Censors. Whilst at school his ruling passions began to emerge. Whilst the interest in religion and left wing politics caused amusement and embarrassment to friends and family, his sexual desires resulted in his expulsion from Lancing during his final term, after making advances to younger boys.

Thanks to private tuition he was awarded a scholarship to Christ Church, Oxford, where he led a decadent lifestyle, living way beyond the means of his monthly allowance. He made the most of his time at Oxford, making contacts and establishing friendships which would stand him in good stead later on in life. He mixed with people as diverse as Aleister Crowley, the Sitwells, Gertrude Stein and W. H. Auden.

He left university without a degree in 1927 and spent time living rough in London, earning money as a street artist before finding work in an all-night café in Soho. In spite of this lowlife existence, he later cited this period as one of the happiest times of his life. He maintained contacts with his Oxford friends, and one of them, Edith Sitwell, who was an admirer of his poetry, was horrified at his predicament. She stepped in to rescue him from the Soho low life by arranging a job for him on the *Daily Express*.

This was to be a major break in Driberg's life. After an initial trial period, he became a permanent reporter on the staff of the paper and remained on the *Express* for the next 15 years, by which time his national reputation as author of the William Hickey column helped him to be elected to Parliament.

His widely read column, entitled 'These Names Make News', focused on gossip from London society; however, it also enabled him to cover great events like the coronation of Pope Pius XII in 1939 and the Spanish Civil War.

In spite of his contacts with the Establishment, he was unable to prevent prosecution for indecency in 1935, following an incident in his 'not quite double' bed with two unemployed Scottish miners. He was able, however, to keep the case out of the newspapers with the assistance of *Express* proprietor Lord Beaverbrook. He attributed his acquittal to one of his character witnesses, Lord Sysonby, whose address at St James Palace had a considerable effect on the minds of the jury. One of the policemen investigating the charges came up to Driberg shortly before the trial and said 'why didn't you tell us who you were?' Driberg would not make the same mistake again.

He was first elected to Parliament as the Independent member for Maldon in a by-election in 1942. He retained the seat as a Labour member in 1945, 1950 and 1951. In 1959 he was elected MP for Barking, a seat he held until he retired from Parliament in February 1974. In Parliament, Driberg was a prominent MP on the Left and a close ally of Nye Bevan in the Labour Party's internecine warfare of the 1950s. He was first elected to Labour's NEC in 1948 and remained a member until 1972.

His interests in Parliament were typically left wing Labour, though he had strong connections to the anti-colonial movement and played a prominent role in the campaign for Burmese independence. To the surprise of many, including himself, he never held ministerial office. Whether this was due to his sexual exploits, his extreme left wing politics or alleged spying for the KGB is uncertain. The Establishment protected Driberg, but they did not trust him.

He remained a prolific writer and journalist throughout his life, writing a weekly column for *Reynolds News*, later the *Sunday Citizen*, until 1967. He wrote biographies of Lord Beaverbrook, art critic Hannan Swaffer and spy Guy Burgess, as well as an in-depth study of the moral rearmament movement. His failure to attain ministerial office excludes him from the ranks of the great Labour politicians of the twentieth century, but as an author and personality and as a prominent left wing backbencher, he has a place in any history of the Labour Party. Created Lord Bradwell in January 1976, he died of heart failure in a London cab near Bayswater on 12 August 1976. He had married Mrs Ena Binfield in 1951, a Fabian friend of John Freeman and George Strauss who already had a son by another man, but even on their honeymoon (to a Brighton hotel) Driberg had sought to ensure they slept in separate rooms. 'She broke her marriage vows! She tried to sleep with me!' he complained to friends. They had lived apart since 1971 and she died in 1977.

Driberg's own autobiography *Ruling Passions* (1977) and Francis Wheen's biography *Tom Driberg: His Life and Indiscretions* (1990) are the key works on his life and both provide excellent anecdotes for dinner parties. He was also the subject of a play, *Tom and Clem*, which ran at the Aldwych Theatre between April and July 1997. His own works include *Guy Burgess: A Portrait* (1960), *Swaff: The life and times of Hannan Swaffer* (1963) and *Beaverbrook: A study of Frustration and Power* (1956).

Colin Dingwall

Anthony Crosland

born 29 August 1918, *died* 19 February 1977

At the age of 22, Charles Anthony Raven Crosland confidently predicted he would achieve for the Labour Party what Edward Bernstein had done for the German SPD. By the end of his life, he arguably deserved this title, having written the most important revisionist book of the century, *The Future of Socialism*, and by setting out a new vision for socialism, economic growth and equality of opportunity which provided the backdrop for successive post-war Labour governments. His intellectual legacy even stretches to the Blair Government that came to office 20 years after his death. Crosland also achieved a significant status as a formidable Labour politician. A close friend of Labour leader Hugh Gaitskell, he build a reputation as a leading reformer, particularly as Secretary of State for Education and for Environment, and as Foreign Secretary in Callaghan's government, he was widely tipped as a possible future Prime Minister.

Yet Crosland's life remains fascinating as much for its failures as for its successes. As perhaps the leading intellectual of his generation, Crosland never achieved the office of Chancellor of the Exchequer that undoubtedly would have provided the greatest test of his skills. Whilst an inspirational figure, his peers on the revisionist wing of the party looked more to his rival Roy Jenkins for leadership than to him. Ultimately, even Crosland's revisionist agenda was brought into doubt. By 1977, the Labour Government of which he was a leading member had been forced to abandon the key elements of the post-war economic consensus which Crosland had cherished. The debate about the merits of revisionism was one which was to continue long after its key exponent had departed.

Charles Anthony Raven Crosland was born on 29 August 1918 at St Leonards-on-Sea. His father Joseph Crosland was an important civil servant in the War Office and his mother Jessie was a college lecturer. Anthony lived with his two sisters at the family home in Golders Green and then Highgate, and enjoyed the relative luxury of a middle-class upbringing.

The most distinctive feature of Crosland's childhood was the family's religious beliefs, which deeply affected his life. The family had for many generations belonged to the Plymouth Brethren, a nonconformist sect with distinctive views about acceptable lifestyles. Taboos included smoking, the theatre and even voting in elections. Crosland certainly drew much from his parents' religious fervour, including a fundamental belief in equality which was to underpin his whole life, but he also developed a passion for attacking shibboleths and puritanical views within the Labour movement which were also derived from this strict upbringing.

He was educated at a private school in Highgate and, on winning a scholarship, at Trinity College, Oxford, which he entered in 1937. Pre-war Oxford provided an atmosphere in which Crosland's political beliefs flourished. The Labour Club, whose large membership included the Marxist sympathiser Denis Healey and Roy Jenkins, was the focal point for his political development, until disagreements over Russia's role in the Second World War led Crosland to form a breakaway 'democratic socialist' club in 1941. In future years, this organisation was to provide a useful forum in which Crosland could meet the Labour Party's leading politicians, many of whom, like Hugh Dalton, were to prove invaluable allies.

After the conclusion of the war, in which Crosland saw active service as a member of the Royal Welsh Parachute Regiment, he returned to Oxford to finish his studies, gaining a first in PPE in 1946. He was soon appointed a Fellow of Trinity College where he taught economics to undergraduates, but Crosland's focus had already turned to Westminster.

His parliamentary career was not without its highs and lows. With the assistance of Dalton, Crosland was elected as MP for South Gloucestershire in 1950, winning a 6,000 majority and retaining the seat a year later, despite the defeat of the Labour Government. But with the boundaries redrawn before the 1955 election, Crosland unwisely moved constituencies and was defeated in Southampton Test. It was not until 1959 that Crosland was returned to Parliament, this time for Grimsby and, after a recount, only by 101 votes. Crosland went on to strengthen Labour's hold on Grimsby and he successfully defended the seat on five successive occasions.

His time out of Parliament in the 1950s was not wasted, however. Indeed, during this period Crosland brought together the many articles and essays he had written over the preceeding years into one work of distinctive and original political analysis. *The Future of Socialism*, published in 1956, was a forceful account of the reasons why Labour needed to change its political and economic approach. Traditional capitalism had changed, he argued, and therefore the levers of traditional socialism, primarily nationalisation, were no longer necessary. Instead

Crosland focused on the remaining pillars of socialism, which he argued were equality of opportunity and the abolition of class divisions. Crosland argued that the increase in public spending necessary to deliver the measures of equality of opportunity was to be paid, not through increased taxation, but through continued economic growth which, writing during the 'long boom' of the 1950s, he was confident would be easy to achieve.

The Future of Socialism was Crosland's greatest work and it helped to shift the political argument within Labour's ranks. Following the achievements of Labour's 1945–51 Governments, the Party appeared to split into the traditional left, who wanted a 'shopping list' of nationalisations, and the old right, who believed socialism was 'what a Labour Government does'. Both groups represented, in the words of Crosland's 1962 book, *A Conservative Enemy* within the Labour Party. In contrast, Crosland offered a revisionist approach which set out a radical course for Labour in a new age. His socialism was still about equality, but the means to deliver equality was now education and improved social and cultural life, not public ownership.

His revisionist works helped to increase his reputation as a formidable intellectual with the Labour Party. However his brash, often arrogant, personality and the small amount of time he spent in Westminster meant that Crosland appeared distant to many parliamentary colleagues. In addition, while he was a loyal supporter of Gaitskell, he made little effort to provide a lead for the revisionist wing of the centre left – notwithstanding his role in the creation of the Campaign for Democratic Socialism in 1960. Both points were to prove extremely significant when Crosland's key supporter, the Labour leader Hugh Gaitskell, died suddenly in 1963 and was replaced by Harold Wilson.

Following the Labour victory in 1964, Crosland gained ministerial office, first at the Department of Economic Affairs and then in 1965 as Secretary of State for Education. It was in this post that Crosland most clearly displayed his clear thinking and forceful leadership within government, notably developing a comprehensive education system which ended the iniquitous 11–plus for thousands of children. It was

Crosland's Woolwich speech of April 1965 that enshrined the 'binary principle', whereby technical colleges would not become universities but would be expanded under local authority control into a planned 30 polytechnics. He was moved to the Board of Trade in August 1967, then again to the Department of Local Government and Regional Planning in 1969, a department that, renamed Environment, he continued to shadow in Opposition (1970–74), returning to government as Secretary of State for the Environment (1974–76).

But throughout this time, Crosland never won real favour with Wilson, particularly as he refused to stop mentioning 'the unmentionable' question of devaluation within Cabinet. The post of Chancellor, which he saw as his immediate objective, remained frustratingly elusive. In addition, Crosland also lost ground with Wilson's enemies, with the mantle of revisionist leader passing to Roy Jenkins. This was reinforced in the early 1970s, as the issue of Europe became more critical within Labour's ranks. Crosland's view was a pragmatic one, based on a need for Party loyalty, and he failed to support the pro-Europeans in the Tory lobby on the debate on the Common Market in 1971, a matter they were not to forget. This was evident first when he stood for the Deputy Leadership in 1972, coming third behind Ted Short and Michael Foot. Jenkins' supporters had still not forgiven him in 1976 when Wilson resigned and Crosland stood unsuccessfully for the leadership, winning only 17 votes.

With his old friend Jim Callaghan winning the leadership, Crosland was rewarded with the post of Foreign Secretary. This meant that he was a leading member of the Labour Cabinet that was forced to agree huge cuts in public expenditure to meet the terms of the IMF loan negotiated in 1976. For Crosland this struck at the heart of his whole analysis. The consensus about economics, the welfare state and the nature of capitalism established in the aftermath of the Second World War was disintegrating. Although when he said 'the party's over' to local authority leaders in 1975 he meant it in a different context, these words were understood as the demise of Crosland's own agenda. David Marquand, a close friend of Crosland, has argued that it is no co-incidence that within weeks of the Cabinet decision, Crosland suffered a massive stroke. He died in Oxford on 19 February 1977.

Crosland's legacy is much debated. Certainly his optimism in the 1950s in the rate of economic growth being sufficient to deliver real measures of equality of opportunity was overstated. This led some critics to abandon his whole approach and to return to public ownership as a solution. But it is significant that key members of the 1997 Labour Government, most notably Chancellor Gordon Brown, have sought to show how Crosland's approach remains enduring. Moreover, Crosland offered more than a political programme: he also offered a new way of understanding socialism. His radical agenda was a synthesis of left and right, and helped to inspire a generation to look beyond the achievements of the Attlee Governments. And for those today who still believe socialism has a future, Crosland's work remains an essential signpost for the way ahead.

Crosland was married twice, first to Hilary Sarson in 1952, which lasted less than a year before they separated, and then to Susan Catling, a journalist, in 1964. His personal life reflected his dearly held libertarian views: he once argued that under socialism many people – including him – would be perfectly happy with 'sex, gin and Bogart'. This passion for freedoms also reflected a rejection both of the Brethren that he had grown up with and the puritanical Fabianism which valued a 'good filing system' above pleasure and enjoyment.

Matt Carter

Norah Runge

born 1884, *died* 6 June 1978

The general election of 1931, which produced the most lopsided House of Commons in modern history, saw some unusual results and the

130–vote Conservative victory in Rotherhithe was certainly one of them.

The winner, Norah Runge, was a formidable worker and campaigner and retained her interest in Rotherhithe until her death, aged 93. Born in 1884 and educated privately, she married J. J. Runge, a sugar broker, in 1906. It was the sugar connection that drew her to Rotherhithe, as her husband was Managing Director of Tate and Lyle – which was a key employer in Bermondsey. Norah Runge was someone who had been taught and believed in public service. During the First World War she was Superintendent of the Soldiers and Sailors free buffet at Paddington Station, serving some eight million meals. For these efforts she was amongst the first recipients of the OBE . She also developed empathy for people of a very different class to her own.

Although living in Westminster, the family retained a close interest in Bermondsey and were patrons of the local Conservative Party. It was this patronage that helped secure the Rotherhithe seat for Norah Runge in the extraordinary election, which resulted in the return of Ramsay MacDonald as Head of the National Government. The Labour MP for Rotherhithe was Ben Smith, a Labour whip, docker's leader and top official with the Transport Workers Union, who went into opposition with Labour on the formation of the National Government.

Norah Runge employed a talented agent, opened a local headquarters (called Runge Hall) and attacked the Labour Party for the economic collapse and looked forward 'to seeing the docks and wharves of Rotherhithe busy to their utmost.' Her victory came after three recounts. One of the other surprise women victors on that October night, Mavis Tate in Willesden West, was also connected to the sugar industry.

Norah Runge threw herself into parliamentary affairs, whilst taking a keen interest in the needs of the constituency. Questions were tabled about the river and the docks and her maiden speech was in a debate calling for local councils to be permitted to grant cinemas licences to open on Sundays, She spoke with understanding of the crowded homes and large families prevalent in Rotherhithe, and was congratulated in the debate by George Lansbury, the Labour leader who commented on the similarities between his constituency and Rotherhithe and how well Mrs Runge had managed to convey this. It is surprising how controversial this proposal was and Norah Runge was quite dismissive of some of her colleagues, particularly with one who suggested that if people wished entertainment 'they could play bridge.' Norah Runge spelt out that Bridge was not exactly the most popular game in Rotherhithe!

She became what would now be called 'a good constituency MP', attending local events as well as speaking on matters that interested her constituents. On other occasions she spoke on greyhound racing and of her personal thrill when one of her dogs won. She became known as 'the White Lady' for the Christmas gifts that she distributed each year to poor families. In one of her last interventions in Parliament she called for streets in poor areas to be kept clear of traffic at designated times to allow children to play in safety.

However, Labour were determined to avenge their 1931 defeat in the 1935 election, where with Baldwin re-instated as Prime Minister the pretension of a National Government was looking decidedly shaky. Ben Smith had been re-selected and made an Alderman of Bermondsey Council to ensure that he had an appropriate platform for his campaigning. Mrs Runge was to complain about 'personal attacks' and her supporters wrote letters of support to the local paper about her charitable work. She also complained about Bermondsey Council 'politicising school governors'. In November 1935, Labour regained Rotherhithe. This was not, however, the end of Norah Runge by a long way.

In 1937 she stood as Municipal Reform Candidate in Rotherhithe for the LCC, polling a respectable vote, but again losing to Labour. Following the election she was put to the Aldermanic bench of the LCC and was to remain at County Hall for the next 24 years, retiring in 1961.

Her interest in Rotherhithe remained and the weddings of both her children were held locally, with receptions at Rotherhithe Town Hall and an overflow 'for ordinary folk' at the Runge Hall. During the 1960s Runge Hall became famed for weekly dances organised by the Bermondsey

Young Conservatives, which as a result of the dances had a membership completely at odds with local electoral support for the Party locally.

During the Second World War she again threw herself into charitable work and organised food parcels for allied prisoners of war and fought Rotherhithe in 1945, losing heavily to Sir Ben Smith who had been Minister Resident in Washington. Sir Ben retired in 1946, having been appointed Chairman of the West Midlands Coal Board and Norah Runge, by then aged 62, and twice widowed, hoped to fight the by-election. The local Party was determined to have 'a younger man' and chose Freddie Burden who went on to drop to third place in the poll and lose his deposit. The defeat, his third, did not affect Freddie Burden's career as he was elected for Gillingham in 1950, serving for 33 years. The winner of the by-election was another docker – Bob Mellish.

Norah Runge's family did have electoral success in 1945 as her son-in-law, Niall Macpherson, was returned as MP for Dumfries and was to serve in the Commons until 1963, when he was elevated to the peerage. He held office under four Prime Ministers.

During the Labour Government, the Runge family were at the forefront of the campaign against further Nationalisation and Peter Runge, her son (who was later to be a founder of the CBI), was the brain behind the 'Mr Cube' campaign against sugar nationalisation. Despite her political activities, she was also vice chairman of the London Conservative Union, and the Labour Government appointed her to the Chair of a Hospital Management Committee in 1948.

Upon retiring from the LCC, aged 77, Norah Runge started a new career, opening an antique shop in Kings Road, Chelsea. Interviewed behind the counter for her ninetieth birthday she suggested that antique 'was something over 100 years old.'

In 1977, during the Queen's Silver Jubilee, she returned to Rotherhithe to present Silver Jubilee Crowns to local children and was remembered affectionately as 'Old Mother Runge' – whilst mentioning that her first husband had proposed to her after singing 'Old King Cole' on New Years Eve 1905.

She died in 1978, aged 93, casting her last parliamentary vote for Peter Brooke in the 1977 Westminster South by-election. Her son, Sir Peter Runge, had predeceased her, but her grandson retained the family interest in the sugar industry.

Reading her maiden speech again, one is very aware how she, as a woman, understood problems that concerned the people of Rotherhithe. For dockers' wives, Sunday must have been difficult, no work in the docks, men paid on Saturday and pubs open until Sunday lunchtime. Sunday cinema for the family, and this was in an era when over 90 per cent of the population went to the cinema at least once a week, may have been a salvation from something far less pleasant in many of the crowded and poor homes.

Norah Runge could easily have been part of one of the 'fashionable sets' of the 1920s instead she dedicated herself to public service. Had she been born later or less devoted to Rotherhithe, then her political career might well have made her far better known.

Peter Golds

Sir Dingle Foot

born 24 August 1905, **died** 18 June 1978

Throughout Britain, particular constituencies and cities have had a long connection with certain families – for instance, the Chamberlains in Birmingham and the Cecils in south Dorset. In Plymouth, politics has been dominated by the Foot family, principally Isaac Foot but also four of his five sons. These include Hugh (later Lord Caradon), John, and the former Labour Party leader, Michael. The eldest, Dingle, had the unique distinction for the Foots of being elected to the House of Commons for both the Liberal and Labour parties. Yet despite his changing party, he never really embraced socialism; he began his political life as a Liberal, and, to quote Simon Hoggart, 'there his heart remained.'

Dingle Mackintosh Foot was born in Plymouth on 24 August 1905, the son of Isaac Foot and his wife Eva, née Mackintosh. He was educated at Bembridge School, Isle of Wight; Balliol College, Oxford (where he obtained a second in modern history); and Gray's Inn, where he was called to the bar in 1930. Whilst at Oxford, he was President of both the Liberal Club (1927) and the Union (1928). It did not take him long to transfer his political skills to the House of Commons. Although he lost his first parliamentary contest (to the Conservative candidate in Tiverton in 1929), he was elected in Dundee in 1931, and again in 1935. In 1940, Winston Churchill appointed him parliamentary secretary to the Ministry of Economic Warfare, where his role in the furtherance of the blockade of Germany and the Axis powers was vital, being sent on important missions to Washington and Switzerland. In 1945 he was part of the British delegation to the San Francisco conference which framed the United Nations' charter. However, his career was cut short in the 1945 general election, when he lost his seat, although in becoming Vice-President of the Liberal Party the following year he remained politically prominent. But he was unable to return to Parliament, coming a close second to the Conservatives in Cornwall North in 1950, and a more distant second in the same seat the following year.

Foot opposed closer links between the Liberals and the Conservatives at a national level, although the two parties cooperated in Dundee to ensure that only one candidate from each party fought Labour for the two-member seat. A 'Samuelite' rather than a 'Simonite' in the 1930s, Foot felt that the both the Conservatives and Labour had put administrative expediency before civil liberties. He perceived a drift to the right by the Liberal Party under Clement Davies' leadership, and did not seek re-nomination as a party Vice-President in 1954, claiming to be 'out of sympathy with its present policy.' A close political ally of Lady Megan Lloyd George, he followed her into the Labour Party in 1956. He felt this was his only way of maintaining political influence, and he (unsuccessfully) urged his brother John to defect too. He soon re-entered Parliament, winning the Ipswich by-election in 1957, and defending the seat successfully in 1959, 1964 and 1966. He lost it by only 13 votes in 1970.

In 1964 he was appointed Solicitor-General in Harold Wilson's first administration, reluctantly accepting the knighthood which went with it. He resigned in 1967, shortly after becoming a member of the Privy Council, to avoid condoning government policy on Rhodesia; he urged that Britain must not rule out 'police action', if necessary, since the guerrillas could not afford to lose the struggle. His 1970 election address, condemning Labour's manifesto commitments on immigration restrictions, may have contributed to his defeat.

Human rights provided the stimulus for much of Foot's legal work throughout the world. He appeared as counsel in Basutoland, Kenya, Ghana and Nigeria, defending Jomo Kenyatta and Hastings Banda amongst others. His relationship with Nigeria proved problematic – he was expelled from there in 1962 while challenging the validity of the Emergency Powers Act on behalf of the western Nigerian premier, Alhaji D. S. Adegbenro, and as a result was refused entry the following year to defend Chief Enahoro on treason charges. Much of his most distinguished legal work took place when he was out of office, or, indeed, Parliament; he became a bencher of Gray's Inn in 1952 and treasurer in 1968, having become a QC in 1954. He continued to practise after 1970, and he died during a case in Hong Kong on 18 June 1978.

Foot's views were strongly based around his beliefs in social justice, civil liberties and racial equality, underpinned by the scrutiny of Parliament over the executive and the rule of law. In this respect he remained a liberal even when he joined Labour; indeed, in 1974, he wrote that Labour had become the party of human rights in a way which it had not been in the 1930s. Although internationalist in outlook, as his legal career suggests, he opposed British membership of the EEC, and voted down the Labour government's proposals for reform of the House of Lords in 1968 on the grounds that it would enhance the government's powers of patronage. However, he was in favour of electoral reform.

His one book, *British Political Crises* (1976), mostly concerned Liberal Party disunity in the early twentieth century, which he described as 'the principal tragedy of British politics in modern times.'

He married Dorothy Mary Elliston in 1933; her social style contrasted with Foot's Methodist background and she was nicknamed within the family as 'Dingle's Tory wife'. They had a long and happy marriage. There were no children.

Aidan Thomson

Frank Owen

born 4 October 1905, *died* 23 January 1979

At the 1997 general election Paul Keetch took Hereford for the Liberal Democrats, thus regaining a seat last won for the Liberals by Frank Owen in 1929. Attracted to the Liberal Party by the fiery radicalism of David Lloyd George, Owen was elected at the age of 23, and went on to a distinguished career as a journalist, editing both the *Evening Standard* and the *Daily Mail* before returning to contest the Hereford seat again in the 1950s. Owen's brilliant, ambitious mind and independent spirit repeatedly made life uncomfortable for many of those he worked with, whether in politics or journalism.

Humphrey Frank Owen was born on 4 October 1905 at the 'Black Swan' public house, then owned by his parents, on Widemarsh Street in Hereford. Owen won a scholarship to Monmouth Grammar School and followed this with a further scholarship to study history at Sidney Sussex College, Cambridge. He graduated with a first class degree in 1927, having represented his college at both rowing and rugby.

Returning to Hereford, Owen secured a job on the *South Wales Argus*, a paper with well-established Liberal sympathies. He threw himself into promoting the cause of the party in the Welsh Marches and in 1928 accepted a researcher's job with Lloyd George. Six weeks before the 1929 general election the Liberal candidate in Hereford (a traditionally Tory seat) stood down due to ill health. Owen was persuaded to take his place, and in a barnstorming campaign took the seat with a majority of just over 1,000 to become the youngest MP in the Commons. His time in Parliament was short-lived, however. At the 1931 election he stood as one of a small band of Lloyd George Liberals opposed to the National Government, in contrast to the Liberal factions led by Sir John Simon and Herbert Samuel. The Tories regained Hereford; Owen was later famously to comment: 'In 1929 the wise, far-seeing electors of my native Hereford sent me to Westminster and two years later in 1931 the lousy bastards kicked me out.'

Owen returned to journalism and rapidly came to the attention of Lord Beaverbrook as a leader writer on the *Daily Express*. Indeed, it was Beaverbrook who introduced Owen to Grace McGillvray, a Bostonian, who Owen married in 1939. In 1938 he became editor of the *Evening Standard* (another Beaverbrook paper), although his outspoken criticism of the policy of appeasement sat uneasily with the opinions of his employer. These arguments were most forcefully advanced in the best-selling pamphlet *Guilty Men,* which Owen co-authored with Michael Foot (then assistant editor at the *Standard*) and Peter Howard in 1938.

When Britain entered the war in 1939, Owen's energies were channelled in a less subversive direction as editor of *South East Asia Command*, the official paper of the army in the Far East. Even in this role his direct, uncompromising style occasionally made life difficult for his superiors. Lord Mountbatten was, however, sufficiently impressed to commission Owen to write the official history of the campaign, *The Campaign in Burma* (HMSO, 1946). Owen ended the war as a Lieutenant-Colonel and was awarded the OBE for his efforts at SEAC.

After the war Owen went to work for the other great press baron of the period, Lord Rothermere, as editor of the *Daily Mail*, but by 1950 he had returned to Beaverbrook's *Express* as a columnist. In 1954, Owen produced *Tempestuous Journey*, his well-known biography of Lloyd George based on the huge collection of Lloyd George papers recently acquired by Beaverbrook.

Owen returned to active politics at the 1955 general election, finishing second to the Conservatives in Hereford, 1,000 votes ahead of the Labour candidate. In 1956 Owen got another chance to contest the seat when the sitting Tory MP, J. P. L. Thomas, was elevated to the Lords, provoking a by-election. The campaign was closely fought by the Liberal Party on the slogan 'Hereford's Son: Second to None', with visits from senior party figures including Jo Grimond, Jeremy Thorpe and Edwin Mallindine. In spite of a significant increase in the Liberal vote, Owen failed to win the seat by 2,000 votes and in 1958 announced he would not stand again. He was succeeded as candidate by Robin Day.

The 1956 by-election was Owen's last foray onto the political scene. He continued to write (including a biography of Colonel Peron and an account of the fall of Singapore) and worked for a time as a television journalist, interviewing Nasser at the time of the Suez crisis, but he was not to regain the national prominence of his newspaper career. His wife, Grace, died in 1968, and Owen himself died on 23 January 1979 in the Worthing Rest Home where he had been living with his sister; he had no children. Gron Williams published a biography, *Firebrand: The Frank Owen Story*, in 1993.

Richard Kirby

Sir Oswald Mosley

born 16 November 1896, *died* 3 December 1980

There are not many politicians in the twentieth century whose lives have been sufficiently eventful and interesting to justify being immortalised in a film or television dramatisation. One thinks of productions such as *Young Winston* or *The Life and Times of David Lloyd George*. Yet in 1998 these rare examples were joined by a four-part drama about Oswald Mosley, entitled *Mosley*. Such a programme serves as testament to the enduring fascination of the tragic and still debated story of Mosley's life.

Oswald Ernest Mosley, the eldest of the three sons of the fifth baronet Sir Oswald Mosley, was born on 16 November 1896 at 47 Hill Street, Mayfair. Aged five, his parents separated and he went with his mother Katherine to live in Shropshire. After West Down private school and Winchester, he attended Sandhurst for the first six months of 1914, was rusticated in June but recalled there at the outbreak of the First World War in August and commissioned into the 16th Lancers in October. In December he transferred to the 6th Squadron, Royal Flying Corps, and from December 1914 until April 1915 was an observer. Trying to obtain his pilot's licence back in England, he managed to break his ankle, leaving him with a permanent limp. After a brief time in the trenches with the 16th Lancers his injury invalided him out of the army and he spent the rest of the war in Whitehall, at the Ministry of Munitions and the Foreign Office.

This proximity to the senior levels of government introduced him to a number of politicians through whom he was able to procure the Conservative candidacy for the Harrow constituency, winning it at the 1918 general election. He further cemented his place in the Establishment by marrying Lady Cynthia Blanche, daughter of Lord Curzon, on 11 May 1920.

Following the war, his self-perception was as part of the vanguard of a new generation of younger politicians seeking to break free of the normal boundaries of political parties and thinking. After making a number of critical speeches in late 1920 attacking excessive military expenditure and the operation of the 'Black and Tans' in Ireland, he became an independent, and was bolstered by backing from his local party. But by 1922 they were demanding assurances of party loyalty

Mosley was not prepared to give and they selected a new candidate; Mosley was however re-elected in that year's general election with a large majority, defeating an official Conservative candidate.

In many ways Mosley personified the flux being experienced by the British party system in the early 1920s and which laid the foundations of the essentially 'two and half' party system which has endured since then. He retained Harrow in 1923 with a reduced majority, which signalled to him that he would need some sort of party base if he were to survive. After initial flirtation with the Liberals, he soon saw the way the wind was blowing and joined the Labour Party in March 1924, a couple of months after its first government was formed by Ramsay MacDonald, who described Mosley that year as 'one of the greatest and most hopeful figures' in politics. In the next general election in 1924 Mosley came within 77 votes of defeating Neville Chamberlain at Birmingham Ladywood, and returned to the Commons in the December 1926 Smethwick by-election.

Whilst out of the Commons he evolved his economic thinking along Keynesian lines. He gained support on the left during the General Strike and with his combination of self-confidence, arrogance and ambition was already being tipped as a future Labour leader.

In 1928 he succeeded to his father's baronetcy and the following year was returned for Smethwick, an election in which Cynthia was also elected as MP for Stoke-on-Trent. In the second Labour government of 1929 he took ministerial office for the first time as Chancellor of the Duchy of Lancaster. Though outside Cabinet, Mosley had a senior post with a key place alongside J. H. Thomas, George Lansbury and Tom Johnston on the Cabinet unemployment committee. Within the government, there was growing tension between the not insubstantial egos of Mosley on the one hand and Thomas and the Chancellor, Philip Snowden, on the other. In 1930 Mosley took it upon himself to pen a memorandum recommending radical changes in policy to deal with the Depression, which included extensive state intervention and a public works programme. On 20 May, following the rejection of his memorandum by Cabinet, he resigned from the government. A further attempt to get these policies adopted by the Labour Party failed at the Annual Conference of October 1930.

Mosley by this point began to believe his own press: his experience of winning parliamentary seats as an Independent, along with his self-belief in his broad political support, talked up by the media, led him to plan the creation of the New Party, which was launched on 1 March 1931. At first this was just a parliamentary venture – Mosley, his wife and four other MPs – and a spectacularly unsuccessful one at that: two MPs remained members for only one day and a third, John Strachey, resigned in June. All 24 of its candidates were defeated in the 1931 election.

Early the following year Mosley visited Mussolini's Italy. He concluded that parliamentary politics had had its day and that the dictatorships springing up around Europe were the way forward. On his return therefore he started planning a fascist movement, British-style, which bore fruit in October 1932 as the British Union of Fascists (BUF). Initially influenced by Italian fascism, the BUF in its early couple of years was relatively successful and great efforts were expended to gain respectability amongst the traditional right, which was achieved amongst some Conservatives.

But this was all undermined by the violence that was clearly on show at the party's June 1934 rally at Olympia. The true face of ugly extremism and anti-Semitism was made plain for all to see, and from later that year anti-Semitism became a major policy theme of the BUF. These events lost the party any middle-class support it might have hoped to get (and quite a lot of its membership), and it took its arguments (and violence) to the streets.

The party ditched its economic policies inspired by Mosley's 1930 memorandum and committed to policies based on totalitarianism, now much more influenced by Nazism. The rapid marginalisation of the BUF was largely complete by 1935, by when it was of little significance and far from political influence and power.

Cynthia had died in May 1933, and in 1936 Mosley married one of the

Mitford sisters, Diana Guinness, at a ceremony in Berlin in the presence of Hitler. Following the outbreak of war, Mosley was interned along with other BUF leaders and sundry suspicious characters on the right under the Defence of the Realm regulations. He was released in November 1943 on health grounds, but any political influence he might have had had now completely evaporated, and for many years after the war the BBC banned interviews with him.

He devoted himself to a series of self-justifying books such as *My Answer* (1946) and *My Life* (1968), along with others that sought to outline his views on various topics such as *Atrocities*, *Britain First*, *European Socialism*, and *Revolution by Reason* and other essays. Living mainly in France for the rest of his life, he became particularly interested in the cause of European unity, but of course based on racial lines, as leader of the Union Movement 1948–66. He made disastrous forays into parliamentary politics in 1959 and 1966, losing his deposit at North Kensington and Shoreditch respectively.

He died in Orsay, France, on 3 December 1980. He left two sons and a daughter by Cynthia, and two sons by Diana. His eldest son is Nicholas Mosley, the 3rd Lord Ravensdale and baronet, a noted author. Another son is Max Mosley, President of the FIA, which oversees Formula One and who came to political light in recent times during controversies on tobacco advertising in the early years of the Blair government.

The debate about Mosley's abilities is in many ways a continuing one. He clearly lacked judgement and was prone to endorsing simplistic theories and strategies. Although he argued that he was part of a new generation leaving behind the old Establishment ideas and politics, he was nevertheless steeped in its traditions with the advantages of birth and position, including great arrogance and total confidence in his own abilities and in his own views. Yet at almost every turn he seemed to take the wrong decision to advance himself or his ideas. A combination of ambition in excess of ability, unfulfilled promise in the 1920s and a fatal impatience makes Mosley a character quite unparalleled in British politics.

The classic biography is *Oswald Mosley* by Robert (Lord) Skidelsky, first published in 1975 with an updated edition in 1990. Nicholas Mosley wrote a two-part biography of his father, *Rules of the Game: Sir Oswald and Lady Cynthia Mosley 1896–1933* (1982) and *Beyond the Pale: Sir Oswald Mosley 1933–80* (1983).

His widow, Diana, died in August 2003.

Matthew Seward

George Wigg

born 28 November 1900, *died* 11 August 1983

George Edward Cecil Wigg was born on 28 November 1900 in Ealing, the first child of Edward William Wigg and Cecilia Comber. His father, the youngest of 13 children, ran a dairy business. The family drifted apart and he was brought up by his mother, described in his autobiography as 'of immense vitality and drive,' in Basingstoke, where he was educated at Fairfield's County School and, as a scholarship boy, at Queen Mary's Grammar School, 'a twentieth-century version of Charles Dickens's Dotheboys Hall', he recalled in his memoirs. The social and educational system of the time thwarted the development of his considerable intellectual gifts. This accounted for his sometimes belligerent attitude towards those he dubbed the 'intellectuals in the Labour leadership.'

Wigg joined the army at 17, joining the Tank Corps in 1919, and spent 18 happy years in the ranks. He served in Turkey at the time of the Chanak incident, in Mesopotamia, where he was befriended by the indomitable Arabist Gertrude Bell, and in Egypt. 'My years in Iraq and Egypt were lonely', he recalled in his autobiography. Though he wrote of his enjoyment of 'racing and riding and swimming … the friendship and life of the sergeants mess', he also valued 'beyond price the privacy of my own bunk, where I could be alone with my books and my thoughts.' He read extensively about the history of the First World War and about the organisation of the armed forces, becoming a great admirer of R. B. Haldane's 'genius' as Secretary of State for War pre-1914. 'Organisation, administration, quartering and supply were my basic interests in military affairs and the core of many of my speeches in the House of Commons. Neglect of these problems brought us near to defeat in both World Wars. In my view the cause of neglect was the ossified class structure of British society.'

Class obsessed Wigg. It was as a soldier that he learned to stand up for himself and to use King's Regulations – as he later used Erskine May, with an ingenuity that I suspect was never shown before and to my certain knowledge never shown since – to confound bullies and cheats.

Stationed in Canterbury in the 1930s, he became involved with the Workers Educational Association (WEA). In 1937 he left the army for a full-time WEA post, working directly for one of his heroes, Sandy Lindsay, Master of Balliol, founder of Keele University in north Staffordshire. On the outbreak of war he was commissioned in the Royal Army Education Corps. He became MP for Dudley in July 1945, serving for 22 years. Substituting for his friend, Dick Crossman, at 24 hours notice, I went to Dudley Constituency Labour Party (CLP) in 1963. Since George terrified us all, Harold Wilson not excluded, it was quite simply the most daunting CLP meeting I have ever experienced. Wigg seemed to have imbued in his CLP members the same inquisitorial skills that he possessed so formidably. Obviously, his constituents thought the world of him – and rightly, since no MP ever raised such hell in Whitehall if he thought there was injustice.

He served as PPS to Emanuel Shinwell, 1945–51, first at the Ministry of Fuel and Power (which was the origin of his distaste for Gaitskell) and subsequently at War and Defence. In October 1964, I was phoned at home – the inevitable call-sign, 'Wigg here' – and asked to propose the nomination of my predecessor but four as MP for West Lothian, Shinwell, as Chair of the Parliamentary Labour Party.

After 1951, from his front-bench seat below the gangway – flanked often by Sidney Silverman – he played a leading part in the Reform of the Army Act. He fought the implications of the defence White Paper of 1957, the Blue Streak project, achieving a mastery of parliamentary tactics – 'Wiggery-Pokery', as Tory Ministers wryly soubriquetised it.

Wigg's autobiography, *George Wigg* (Michael Joseph, 1972), gives an account of the Portland and Vassall trials of fascinating insight. As a new MP, I sat in the Chamber, uncomfortable at the *ad hominem* onslaught on Profumo, yet spellbound. This was not the silly name-calling and sound-bites of the year 2000 – it was devastating, intensely felt Parliamentary investigation into wrong-doing. Norman Shrapnel wrote: 'Above all one remembers him through the Macmillan years in endless running battles with what seems in retrospect like whole battalions of defence and service ministers … his scorn for the stock uninformative reply was peppered with rich serviceman's comment … "half-baked nonsense!" he would shout at Mr Soames, sometime Secretary of State for War … He would make speeches about the army at enormous length – longer, people were already beginning to think, than it would take to fight a contemporary all-out war … He resented an army in which, as he appeared to think, the well-being of soldiers was so often disregarded that all too often they would desert and go off to fight by-elections.'

In 1963, on the death of Gaitskell – 'while there is death there is hope', boomed George – he became a manager for Wilson's leadership campaign, being appointed Paymaster General and a Privy Counsellor by Wilson in 1964. What he did was a mystery to most of his colleagues. All I know, staying with R. H. S. Crossman in 9 Vincent Square Mondays to Fridays, was that Wigg phoned about 8am most mornings. He was interminable. Quite often Crossman would come down to an overcooked breakfast I had prepared and sigh, 'That was George – he's been on to Harold, haranguing him for 40 minutes this morning.' Wigg had a unique relationship with Wilson 1964–67 – albeit as a devourer of Prime Ministerial time.

Mercifully, in 1967 Wigg accepted with alacrity the chairmanship of the Horserace Betting Levy Board, on which he had served 1958–64, and resigned his seat to accept a peerage. No sinecure! Betting and horses had been a passionate interest. From the unlikely quarter of my constituent, the sixth Earl of Rosebery, KT PC DSO MC, owner of Derby winners, whose colours were famous at Newmarket and elsewhere for 30 years, came a glowing judgement: 'George knows what he is talking about!"From a dour aristocrat and wartime Cabinet Minister, that was an accolade. He served until 1972.

My last memories of George are of going regularly to see him in his basement flat at 83 The Green, Clapham Common, for advice on opposition to Mrs Thatcher's Falkland's War – a reckless adventure that lost serviceman's lives for no long-term purpose. George never mellowed to his dying day: 11 August 1983. He was survived by his wife and three daughters.

Tam Dalyell

George Brown

Lord George Brown

***born** 2 September 1914, **died** 2 June 1985*

George Brown was Deputy Leader of the Labour Party 1960–70 and, as First Secretary of State and then Foreign Secretary in Harold Wilson's Government, Deputy Prime Minister from 1964 to 1968. He entered Parliament in 1945 for Belper, and quickly made his mark. He was Minister of Works and a Privy Counsellor in 1951 and rose steadily though the party during its 13 years in opposition. He challenged for the leadership on Hugh Gaitskell's death in 1963 but lost to Wilson by 144 votes to 103.

George Brown was in every sense a colourful character. He had a natural instinct for politics and a forceful personality. He had a first-class mind and could be passionate in debate. He was easily recognised by the public, which enjoyed his style and forgave him his shortcomings. Most of these resulted from a volatile temperament often fuelled by too much to drink. In the end he threw away his career. He was only 56 when he lost his seat but he made no significant contribution to politics thereafter. He sat in the House of Lords but left the Labour Party in March 1976. He was an embarrassment rather than an asset to his old friends who founded the SDP when he chose to join them in 1981.

George Alfred Brown was born in Southwark on 2 September 1914, the son of a lorry driver. He left school at 16 and became a fur salesman. He then graduated into a full-time official of the Transport and General Workers Union which sponsored him for Parliament. Already, at the Labour Party conference of 1939, he had made a striking debut with a speech in favour of the expulsion of Sir Stafford Cripps. When, six years later, Hugh Dalton, then Chancellor of the Exchequer, held a Young Victors party for new Labour MPs, George Brown was amongst 12 of his most promising contemporaries, nine of whom were to become ministers. Appointed PPS to Minister of Labour George Isaacs in 1945, and subsequently to Hugh Dalton in 1947, he served as Joint Parliamentary Under-Secretary at the Ministry of Agriculture from October 1947 until his appointment as Minister of Works in April 1951.

In the years of opposition after 1951, George Brown rose steadily in the party. He was elected to the shadow cabinet in 1955 and in November 1956 became its spokesman on defence, after brief stints shadowing first agriculture and then labour. When the Soviet leader Nikita Khruschev came to London and was entertained by the National Executive Committee, George Brown had a noisy exchange with him that upset his colleagues but brought him into the public eye as a man of strong views, boldly expressed. In 1961 he became Shadow Home Secretary. He was a commanding speaker both in and out of Parliament and won praise for an impromptu civil liberties speech against the expulsion of African asylum seeker, Chief Enharo. Later, in 1962, he showed great skill in his robust advocacy of the case for

Britain joining the Common Market at the end of a notable debate at the party conference.

George Brown was the obvious candidate of the right and centre of the party to succeed Hugh Gaitskell as leader. But he had already acquired a reputation of being unpredictable and sometimes 'overwrought'. A number of his natural supporters in the Parliamentary Labour Party preferred Jim Callaghan, or believed that Wilson, although the candidate of the left, was a safer all-round choice. In the event, Wilson's election was a blow to George Brown from which he never quite recovered. Wilson treated him fairly, recognising his qualities and his standing in the party and with the public. But Brown was suspicious and often imagined slights where there were none.

Initially, however, after a short pause to recover from the immediate shock of defeat, he knuckled down to widen his horizons, particularly on home affairs, and to prepare himself for government. When in October 1964 Wilson became Prime Minister, Brown, together with Jim Callaghan, made up the triumvirate upon which the Government was to depend.

Brown threw himself with immense energy into creating the Department of Economic Affairs, bringing together career civil servants and a very talented group of outsiders from business and academia. Within two months he had persuaded the CBI and the TUC to agree to a Declaration of Intent committing themselves to a voluntary incomes policy. Within a year there was a National Plan for sustained economic growth and Economic Planning Councils had been set up in almost every region. It was a huge personal achievement, the result of working immensely long hours, breaking every convention to get his own way and successively bullying and charming and ultimately exhausting those whose support he required.

But the parlous economic state of the country was an enemy of the DEA's work. Short-term problems defeated long-term strategies. The situation was aggravated by the Government's failure to devalue the pound immediately after the election, a course which Brown advocated but Wilson and Callaghan opposed. The National Plan was out of date and hopelessly optimistic by the time it was published and a voluntary policy gave way to a statutory incomes policy in the summer of 1966. Regional Economic Planning Councils did some useful work but eventually lost their momentum. Within two years, the DEA was in decline and George Brown confessed to his friends that he was over the hill.

But when he was moved to the Foreign Office in August 1966 it was no humiliation. George Brown had long believed in Britain's membership of the European Economic Community and now was his chance to support the Labour Government's bid to enter. He was proud to follow in the footsteps of Ernest Bevin, a trade union leader who had become a great Labour Foreign Secretary. He soon acquired a reputation for being rough with officials and rude to their wives, and he did not much enjoy the confident ambience of the Foreign Office. But he gave his mind to difficult, detailed problems in the Middle East (including Britain's withdrawal from Aden) as well as the macro issues of the Cold War and Britain's relations with the United States at the time of Vietnam. He might have been an outstanding foreign secretary in a different era when heavy drinking and threats of resignation would have remained a private matter. But when in March 1968 he finally resigned, the event was no great surprise and, for some, a considerable relief.

In 1970, despite favourable opinion polls, Labour won its smallest share of the national vote for 35 years. In Belper there was a 5 per cent swing to the Conservatives, which was sufficient to push George Brown out. In his younger days he would have fought a by-election at the earliest opportunity and played a full part in rebuilding Labour in opposition. But he knew that he was well into the autumn of his political life and would never again command the same influence and status. He was created Lord George-Brown in 1970. He did some campaigning for friends in the elections of 1974, and the following year he supported a 'Yes' vote in the referendum on Britain's continued membership of the Common Market. But for the most part during the 1970s he earned a good living from newspaper articles, business ventures and his celebrity status. Finally, ill and in obvious decline, and having left his wife Sophie after over 40 years of marriage, he retired to a remote cottage in Cornwall and died in a Truro hospital on 2 June 1985.

The obituaries were a reminder of his larger-than-life career. 'Explosive and unpredictable but the nation loved him' was the *Daily Telegraph's* verdict. 'Hero-figure, fall guy, public entertainer' said the *Guardian*. In the *Financial Times* a former Cabinet Secretary described him as someone 'who always seemed to be at war with himself. ..finally betrayed by the defects of his personality'; and *The Times* honoured him with a leading article as 'The Nearly Man'.

George Brown was ultimately a tragic figure and his a wasted life. But for many years he brought his outstanding talents to the service of the Labour movement, winning the admiration of his friends and the respect of many who differed from him. George Brown's autobiography was called *In My Way* (1972).

Bill Rodgers

Peter Bessell

born 24 August 1921, *died* 27 November 1985

The maverick Cornish Liberal politician, failed businessman and small-time conman Peter Bessell will probably be best remembered as the main prosecution witness in the 1979 trial of Liberal Party leader, Jeremy Thorpe. As Bessell had assiduously courted Thorpe during his political career, this was viewed by Thorpe's numerous friends as a dastardly act of treachery. However, Bessell proved to be an incredible witness; he was in fact a self-confessed habitual liar. Moreover, it soon leaked out that he was to be paid £25,000 by the *Sunday Telegraph* for his story, a figure that would be doubled if a conviction was secured. There was widespread outrage at this example of chequebook journalism. Paradoxically,

Bessell's involvement in the trial may well have aided Thorpe's acquittal.

Peter Joseph Bessell was born in Bath, on 24 August 1921, as the only child of a lady's dressmaker and part-time investment adviser, Joseph Edgar Bessell, and his wife, Olive. The couple divorced when Peter was just five years old, the boy remaining with his father and paternal grandparents. As he was considered a sensitive child, he was tutored privately at home for the next two years, before going on to an undistinguished spell at the local school. The household was loving but strict, adhering to Victorian Christian values. By now blessed with the gift of the gab, at the age of 18 Peter became a Congregational lay preacher – a role he played until 1970, despite developing tastes that were totally out of keeping with any religious vocation.

During the Second World War, he registered as a conscientious objector (a position he later renounced), and was sent by the Ministry of Information to lecture to British and Allied troops. But he was already tempted by the sort of affluent lifestyle that would only be possible if he became a successful businessman. He seems to have helped his father for a while, before setting up his own tailoring business in Paignton, Devon, and branching out into dry-cleaning.

It was in Torbay that he first became involved with the Liberal Party, partly for social reasons. In 1953, as part of the area's Coronation celebrations, he organised a pageant with such verve that he gained a reputation as someone who could get things done. Accordingly, when the Liberal prospective parliamentary candidate for Torquay stood down on the eve of the 1955 election, the local association turned to Bessell to step into his shoes. He came third, with a dispiriting 14 per cent. But the Conservative MP died within a matter of months, causing a by-election, where Bessell's vote was boosted to 24 per cent.

During that by-election campaign, Bessell first came into close contact with Jeremy Thorpe, an ebullient young lawyer who was already seen as a rising star within the then tiny Liberal Party – a situation confirmed when he won North Devon in the 1959 General Election. By then, Bessell had himself moved to a more winnable seat: Bodmin, in Cornwall. The two men developed a close working relationship; though different in character, both were showmen. Whereas Thorpe had real charisma, and a brilliant sense of political gimmickry, Bessell preferred to pose as an immensely suave, smartly-dressed, clever businessman who was brimming with creative ideas. He managed to charm large sums of money out of investors on both sides of the Atlantic, to back such ventures as motels and a factory for making plastic egg-cartons.

While on numerous trips to the United States, Bessell observed US-style political campaigning techniques, which he introduced back home. Cornwall had seen nothing like it before. Yet at the same time, he succeeded in manufacturing Cornish credentials for himself, largely by focusing on local issues. He joined the Cornish nationalist organisation Mebyon Kernow, and remained a member even after he was elected to Parliament in 1964.

In parliament, he quickly established a reputation as a maverick, with a distinct touch of populism. For example, he gained considerable publicity in the more conservative press by attempting (unsuccessfully) through parliamentary means to save the long-running radio soap opera *Mrs Dale's Diary,* which the BBC had decide to axe. Unusually for a Liberal, he was pro-hanging and anti-Common Market. Moreover, as the United States became ever more deeply involved in the Vietnam War, he became a vociferous supporter of the war against Communism. This put him at loggerheads with fiery Young Liberals, who portrayed him as a hate figure. In contrast, his stance on the war boosted his stock in Washington. Years later, he claimed that he had worked for U.S. intelligence at this time, though this was probably just another of his flights of fancy.

After becoming an MP, Bessell strengthened his relationship with Thorpe, in the correct belief that Thorpe would succeed Jo Grimond as leader of the party, which happened early in 1967. By then, Bessell not only knew of Thorpe's secret sex life, but had become deeply involved in attempts to limit the damage that could be done to Thorpe and the Liberal Party by allegations from a former male model, Norman Josiffe (later Scott), that he had had a homosexual affair with the Liberal leader. Bessell later wrote up his version of these events in a rambling, self-serving memoir of dubious veracity, entitled *Cover-Up* (1981). As Bessell was himself a serial heterosexual philanderer, who not only married three times, but also frequented prostitutes, he had no difficulty whatsoever in tolerating Thorpe's peccadilloes, unlike several of their Liberal parliamentary colleagues.

Following his defeat at the 1970 general election, Bessell emigrated to the United States, where he set himself up as an investment consultant. He developed a wide range of business interests, several of which went spectacularly bust, putting him in a precarious financial position personally. Though many investors at first fell for his elegant British manner, after a while among some of those who had lost money because of him he acquired the nickname 'Joe Disaster'.

The Thorpe trial offered Bessell the opportunity to get back into the limelight in Britain and, he hoped, to earn some useful money. The prosecution offered him immunity in return for his evidence, which they believed would be damning enough to secure a conviction. In the event, Norman Scott – who was described by the judge as 'a crook, liar, parasite and a fraud' rather stole the show in his pathetic awfulness, but Bessell also came over badly. Thorpe's defence counsel, George Carman, dismissed his evidence as 'pure fantasy'.

Publicly humiliated, Bessell returned to the United States, where he kept a low profile, apart from the publication of his book, which evoked little interest. He died in Los Angeles on 27 November 1985, leaving a widow, Diana, and two children from earlier marriages.

Jonathan Fryer

Emanuel Shinwell

Lord Shinwell of Easington

born 18 October 1884, *died* 8 May 1986

Emanuel 'Manny' Shinwell made his reputation as a socialist orator, reared in the tough politics of Clydeside in the early twentieth century. He was a prominent figure in the Labour Party for more than half a century, serving in the governments of the 1920s and 1940s and acting as chairman of the PLP in the 1960s.

Shinwell was born in Spitalfields in the East End of London on 18 October 1884, the eldest of 13 children of Samuel Shinwell, a clothing manufacturer. He left school at the age of 11 and was apprenticed to the tailoring trade, but for several years he drifted through a variety of poorly paid jobs.

As a young man he moved to Scotland, where he became actively engaged in politics, joining the Independent Labour Party in 1903. At the age of 22 he was elected to the Glasgow Trades Council, of which he was twice president, and he devoted much of his time to the development of trade unionism among the seamen of the Clyde ports. Employment in the shipping industry meant he was in a reserved occupation during the First World War, which he initially supported, though by 1917 he backed the campaign for a negotiated peace.

Shinwell first came to national prominence on 'Red Friday' in January 1919, when he was one of the organisers of a strike (aimed at securing the introduction of a 40–hour working week) that saw violent clashes with the police in Glasgow. He was arrested and imprisoned for five months – on the charge of inciting a riot – though accusations that he was a 'revolutionary' were at odds with his moderate demands throughout the dispute.

After seven years as a Glasgow councillor Shinwell was elected as MP for Linlithgow in 1922 – a seat he first contested, unsuccessfully, in 1918.

He was soon known for his effective debating skills, honed by assiduous reading that gave him a command of language unusual among those with little formal education. He was an enthusiastic supporter of Ramsay MacDonald and served for a few months as Parliamentary Secretary to the Department of Mines in the first Labour government, but he lost his seat at the 1924 election, only to regain it at a by-election in 1928. He was Financial Secretary to the War Office in 1929–30, and then returned to the Mines Department until he lost his seat when Labour was heavily defeated at the 1931 general election.

Shinwell's volatile nature was evident in two episodes during the 1930s. Angry at what he regarded as the betrayal of the party's leaders in 1931, he launched a vitriolic campaign against Ramsay MacDonald at the 1935 election, winning the contest for the Seaham constituency in Durham (which he held until 1950) and driving his old chief out of politics at the same time. Three years later, provoked by the comments of his opponents, Shinwell crossed the floor of the House and hit the Conservative MP Commander Robert Bower, a former naval boxing champion, before storming out of the chamber.

After the formation of the wartime coalition in 1940, he turned down the offer of a junior ministerial post and became instead a vocal critic of Churchill's conduct of the war. He did little in these years to endear himself to colleagues. His alliance with the Tory war critic Lord Winterton earned the label 'Arsenic and Old Lace', and his attacks on Labour ministers for not pressing hard enough for socialist policies inside the coalition aroused resentment among many in the PLP.

He was nevertheless considered sufficiently worthy – or too much of a loose cannon – to be offered a senior post when Labour came to power in 1945. Attlee appointed him as Minister of Fuel and Power, and he set about the task of implementing Labour's commitment to nationalise the mines. His bill was the first to come forward in the government's extensive nationalisation programme, but expectations that a change of ownership would boost production were dashed when the vesting date of 1 January 1947 found Britain facing a fuel crisis.

Shinwell gave several advance warnings of possible coal shortages, but he always denied that this would cause dislocation across industry or factory closures. He therefore faced a storm of criticism after announcing that much of industry would have to shut down temporarily. Amidst the snow and ice of a freezing winter, 'Shiver with Shinwell' became a potent slogan for the Tory opposition, and after a series of poor performances in the Commons he was fortunate to survive in office.

In October 1947 he was moved to become Secretary of State for War. Shinwell bitterly resented this demotion to a post outside Cabinet rank, but he proved to be more adept at dealing with military matters than he was at handling the problems of industry. By March 1950 he had returned to the Cabinet as Minister of Defence, a post in which he adopted a hawkish posture on the need for large-scale rearmament following the outbreak of the Korean War.

Shinwell's influence within the party waned when Labour lost office in 1951. He was MP for Easington after 1950 (through to 1970), but after nine years he lost his seat on the NEC and failed in his attempts to gain re-election in the early 1950s. In 1955 he left the shadow cabinet and published – apparently without any trace of irony – an autobiography entitled *Conflict Without Malice*. By this time he was assuming the mantle of a Labour veteran, speaking his mind by defending the principle of public ownership and arguing for Britain to contract out of the 'club' of nuclear powers.

When Labour returned to power in 1964, ministerial office was out of the question for Shinwell at the age of 80, but his continuing vigour and enthusiasm for politics were such that he was elected chairman of the PLP. For a while the one-time rebel proved successful at containing a new generation of critics, though murmurings against him increased as Wilson's government lost its sense of direction and popularity. Unable to enforce discipline as strictly as he wished, Shinwell resigned in 1967 and returned again to the back benches, where he spoke forcefully against the principle of British membership of the EEC.

He was made a life peer – Baron Shinwell of Easington – in 1970, and into his nineties he remained an outspoken member of the House of

Lords, well informed on the major issues of the day. He surprised many commentators when he resigned the Labour whip in March 1982, protesting against the left wing drift in policy. He remained a party member, but thereafter sat with the Independent group in the Lords.

Shinwell was married three times. His first wife, Fay, died in 1954 after more than 50 years of marriage. In 1956 he married Dinah Meyer, from Denmark, who died in 1971. A year later he married Mrs Sarah Hurst, who also predeceased him, in 1977. He celebrated his hundredth birthday in 1984 in the Royal Gallery of the House of Lords. Much of the conversation was about the miners' strike of the day, and thoughts went back some 60 years to the time when Shinwell supported the miners during the 1926 General Strike.

By the time he died in London, aged 101, on 8 May 1986, Shinwell's firebrand years were a distant memory and he had become a figure of affection among political friends and enemies alike. In many ways he shared the virtues and shortcomings of the early generation of Labour leaders. He was a tough and instinctive champion of the underdog, a quick-witted and skilful platform speaker. But in office he lacked administrative expertise and the capacity to plan ahead. As one of his juniors commented, as a minister – as in life – he acted on impulse, in fits and starts.

Kevin Jefferys

Harold Macmillan

Lord Stockton

born 10 February 1894, *died* 29 December 1986

Harold Macmillan was Prime Minister (from 1957 to 1963) in a world very different from our own. It was a world of consensus politics – now derided as much by Conservatives as by the left. 'For me,' Mrs Thatcher said in 1981, 'consensus seems to be the process for abandoning all beliefs, principles, values and policies.' Yet under Macmillan, unemployment was neglible and prices stable: government worked amicably with organised labour, and the living standards of trade unionists increased far more rapidly than they were to do in the 1970s and 1980s. Affluence and a rising standard of living were taken for granted, and Britain's political and constitutional system was widely admired as a symbol of stability and ordered progress.

Harold Macmillan dedicated his political career to humanising the Conservative Party, and he could say after his election victory in 1959, 'The class war is obsolete.' By then, the hard-faced Conservatism of the pre-war years, to be resurrected again in the late 1970s, was but a distant memory.

In the 1930s, Macmillan had been one of the few Conservatives to stand out against the narrow orthodoxies of the day in both domestic and foreign policy. He rebelled against the doctrine that the humiliation and misery of prolonged unemployment were the product of impersonal forces which governments could do little to alleviate and he allied himself with Churchill in his campaign for armed resistance to Hitler. Until war came he remained a lone and eccentric backbench rebel. But his fortunes changed when Churchill became Prime Minister in 1940. At the age of 46 Macmillan became a junior minister. 'You and I owe Hitler something', he told Churchill. 'He made you Prime Minister and me an Under-Secretary. No power on earth, except Hitler, could have done either.' It needed a world war to bring Macmillan into government, it took Suez (in 1956) to make him Prime Minister. The crisis itself called Macmillan's judgment severely into question, for it was he who hysterically insisted that he would pawn every picture in the National Gallery rather than accept humiliation at the hands of Nasser it was he who pressed for military action without any assurance of American support: and eventually it was he who, having miscalculated the financial position, threatened to resign if there was not an immediate cease-fire.

In Harold Wilson's caustic phrase, Macmillan at Suez was 'first in, first out.' Yet he emerged from the wreckage as a resolute figure. His rival, R. A. Butler, always doubtful of the wisdom of armed intervention, only enhanced his reputation as an appeaser.

Entering Downing Street in January 1957, Macmillan succeeded to a grim inheritance, for Suez had left the Conservatives dispirited and demoralised. He told the Queen that he did not think his administration could last for more than six weeks. Yet recovery was rapid, and in October 1959 the Conservatives were returned to power. It was the first time in the period of mass suffrage that a government had actually increased its majority twice in succession.

Macmillan's achievement was partly one of style. A nervous and sensitive man, his public posture of unflappability served to reassure the electorate that Britain remained strong and secure. Yet, as a radical realist, Macmillan re-orientated British foreign policy, repairing the 'special relationship' with the United States, and, with his 'winds of change' speech at Cape Town in 1960, distancing himself from apartheid. He speeded the process of decolonisation, and was the first British Prime Minister to appreciate that Britain's future lay with Europe.

But baulked of his ambition to lead Britain into the EEC by de Gaulle, Macmillan's greatest achievement in foreign policy lay in hastening the thaw in relations with the Soviet Union in the post-Stalin, post-Dulles world. The nuclear test-ban treaty of 1963 represented the culmination of his efforts, eliciting tributes from both Kennedy and Khruschev to his skill and patience as a negotiator.

In domestic policy, Macmillan's central concern was to avoid mass unemployment. As MP for Stockton between the wars, he had learnt 'lessons which I have never forgotten. If, in some respects, they may have left too deep an impression on my mind, the gain was greater than the loss.' In the 1930s, he had been an advocate of planning and his book *The Middle Way*, published in 1938, laid the foundations for a form of society neither socialist nor classically capitalist, but combining freedom of enterprise with public control so as to secure the benefits of both.

In 1951 Macmillan had become Minister of Housing, achieving the target of 300,000 houses a year and so helping to create the 'property-owning democracy' which lay at the heart of Conservative thinking. Yet in economic affairs, the Conservatives seemed the party of economic liberalism and not planning. Assisted by the fall in world commodity prices and an improvement in the terms of trade, controls could be removed without inflation resulting. From 1955 onward, however the British economy was bedevilled by a series of exchange crises which seemed to show that sterling could only be defended in a period of fixed exchange rates through strict control of the money supply. This was a policy favoured by Macmillan's first chancellor, Peter Thorneycroft, and by his junior ministers, Nigel Birch and Enoch Powell, the latter providing the doctrinal foundation for polices thought obsolete in the 1950s but newly-fashionable 20 years later. Macmillan was not impressed. 'When I am told that inflation can be cured or arrested only by returning to substantial or even massive unemployment, I reject that utterly.'

Dismissing the resignation of his entire Treasury term in January 1958 as 'little local difficulties', he sought for an alternative which could ensure both full employment and price stability. That alternative was to be found in the planned pursuit of economic growth, buttressed by an incomes policy.

In the early 1960s, Macmillan adopted a new approach to the economy. In 1961 Selwyn Lloyd, as chancellor, announced the birth of Neddy, declaring: 'I will deal first with growth in the economy. The controversial matter of planning at once arises. I am frightened of the word.' The move to planning, and the struggle to establish a voluntary incomes policy through the National Incomes Commission, were an attempt to realise the philosophy of the Middle Way in the very different conditions of the 1960s. Regional planning machinery was established, 'Little Neddies' set up to plan individual industries, and Macmillan's successor, Sir Alec Douglas-Home, accepted the recommendations of the Robbins Report with its commitment to university expansion.

By the time they left office in 1964, Conservative economic policy had been transformed. In place of the crude attempt to control the economy through the structure of interest rates, there was a whole complex of economic regulators. In place of the rule-of-thumb nostrums of the Treasury, a planning staff had been established, and economic experts were beginning to be introduced into Whitehall. In the words of Andrew Shonfield: 'It may be said that the intellectual and administrative preconditions for modern capitalist planning had been created, or were in course of being established'. For much of this achievement, Macmillan deserves the credit.

Until struck down by illness in October 1963, Macmillan seems to have intended to lead the Conservatives into another general election, one which they might well have won.

During the long years of retirement, Macmillan mostly refrained from public comment on political matters, although he spoke a number of times in favour of European unity. In 1976 he called, as he had done in the 1930s, for a coalition government to secure economic recovery. In 1980 he gave a broadcast in which he criticised, in carefully coded language, Mrs Thatcher's policy of deflating in the middle of a world recession.

He remained a sardonic and good humoured spectator of contemporary affairs, taking pleasure in the various honours which came his way, especially the chancellorship of the University of Oxford, an office to which he had been elected in 1960 and which gave ample scope for the display of his characteristic qualities of wit and generosity.

In 1984 Macmillan accepted a hereditary peerage, becoming Earl of Stockton, and his maiden speech in the Lords in November 1984 was a masterly restatement of his Middle Way philosophy while its combination of vision and professionalism delighted the House.

Macmillan's legacy to British politics was complex. The methods of economic management which he advocated were continued by the Wilson and Heath administrations, but they did not succeed in stemming Britain's economic decline. Macmillan never confronted the deeper sources of Britain's economic difficulties, but then neither have his successors.

In foreign affairs, Macmillan was unable to secure a new role for Britain and, although Britain entered the EEC in 1973, it has still not fully come to terms with Community membership. The hopes which detente aroused remain, on the whole, unfulfilled while Macmillan's part in returning Russian prisoners of war to Stalin in 1945 will need explanation to his biographer. Macmillan's failure was in part a result of the ambiguous and indirect methods which he felt bound to pursue. He had to reassure the Tory right that he was maintaining national prestige while in reality undertaking a policy of colonial withdrawal he had to mouth the rhetoric of economic liberalism while remaining at heart a dirigiste. Unable or unwilling to confront the electorate directly, he could not mobilise popular support for his aims and, like Disraeli, the Conservative leader whom he most resembles, he found Britain 'a very difficult country to move,' with more disappointment than success attending the attempt.

More imaginative and far-sighted than most of his generation, Macmillan stood for much that is best in British political life – its decency and tolerance, its dislike of puritanism and cant. If on occasion he was prone to worldliness and cynicism, he nevertheless helped to create a society which provided, for the vast majority of British people, a happier and more secure life than they had ever known. It was an achievement that seemed easier in the 1950s than it does today, at a time when his political successors have dismantled so much of his legacy.

Vernon Bogdanor

John Stonehouse

born 28 January 1925, *died* 15 April 1988

Infamous as remains the story of the disappearance of Lord Lucan in the early 1970s, the consequences of his apparent discovery by Australian police in December 1974 proved to have far more profound consequences. The Victoria State police, it turned out, had initially made a mistake. Joseph Arthur Markham and Clive Mildoon, the one man with two false passports they arrested in Melbourne on Christmas Eve, was not Lord Lucan but the Rt Hon. John Thomson Stonehouse, Labour MP for Walsall North since 1974 (and for Wednesbury since a by-election of 1957), who had been missing, presumed dead, since his disappearance off a Miami beach on 21 November 1974.

Stonehouse, the then chair of the ASTMS union group of MPs, was a not insignificant political figure and had been regarded in the 1960s as a rising protégé of Harold Wilson, who had even once lent Stonehouse and his family the Wilson holiday bungalow on the Scilly Isles. After his arrest and extradition, an Old Bailey trial revealed his involvement in financial irregularities at the British-Bangladesh Trust Bank which had underpinned his £1 million debts and £100,000 horde in a Swiss bank account. His conviction on 18 charges of theft and false pretences and imprisonment in Wandsworth prison were a profound embarrassment to the then Labour government. In the consequent by-election of 4 November 1976 the seat was lost to the Conservatives on a 22 per cent swing, even though Stonehouse himself had already resigned the Labour whip and renounced the party in April of that year, depriving the Callaghan Government of a Commons majority on its first day in office.

Born in Southampton on 28 January 1925, the youngest of four children, his family were enthusiastically involved in local Labour politics. His father, William Mitchell Stonehouse, a Post Office engineer, was secretary of his local trade union branch, and his mother Rosina was a Southampton councillor and alderman (1936–70), president of the local Co-op society and Mayor of Southampton in 1959. His elder sister recruited him into the Woodcraft Folk, where he was nicknamed 'Falcon'. He grew up in a Southampton council house and attended Tauntons School, where he was taught English by Horace King, later Labour MP for Southampton Test and Speaker of the House of Commons (1965–70). At 16, King told him he had little ability and ought to become an apprentice butcher; instead, in 1941 he joined the Southampton Probation Department as a clerk and typist. Leaving for the RAF in 1944 he trained as a pilot in the USA before going to the LSE in 1947, where he was Labour Club Chairman, graduating with a BSc (Econ) in 1951. At the LSE Harold Laski encouraged him to put his name forward for Parliament. Stonehouse, still in his mid-twenties, was Labour's unsuccessful candidate at Twickenham in the general election of 1950 and for Burton in the election of 1951. In 1948 he married Barbara Smith, with whom he had a son and two daughters.

Before his election to Parliament in the Wednesbury by-election of February 1957 (caused by the deselection of the sitting Labour MP, former minister Stanley Evans, over his support for Suez), where he defeated Tory candidate Peter Tapsell, having already beaten the favourite, Ray Gunter, in the selection, Stonehouse worked at home and abroad in the Co-op movement. From 1952 to 1954 he lived with his wife and young family in Uganda, building the African Co-op movement and establishing the credentials which would make him Vice-Chairman of the Movement for Colonial Freedom under Chairman Fenner Brockway. On a visit to Rhodesia in 1959, his speech calling for black Africans to 'lift your heads high and behave as though the country belongs to you' led to his arrest and forcible deportation by the minority white Rhodesian government, experiences he chronicled in *Prohibited Immigrant* (1960).

Closer to home he became Director of the London Co-operative Society (1956–62) and its President (1962–64), narrowly beating a Communist candidate in the election.

Wilson appointed him Under-Secretary of State at the Ministry of Aviation in 1964, under Roy Jenkins, where he set about vainly promoting the virtues of the British Super VC Ten versus the rival Boeing 707. In April 1966 he was moved sideways to the Colonial Office, where he furthered the process of granting independence to Mauritius and Botswana. In January 1967 he became Minister of Aviation in his own right, taking on responsibility for Concorde and Airbus, Anglo-

French projects that persuaded him to drop his previous opposition to Britain joining the EEC. With the merging of the Aviation Ministry into the Ministry of Technology in February 1967, six weeks into his appointment, Stonehouse became Minister of State at MinTech under Tony Benn, retaining responsibility for aviation. Created a Privy Counsellor in June 1968, in July he succeeded Roy Mason as Postmaster General (redesignated Minister of Posts and Telecommunications from October 1969) where he unsuccessfully tried to ditch what he regarded as the technological white elephants of his ministerial predecessors: namely postcodes and Girobanking.

It was then, however, that his career peaked: though he finally got to run his own ministry, he never made Cabinet, and after Labour's defeat at the 1970 election he was dropped from the front bench. Perhaps it was the Czech spy scandal that finally raised doubts in Wilson's mind about Stonehouse's reliability (in 1968 Stonehouse was named by a defector – though cleared – of being an informer for the Czech Secret Service). As Stonehouse himself wrote in his memoir, it was deeply ironic that as Minister for Posts and Telecommunications, unbeknown to him, his telephone was bugged on the orders of the Home Secretary. Nevertheless, the doubts of senior Labour figures like Barbara Castle and Roy Jenkins seem to have had no appreciable impact in retarding Stonehouse's prior career progression (Jenkins had resisted Stonehouse as his deputy at Aviation in 1964, preferring Tom Bradley, but Wilson had insisted on Stonehouse). Dick Crossman's views were typical of those like Castle and Jenkins whose doubts were ignored. He noted in his diary of 23 January 1969:

A tall, dark rather sleek young man … [Stonehouse] has this rather insolent, handsome face, and when he is nervous an incipient stutter. I have always had the profoundest suspicion of his moral reliability. I met him first in Kampala in 1954 when I was reporting on the Mau Mau. He was Secretary of the Uganda Producers' Co-operative, which closed down in a great stink and he had to fly the land … He certainly used pretty rough tactics in 1962 when he got himself made President of the London Co-operative … When Harold gave me the job of investigating that great scandal at the Ministry of Technology, I found that there was no doubt that John Stonehouse had behaved in the most extraordinary way … I have watched him in every job – for some reason he gets advancement – and I think he is a kind of dangerous crook, overwhelmingly ambitious but above all untrustworthy.

He was released from prison in 1979, having served three and a half years, half his sentence, during which time he underwent heart surgery after suffering several heart attacks. Having divorced his first wife in 1978, in 1981 he married his mistress and former Commons secretary Sheila Buckley, with whom he had planned to start his new life in Australia. They had one son. His memoir, *Death of an Idealist*, had appeared in 1975 and three novels were published from 1982 to 1987: *Ralph* (1982), *The Baring Fault* (1986) and *Oil on the Rift* (1987). In 1985 he founded a company manufacturing electronic safes. He collapsed at his home in Totton near Southampton on 15 April 1988 and was dead on arrival in hospital.

Greg Rosen

Sir Richard Acland

born 26 November 1906, *died* 23 November 1990

Herbert Asquith once said that mankind was divided into three species – 'Men, women and Aclands'. The utopian idealist Dick Acland kept up the tradition of a long line of independent-minded personalities involved in British politics, and his own brand of Christian Socialism played an important footnote in the unusual political circumstances of the 1930s and '40s.

Acland was born on 26 November 1906 in Broadclyst, Devon, the son of Sir Francis Acland, the fourteenth baronet, who was at that time

Liberal MP for Richmond in Yorkshire, and was later a minister under Lloyd George. The Acland family had a rich historical lineage. The baronetcy was created in 1644 when the Aclands' garrison was the only one in Devon that stayed loyal to King Charles I. Other members of the family included one who went to fight for Britain in the American War of Independence only to swap sides when he got there; another was the only Tory MP to vote for the Great Reform Act, and Acland's grandfather was Education Minister in Gladstone's last government.

Educated at Rugby School and Balliol College, Oxford, Acland qualified as a barrister, practising until 1934. In the family tradition, he unsuccessfully contested as a Liberal the local seats of Torquay in 1929 and Barnstaple in 1931. He was elected for Barnstaple in 1935, a seat he held for the next ten years.

But he did not remain a Liberal. In the 1930s he moved to support the fight against fascism and appeasement, getting involved with the Left Book Club and moves for a Popular Front. As a result, he found himself associating frequently with diverse figures such as Harold Laski and the Communist Harry Pollitt, joining forces with Stafford Cripps and Nye Bevan to achieve the famous 1938 Bridgewater by-election victory for an Independent Progressive. These political stances led to Acland's shift to supporting the economic solutions offered by the left, and combined with his non-conformist tradition he developed his own distinctive brand of Christian Socialism. In 1936 he married Anne Alford, and they went on to have three sons. He succeeded to his father's baronetcy in 1939.

His views were exemplified in his best-selling 1940 Penguin paperback *Unser Kampf*, which called for extensive common ownership of land and industry, and emphasised the moral dimension to the war. He published a series of pamphlets including *What It Will Be Like* and *How It Can Be Done*, and set up a radical group based on one entitled *Forward March*. In 1942 this combined with the 1941 Committee, a group concerned with more mechanistic aspects of the war effort and inspired by the radical wartime broadcasts of J. B. Priestley and whose chief patron was

Picture Post owner Edward Hulton; together the two formed the Common Wealth Party. The party advocated Acland's common ownership principles, arguing for mass nationalisation, immediate independence for India and aid for the Third World.

The most significant role played by Common Wealth was its breaking of the wartime by-election truce whereby the main parties had agreed not to contest each other's vacant seats. Common Wealth dived in and put up candidates against what it saw as 'reactionary' candidates, and scored three dramatic successes, with Acland being joined in the Commons by Common Wealth MPs for Eddisbury, Skipton and Chelmsford.

For a time, Common Wealth tapped in to the aspirations of voters for the future once the war was over. With the wide-ranging reforms suggested by the 1942 Beveridge Report backing it up, the Christian-based idealism of Acland filled a gap. Acland was an effective campaigner, but even his efforts were overwhelmed by Labour's 1945 landslide. In that election all but one of the Common Wealth candidates (including Acland himself in Putney) were defeated. Acland promptly joined Labour, and Common Wealth rapidly disappeared – its only MP joined Labour straight after the election. Common Wealth had served two purposes as far as the Labour Party's future was concerned – it laid the ground (and in some ways, heralded victory) for the radical reforming agenda of the Attlee government and helped to instil the belief that such reforms, including Beveridge, were both necessary and desirable in the post-war reconstruction. On a more mundane level, the party acted as a conduit through which people like Desmond Donnelly, George Wigg and of course Acland himself found their way into the Labour Party.

Following his switch to the Labour Party, Acland was chosen as the 'clean' Labour candidate in the 1947 Gravesend by-election to replace the sleaze-tainted Gerry Allighan, who had been expelled from the Commons for a breach of parliamentary privilege. It is suggested that Herbert Morrison personally picked Acland to be the candidate. The by-election was eventful; *The Times* recalled Kent miners parading through the streets of Gravesend by the light of their lamps, and on Acland's victory Morrison sang 'Oh What A Beautiful Morning' to the assembled press.

Back in the Commons, Acland served as Second Church Estates Commissioner from 1950 to 1951. He soon fell in with the Keep Left crowd, which opposed Ernest Bevin's Cold War policies, and it was defence which led to Acland's final change of allegiance. When the British development of a hydrogen bomb was announced in 1955 and was not opposed by Labour, Acland resigned his seat in protest. He sought to stand as an Independent against a Labour candidate in the ensuing by-election, but the Conservative government called the 1955 general election soon after. In the resulting contest, Acland split the vote and denied Labour candidate Victor Mishcon the seat, handing it to the Tory Peter Kirk.

After this defeat and a brief spell teaching at Wandsworth Grammar School, Acland retreated to the family's spiritual home of Exmoor, and became a lecturer at St Luke's College of Education in Exeter until 1974. He kept up his campaigning for peace and equality, and into the 1980s was speaking out on the plight on the Third World. Acland continued publishing pamphlets and books on a variety of subjects throughout his life, including *Forward Speaking*, *Nothing Left To Believe?*, *Why So Angry?*, *We Teach Them Wrong*, *Sexual Morality*, *Curriculum or Life*, *The Next Step* (1974) and *Hungry Sheep* (1988). He died on 23 November 1990, at a time when British politics was dominated by the Conservative leadership contest.

Two other small legacies have flowed from Acland. In 1943, in keeping with his principles of common ownership, he donated the ancestral estate of Killerton to the National Trust. The house was subsequently rented back from the trust as a hall of residence for St Luke's College, with Acland as Warden. After his death, debate over whether stag hunting should be banned on the land (contrary to Acland's wishes) was a great controversy at Trust AGMs. And in Gravesend, Acland donated the classic bell wether seat to psephologists – since the Tories won in 1955, Gravesend and its successor Gravesham has been the only parliamentary seat that has always gone the way of the overall winning party.

Acland was an idiosyncratic figure, forged in the unusual politics of his time. But he appears to be universally remembered as a decent, principled idealist in the Liberal aristocratic tradition. The abiding impression is one of a political life dominated by politics as a moral crusade; in Acland's own words, 'Do not ask 'Is it expedient?' Simply ask 'Is it right?''

Matthew Seward

Eric Heffer

born 12 January 1922, *died* 27 May 1991

Eric Heffer was born into a lower-middle-class home in Hertford on 12 January 1922. His father had a small shoe repair and boot-making business, whilst his mother was a freelance cook (or 'caterer', in today's parlance). He was educated in local schools – Bengeo Church of England Primary, and Longmore Senior School. He had a happy childhood and youth, without the deprivation then commonplace in many parts of the country.

Leaving school at fourteen years of age, Eric had various jobs including apprentice electrician, leatherworker, and, finally, as an apprentice carpenter. Conversation at home often turned to politics, and when hunger marchers passed through Hertford in 1936, it had a profound effect on the young Heffer. His burgeoning political consciousness fitted well with his incipient trade unionism, and his religious convictions. This matrix was to be his lifelong anchor.

Having initially joined the Labour Party, Eric resigned at the age of 17 to join the Communist Party. As Eric wrote: 'To me, Stalin was the greatest of men.' He remained a member of the Amalgamated Society of Woodworkers until, in 1942, he was called up into the Royal Air Force. After various postings, he was sent to a maintenance unit in Fazakerley (in the Walton constituency) where he was to meet his future wife, Doris, and where he was to make his political future.

Before and during his conscription, his life was a frantic round of political and trade union meetings and activities. His marriage in 1945 to Doris led initially to a return to Hertford, to live with his parents; but it did not work out. He and Doris returned to Liverpool, but not before he unsuccessfully contested a Hertford council seat in 1946. Working as a carpenter, Eric threw himself into political and trade union activism, leading to his expulsion from the Communist Party after ten years' membership. He lost not only his political allies but his circle of friends. Within six months, he had rejoined the Labour Party in the Toxteth constituency.

Locally, he made his mark, sitting on the executive committee of the Liverpool Trades Council from 1950 to 1964, and chairing it twice – in 1959 and in 1964. He also became a member of the executive of the North West Regional Labour Party, giving him a wider audience. However, he once again resigned from the Labour Party, in 1954, to join the Socialist Workers Federation. This, in turn, collapsed in 1957, leaving Eric to join the Labour Party for the third time.

Within three years, he became a councillor for the Pirrie ward (1960–66), and chairman of Liverpool City Council's Direct Works Department in 1962. Yet a bigger stage beckoned. In 1963, he came from behind to win the Labour Party nomination as candidate for Liverpool Walton. In October 1964, he defeated Tory incumbent, Sir Kenneth Thompson, by nearly 3,000 votes. Eric fitted the House of Commons like a glove, and was to enjoy no finer compliment than to be described as a parliamentarian.

Between 1964 and 1974, Eric Heffer was a backbench journeyman, learning his new parliamentary trade. Harold Wilson appointed him

Minister of State in the Department of Industry in 1974, but was to sack him twelve months later for speaking in the House against the government on the Common Market. Eric immediately became an icon of the left, and was voted onto the National Executive Committee of the Labour Party.

This ushered in Eric's era of national celebrity. On the NEC from 1975 until defeated in 1986, he was Labour Party Vice-Chairman 1982–83 and Chairman 1983–84. During this period he secured election to the Shadow Cabinet for three consecutive years from November 1981, serving as European Affairs spokesman until October 1983 and as Housing and Construction spokesman until he failed to secure re-election to the Shadow Cabinet in October 1984. He also stood unsuccessfully against Neil Kinnock in the contest to succeed Michael Foot as Party leader in 1983. A later attempt for high office, alongside Tony Benn in 1988 challenging Kinnock and Hattersley, was another miserable failure.

Eric never recovered from his ignominious walk-out from the platform during Neil Kinnock's 1985 Conference attack on Militant. Later attempts for both a Shadow Cabinet place and an NEC place, in 1988, convinced him that his time had passed; and in November 1989 he announced his retirement at the following general election. In fact, he died of cancer on 27 May 1991.

A convinced Christian and a unilateral nuclear disarmer, Eric Heffer had been a founding member of the Tribune Group of MPs. He wore his opinions on his sleeve and was famed for his protests. Indeed, one protest led him to storm out of an NEC meeting, but he chose the wrong door, ending up in a cupboard rather than a corridor – an appropriate metaphor for a complex career. His autobiography, *Never A Yes Man,* was published posthumously in 1991.

Peter Kilfoyle

Alice Bacon

Baroness Bacon of Leeds and Normanton

born 10 September 1909, *died* 24 March 1993

Alice Bacon was born into a Yorkshire mining family and into the Labour movement on 10 September 1909. Her father, Benjamin, was a miner and a West Riding county councillor. She went first to elementary schools in Normanton and then to Normanton Girls' Grammar School. During this time she was a leading light of the Labour League of Youth, which introduced her to national politics at a young age.

Bacon trained as a schoolteacher at Stockwell training college and as an external student at London University, and then worked as a secondary school teacher. During her political career she was often described as having the manner of a schoolmistress, with a didactic, commonsensical approach to speaking, which could be effective and persuasive but rankled with Labour intellectuals such as Richard Crossman, who could not abide her flat Yorkshire vowels. Denis Healey described her as 'a bonny Yorkshire lass of immense common sense and strong character, she had more than a touch of Jane Eyre about her. No Rochester ever entered her life, but she had a personal devotion to Hugh Gaitskell which went beyond politics.' Education was always one of her main political interests, at a time when it was regarded as a political backwater, and she was an early advocate of comprehensive schools.

Her contribution to Labour history was mostly through her long service on the National Executive Committee; she first won a place in 1941 and served continuously until she stepped down from parliament in 1970. She was chair of the Labour Party in 1950–51. Alice Bacon was elected MP for Leeds North East in July 1945, overturning a large Conservative majority, and following boundary changes which added suburban Tory territory to North East she moved in 1955 to Leeds South East, where she remained until 1970.

Alice Bacon was one of Gaitskell's staunchest supporters on the NEC and not unwilling to get involved in his 'dirty work', including the attempted expulsion of Bevan in 1955; she was also a notably disciplinarian chair of the Organisation Subcommittee. She and the National Agent, Sara Barker, would suspend and reorganise constituency parties suspected of Trotskyite infiltration with a fervour that would make New Labour's efforts at enforcing its will on local parties seem timid. She seriously proposed that the right and the Bevanites should use different lifts at Transport House when turning up for NEC meetings. As well as being a fierce battler in the bitter internal Labour politics of the 1950s, Bacon was also involved in policy development, fraternal visits and Labour's general election campaign committees in 1959–66.

Bacon was appointed Minister of State, second in command at the Home Office, in October 1964, having been a Shadow Home Office Minister since 1959. For the first year the department was under the benign but ineffective regime of Frank Soskice, and Bacon made much of the running on the biggest Home Office issue, immigration control. She oversaw the introduction of the 1965 Immigration Act and persuaded the 1965 Labour conference to endorse this moderately restrictive (but nowhere near as illiberal as the 1968 Act) measure. She then served under Roy Jenkins, her remit including drugs policy. She expressed her strong personal disapproval of cannabis, but established the liberalising Wootton committee to investigate the drug laws. She joined the Privy Council in 1966.

On 29 August 1967 Alice Bacon moved to Minister of State at the Department of Education and Science, under Patrick Gordon Walker and Ted Short, where she helped administer Labour's policies of comprehensive schooling and expanding higher education. She was not a Wilson loyalist on the NEC; she participated in the plots against him in 1968 and 1969 over the new General Secretary and *In Place of Strife*. Her decision to stand down from parliament in 1970 was in order to take care of her aunt, who had previously cared for Bacon's own parents in their old age. She went straight to the Lords as Baroness Bacon of Leeds and Normanton and contributed actively to the Labour cause in the 1970s and early 1980s, particularly on Home Office matters, education and local government. She died on 24 March 1993. Alice Bacon's was a notably unselfish life, devoting her energies to the Labour Party, Hugh Gaitskell and the improvement of educational and social conditions.

Lewis Baston

Ian Mikardo

born 9 July 1908, *died* 6 May 1993

Ian Mikardo – always Mik to his friends – was born in 1908, in Portsmouth. Both his parents had come to Britain in the last decade of the nineteenth century in that massive Jewish exodus from the Tsarist empire. His mother was from Ukraine, his father from Poland. A family tale, which Mik enjoyed, was that his father, on landing at the London Docks, and speaking no English, was for some months under the impression that he was in New York. The recognition of the plight of strangers in a strange land, stemming from his own background, was a very powerful formative influence in Mik's eternal opposition to anti-semitism and racism in all its forms.

His mother wanted her son to become a rabbi, and indeed he briefly studied at a Rabbinical college – but later transferred to Portsmouth Grammar School, where his headmaster, recognising a formidable talent in the young Mikardo, presciently predicted that he would go far – perhaps one day become an MP.

In 1930 Mik met Mary Rosette, to be his lifelong partner for over 60 years – and he also joined the Labour Party and Poale Zion, the Zionist

Workers' Movement. Throughout the thirties Mik was active in the Labour Party an in the trade union movement, in unions which pre-dated ASTMS, of which he rose to be its first president. During the war he spent his time in aircraft factories, as a consultant.

He first came to national prominence at the 1944 Labour Party Conference. The tale is now well known. Proposing a resolution on behalf of Reading Labour Party, which had recently adopted him as its prospective parliamentary candidate, Mikardo was responsible for defeating the platform with a call for far wider ranging nationalisation measures than the leadership of the Party had wanted. As he left Central Hall Westminster, the Conference venue, he was stopped by Herbert Morrison. 'Young man, you did very well this morning. That was a good speech you made, but you realise, don't you, that you have lost the General Election?' Mik enjoyed telling this story, too. In the 1945 landslide he was elected as MP for Reading.

During that period of the post-war Labour Government, Mik was at his most active as a propagandist and pamphleteer, *Keep Left* (1947) and *Keeping Left* (1950) – with Dick Crossman, Michael Foot and Jo Richardson – being his most famous.

From Reading came another of Mik's lasting contributions to the Party – the 'Reading system'. Prior to this, canvassing and mobilising the vote of election day had tended to be a rather hit-and-miss affair. Mikardo, fully aware that the Reading seat was far from safe, developed a more scientific, more systematic method of recording canvass details – to best maximise the Labour vote. The system, in its essentials, is still in use today. Its initial success was that it saw Mikardo home in Reading, against the trend, in 1955.

Not even scientific canvassing could save the Reading seat for Labour in 1959, and in that year Mikardo lost his seat in Parliament, and also on the National Executive Committee, to which he had first been elected in 1950. This was a double blow, for it was the year before he had been due to become Chair of the Party. However, he was back on the NEC the following year, and was fulfilled as Chair of the Party ten years later –

when, in 1970 and 1971 he chaired no less than three Party Conferences – the only person ever to have done so.

He returned to Parliament, fittingly for a seat in London's East End, in 1964; and continued to represent seats in Tower Hamlets, variously named as a result of boundary changes – Poplar; Bethnal Green and Bow; and Bow and Poplar – until his retirement in 1987.

During the Wilson Government of 1966–70, Mikardo was enormously influential as Chairman of the Select Committee on Nationalised Industries. It was a source of great sadness to his friends and admirers that he never achieved ministerial office – for his organising talents were prodigious.

He served briefly as the Chairman of the Parliamentary Labour Party in 1974. Throughout the sixties and seventies, on the NEC he was hugely active, often behind the scenes, in shaping the policies of the Party. He was Chairman of the Party's International Committee 1973–78, and Honorary President of the Socialist International 1983–93.

Ian Mikardo inspired a generation, perhaps two generations, of Labour Party activists. He was a generous and supportive colleague, despite his apparent abrasiveness. The question Churchill is alleged to have asked – is answered resoundingly by all who knew him well – he was much nicer than he looked.

Alan Haworth

Jo Richardson

born 28 August 1923, *died* 1 February 1994

Jo Richardson died yesterday after a long and painful illness. She was 70. Born in 1923 in Newcastle upon Tyne, Josephine Richardson was the daughter of a methodist commercial traveller, who stood as a Liberal candidate in Darlington in the 1930s. Her mother was an ardent

Congregationalist. Much of Jo's subsequent political interests and sympathies with the position of working class women no doubt derive from her experience of the difficulties faced by her mother, after the premature death of her father.

She was educated at Southend School for Girls, and although of great intelligence and ability, was unable, for financial reasons, to continue into higher education.

In 1945 she joined the Labour Party and became private secretary to Ian Mikardo, who had just been elected as MP for Reading. Over the next 15 years she combined the roles of constituency secretary and political organiser – providing administrative back-up for the Keep Left Group, the Bevanites, Victory for Socialism and, later, the Tribune Group.

In 1951 she was elected to Hornsey Borough Council, and became the full-time secretary and working partner in Ian Mikardo's business company, which specialised in east-west trade.

She contested Monmouth against Peter Thorneycroft in 1951, and again in 1955. In 1959 she fought the marginal and exceptionally large seat of Hornchurch, where she was beaten despite having polled over 27,000 votes. In 1962 she won a seat on Hammersmith Borough Council and in 1964 contested Harrow East in the general election.

In 1973 she was finally selected to fight a safer seat, at Barking, where she replaced Tom Driberg. The selection was hard fought, and Jo won the nomination by a single vote on the fifth and final ballot. She entered Parliament in 1974.

Her parliamentary initiatives were legion. In her maiden speech she supported better pay for primary and nursery teachers. She wanted to nationalise the banks and insurance companies, of course, and sponsored various acts to prevent violence against women and aid battered wives. She was an lifelong champion of women's rights, particularly the rights of working class women – 'those who never get to first base, those who are poor, have kids, whose lives are drudgery.'

In the eighties she was heavily involved and particularly influential in resisting the many attempts which have been made to weaken or undermine the 1968 Abortion Act – through Private Members' Bills introduced by John Corrie, James White, David Alton, and Ann Widdecombe and others.

She was not, though, compartmentalised, having served, in the seventies, variously on the Select Committees on Home Affairs, Nationalised Industries, Expenditure and Procedure.

In 1979 she was elected to the National Executive Committee, replacing Barbara Castle. She served on the NEC for the next 12 years, and was Chair of the Party at the Blackpool Conference in 1990.

For a number of years in the mid 1980s she was the only woman in the Shadow Cabinet. She was appointed as spokesperson on Women's Rights by Neil Kinnock in 1983, a position held until losing her seat in the Shadow Cabinet in 1992. Had she been in good health and had there been a Labour Government at the last election Jo would quite certainly have been the first Minister for Women's Affairs in Britain. Alas, that was not to be.

Jo Richardson's memorial is the intense loyalty and affection of the vast majority of the Labour Movement – shared by not only women, and not only those who held her views on particular issues, but by everyone who knew her. She was deeply loved. Jo suffered very badly from arthritis for a number of years, and last year underwent a major spinal operation, from which she never fully recovered. She continued to come to the Commons, from her hospital bed, for those key votes, determined to the last never to give up, and never to give an inch. She came to vote against VAT on domestic fuel in the week before her death, and was 'nodded through' in the same way as with the key votes against the Government last summer. It was symptomatic of her lifelong qualities.

Alan Haworth

Ron Leighton

born 24 January 1930, *died* 28 February 1994

Ron Leighton had been Member of Parliament for Newham North East, since 1979. He was born in London in 1930, the son of a London Underground driver. He was educated at schools in Barking, and, later, at Ruskin College, Oxford. He spent most of his working life in newspaper machine rooms, starting on the *News of the World* and later moving to the *Sun*. He was an active trades unionist, in the printing union NATSOPA (later SOGAT), and a life-long campaigner against the Common Market, European Community, and European Union.

He joined the Labour Party in 1945, at at the age of 15. In 1964 he contested Middleton and Prestwich. In 1967 he became Secretary of the Labour Common Market Safeguards Committee, and in 1970 Director of the All-Party Common Market Safeguards Campaign. In February 1974 he contested Horsham and Crawley. In the 1975 EC Referendum Campaign he was the National Organiser of the 'No' Campaign.

He entered Parliament in 1979 in unusual circumstances. The Labour PPC for Newham North East quit as candidate several days into the election campaign, and a replacement candidate was needed in a very big hurry. A short list of three was hurriedly drawn up on the authority of the National Executive Committee, and Ron narrowly beat the supposed front runner, Dick Clements, then editor of *Tribune*.

On election day he had the unusual satisfaction, in 1979, of being one of the tiny number of Labour 'gains', as he replaced Reg Prentice, who had been sitting as a Conservative MP for Newham North East, having crossed the floor of the House during the previous Parliament.

He will be best remembered as Chairman of the Employment Select Committee, from 1984 to 1992. His nine years of Chairmanship were not uncontroversial; it included his Committee's strong criticism of the Government's decision to ban trades unions from GCHQ; its strong support for the 600 black-listed miners against the National Coal Board; and its critical look at the claims of the London Docklands Development Corporation to have created employment. These investigations featured such prominent witnesses as EC Commissioner Papandreou, Arthur Scargill and Sir Ian MacGregor.

He was a staunch friend of trades unionists and workers in struggle, not just through his work on the Select Committee, but on the streets as well. In particular, former colleagues from the print unions have saluted his support of the pre-Wapping workforce of News International, whose sacking he strongly condemned. He was present on the picket lines in Wapping on many occasions, and in particular on the night of the infamous 'police riot'. He pursued these matters with characteristic vigour with the Commissioner of the Metropolitan Police, and successive Home Secretaries.

Although his friends had been increasingly worried about his health, he had continued to attend the Commons right up until the week before his death, when he attended the votes on the Sunday Trading Bill and also voted for the reduction of the age of consent.

Alan Haworth

Bob Cryer

born 3 December 1934, *died* 12 April 1994

The accidental death of Bradford South's assiduous Labour MP, Bob Cryer, aroused shock among limited circles of his colleagues. As a hard-line supporter of the Campaign Group, his 1990–91 attacks on the Gulf War lost him 30 per cent of his supporters on Labour's back benches. Whereas he used to chalk up 42 votes in the annual poll for Labour's Shadow Cabinet, from 1990 on he only polled 29. Indicative was the reaction of soft-Left journalist Ian Aitken, who referred to him as 'Dennis Skinner without the charm'.

Bob Cryer tried to skin his opponents, as when he asked John Major last November whether he would 'clear out the cesspit of the present Government by sacking all those ministers who conspired to pervert the course of justice in the Matrix Churchill case in order to cover up a Government policy encouraging the sale of machinery to Iraq'. The Prime Minister dismissed him as 'one of the foremost conspiracy theorists in the House and an acknowledged expert at muckraking'.

Cryer got under the skins of ministers and Labour front-benchers who backed the UN effort to oust Saddam Hussein from Kuwait when he helped turn the CND sympathies of the Campaign Group into a type of aggressive pacifism over the Kuwait crisis. On numerous occasions between September 1990 and February 1991 he voted against the Gulf War, even claiming that the UN action against Saddam Hussein was illegal because China had abstained. When he returned to the subject in January 1992, claiming that UN actions against the Baghdad dictator were 'selective' and 'misguided', Defence Secretary Malcolm Rifkind snarled that Cryer 'might see himself as a friend and ally of Saddam Hussein'.

The only minister who highlighted Cryer's other face was the Attorney General, Sir Nicholas Lyell, who described his 'almost unrivalled knowledge of the procedure of the House, and that knowledge is greatly respected.' This was a reference to Cryer's curious role as Chairman of the Joint Select Comittee on Statutory Instruments, a job he held since 1987, and before that between 1979 and 1983. However much he detested the 'Establishment' and particularly the royal family, there was something in him which obliged him to be useful.

This almost split personality was shown in his role as MEP for Sheffield between 1984 and 1989. Cryer detested the European Community and everything it has stood for, voting against it on every occasion, particularly during the passage of the Maastricht treaty. But he had to understand what it was he hated.

What he genuinely loved was railways, particularly the Keighley and Worth Valley Light Railway, in which he had five £10 shares which, he proudly proclaimed, had never produced a dividend.

He was also an agnostic, who loved the 'beauty and majesty of churches in the townscape'.

Bob Cryer was the son of John Arthur Cryer, a fitter, and was educated at Albert Road School, and Salt High School, both in Shipley, and then at Hull University, where he took a Bachelor of Science degree in Economics.

Although he initially worked as a personnel officer, he quickly became a teacher in Hull, Keighley and Bradford and then a lecturer in Keighley, Dewsbury and Blackburn colleges.

A tall, lean, ginger-haired figure, he had a very puritanical approach, to alcohol as well ('I am not a drinker of alcohol'). Although a cricketer who played for the Yorkshire Universities XI and in the Aire/Wharfe League), he never shared this enthusiasm with cricket-loving Conservatives.

He became a conscientious objector against nuclear weapons in l958, at 24, joining the CND National Council in 1985. He joined the Labour Party in 1958 as a fully-committed nuclear pacifist.

He got the candidacy bug soon, contesting hopeless Darwen in 1964. He succeeded in capturing Keighley from Joan Hall in February 1974. He was named Under-Secretary for Industry in September 1976, but like other hard-Left wingers – including the late Eric Heffer – he did not like being a Minister. In November 1978 he resigned in protest against Government secrecy, but specifically against the Government's refusal to continue funding the Kirkby Co-operative.

He managed to hang on to Keighley by a slender 78 votes in 1979, but lost it in 1983, becoming the MEP for Sheffield the next year. He was returned for Bradford South in 1987.

Back on the back benches, he played the role of a puritanical hard-Leftist. With Arthur Scargill he criticised James Callaghan for having supported right wing policies which allegedly caused its defeat in June

1979. In December 1979 he again opposed subsidies to the Press Gallery. He demanded the sacking of Bill (now Lord) Rodgers for his support of Cruise missiles before he became a co-founder of the SDP. He attacked Denis Healey as part of his campaign for his hero, Tony Benn, who narrowly lost the Deputy Leadership to Healey in September 1981. Once back in the Commons in 1987 he immediately identified himself with the Campaign Group, which put him on its slate. But he was such a sectarian Left winger that he never managed to win support outside that narrow group.

Andrew Roth

John Smith

born 13 September 1938, *died* 12 May 1994

The paradox about John Smith, the fifteenth Labour Party leader, is that throughout his career he was regarded as being on the party's right wing, but posthumously he became an almost iconic favourite of the left. The view of Smith's admirers is that, if he had lived, he would have won the 1997 election and would have been a more radical Prime Minister and more emollient party leader than Tony Blair. The harsher view, taken by more partisan Blairites, is that he threw away the 1992 election and might have done the same again in 1997.

Smith remained doggedly consistent through his long career in his belief in social democracy as expounded by Hugh Gaitskell and Anthony Crosland. To the Bennite left, he was barely distinguishable from the founders of the SDP, but by the late 1990s his views on redistribution through taxation seemed 'old Labour'.

The son of the headmaster of a village school, born 13 September 1938, he grew up in the tiny town of Ardrishaig, in West Scotland. After Dunoon

Grammar School, he read Law at Glasgow University, where he was the leading figure in a promising Labour Club (he was Chair in 1960), whose other stars included a future Scottish Secretary and First Minister, Donald Dewar, and a future Lord Chancellor, Lord Irvine. Having been talent-spotted by officials at the party's Scottish head office, Smith was a parliamentary candidate at the age of only 22, in a by-election in East Fife in 1961, a safe Tory seat in which he did well to come second. He unsuccessfully re-fought the seat at the 1964 general election. He then took a break from politics to establish himself as a lawyer and start a family. In 1967 he married a contemporary at Glasgow University, Elizabeth Bennett, and had three daughters, Sarah, Jane and Catherine. For the whole of Smith's political career, the family home was in Edinburgh, not London.

Smith returned to politics by winning North Lanarkshire with a majority of 5,019 in the 1970 election. He was considered to be a reliable and hard-working backbench MP with a fine grasp of detail, but no firebrand. His political tactic was – as his friend Roy Hattersley put it – to be 'on the right but not deeply involved in the right.' He avoided making enemies and generally did as directed by the whips, except on one significant occasion: in 1971, he was among several dozen pro-marketeers, led by Roy Jenkins, who broke a three-line whip and secured the UK's entry to the Common Market.

He was quickly forgiven for this, and for turning down the first government job offered him by Harold Wilson in 1974, as a Scottish law officer. After serving briefly as PPS to Scottish Secretary Willie Ross, in October 1974 he was appointed an Under-Secretary of State at Energy, with special responsibility for the new North Sea oilfields. Eight months later he found himself working alongside Tony Benn, who respected him enough to demand his promotion to Minister of State level in December 1975 (and to vote for him in the 1992 leadership election). Together they created the British National Oil Company. Smith vehemently protested when the company was later privatised by the Conservatives.

In April 1976, James Callaghan sent Smith to work as deputy to Michael Foot, Leader of the Commons, as Minister of State at the Privy

Council Office. His job was supervising the extremely complex legislation to create devolved assemblies for Scotland and Wales. The number of parliamentary days the legislation required was a post-war record, but Smith finally saw it through. By the time devolution was killed off by referendums in the two countries, he had been promoted Secretary of State for Trade (as of 11 November 1978), making him the youngest member of the Cabinet, just after his fortieth birthday.

In opposition, Smith set a unique record as the only person to be re-elected to the Shadow Cabinet every year for three whole parliaments, until he became party leader. This was despite his threadbare record in the early years, when much of his time was spent reviving his law practice. As Shadow Secretary for Trade, Prices and Consumer Protection (1979–82), during 1981 he made only two brief speeches to the Commons. In 1982, he did not speak at all until after he had been promoted to the post of Shadow Energy Secretary in December. In 1983, he qualified as a QC.

He became a much more significant figure in the Labour Party after the 1983 general election and the subsequent resignation of Michael Foot. A boundary change in that election meant that he was returned as MP for Monklands East, with a majority of 9,799. He ran Roy Hattersley's campaign for the party leadership. Under pressure from unions like the GMB and AEUW, Neil Kinnock appointed him Employment spokesman in October 1983, then promoted him to be Trade and Industry spokesman a year later. His reputation as one of Labour's best parliamentary performers was established during the Westland crisis, an argument over the future of a Cornish-based helicopter firm, during which Smith played a large part in forcing the resignation of Leon Brittan, his opposite number in the Cabinet.

After the 1987 election, Smith was appointed Shadow Chancellor, which made him deputy leader of the party in all but name, and the most obvious putative successor to Neil Kinnock. He was privately approached by some MPs who wanted him to run against Kinnock, but turned them away. Perhaps understandably, his relations with the leader were cool, and deteriorated until their inability to get on became an impediment to Labour's election chances. The origin of the problem was that Kinnock wanted to hurry ahead with a radical policy review, whilst Smith was reluctant to commit himself early, and moved only when he felt that the time was right.

An example of how nimbly he could move, when he thought it necessary, was during the Cabinet crisis which led to the resignation of the Chancellor, Nigel Lawson, brought on by Margaret Thatcher's opposition to Europe's Exchange Rate Mechanism (ERM), the prelude to the euro. Labour had always opposed British membership of the ERM, but in the middle of a parliamentary speech in October 1989, Smith casually announced a new policy, which favoured joining if certain 'prudent' conditions were met. The switch, which had not been agreed by the Shadow Cabinet, was adroitly timed to maximise the advantage of the Lawson-Thatcher rift. Smith was notably vague about what the 'prudent' conditions for ERM membership might be.

His popularity in the party was undiminished by the political risk he took in January 1988, during a free vote on abortion. Smith and the Monklands West MP Tom Clarke, his Parliamentary neighbour, were the only members of the Shadow Cabinet to support a proposal to tighten the abortion law by reducing the upper time limit to 18 weeks.

Politically, he may have been assisted by the sympathy he attracted after he had suffered a heart attack at the age of 50, just after the 1988 annual party conference. It might have killed him but for the lucky chance that it hit him whilst he was in hospital, after being cajoled by Mrs Smith to go in for a check-up. It took him out of politics for the latter part of 1988 and the early part of 1989. Whilst he was convalescing, he came second in the Shadow Cabinet election, topping the poll the next year.

At the time, Smith appeared to be a cautious Shadow Chancellor, keen to make Labour acceptable to business, and anxious not to repeat the expensive manifesto commitments which had bedevilled Labour's 1987 election campaign. He imposed a rule that no shadow minister was allowed to enter into a new spending commitment. However, he did not demur from expensive promises to raise pensions and child benefit, and to pay for them he proposed what amounted to a 19p in the pound income tax increase for the highest paid. This threatened increase, freely misinterpreted by the Tories and their supporting newspapers so that even the relatively low-paid imagined that it applied to them, was possibly the single biggest cause of Labour's 1992 defeat.

Nevertheless, when Neil Kinnock retired, it was almost a foregone conclusion that Smith would be his successor, despite the mistrust he had aroused among modernisers like Tony Blair. He easily saw off his only challenger, Bryan Gould, an opponent of ERM, and was virtually able to choose his own deputy in Margaret Beckett.

His brief leadership was characterised by what one admirer called 'masterly inactivity'. It frustrated the modernisers, who wanted to push ahead with party reforms and with another drastic revision of party policy. Smith was not to be hurried. He displayed a fondness for setting up commissions and committees to mull over difficult issues. The most prominent was the Social Justice Commission chaired by Lord Borrie, which produced a long, erudite and widely read report on reforming the welfare state, with little obvious impact. There were other commissions or committees handling topics like economic policy, electoral reform, and the role of the trade unions within the Labour Party.

On this last issue, Smith again displayed his capacity for moving quickly and decisively when he chose. The committee was examining the time-honoured method of using union 'block votes' in the election of party leaders and selection of parliamentary candidates. With union full-time officials around the table, there was no sign that it would produce any radical reform until Smith made a sudden appearance at its meeting in July 1993 to pronounce that nothing less than a one-member, one-vote (OMOV) system would do.

At the time, Smith seemed to be heading towards certain defeat, because a rule change had to be agreed by the annual party conference, which was itself dominated by union block votes. Three of the four biggest unions were opposed to introducing OMOV. Yet Smith persisted, against the odds, cajoling and exhorting the leaders of the smaller unions and privately hinting that he would resign if he lost. In the end, the reform was agreed by a tiny majority at the party's annual conference in October 1993. It was possibly the single most important change to the Labour Party's rule book in its entire history, whose most obvious bene-ficiary was Tony Blair. John Smith, meanwhile, was hit by a second and fatal heart attack in his London flat early in the morning of 12 May 1994.

Andy McSmith

Fred Mulley

Lord Mulley of Manor Park

born 3 July 1918, *died* 15 March 1995

Now remembered most colourfully as the Defence Secretary who fell asleep during the Queen's Silver Jubilee flypast, Fred Mulley was one of the unsung workhorses of the Wilson and Callaghan governments, remaining on Labour's front bench throughout the period 1964–79, though never becoming an elected member of the shadow cabinet. A cautious, unflamboyant and hard-working government loyalist, he was the epitome of the so-called 'safe pair of hands'. A solid pillar of the pro-European, pro-NATO social-democratic right, he was a prime deselection target of the militant left in the aftermath of the 1979 election defeat. Mulley combined his parliamentary work with his role as APEX member of the trade union section of Labour's NEC 1958–1980, in which capacity he was in 1974–75 chair of the Labour Party and of the Special Conference called in April 1975 on the EEC. In 1971 he and USDAW President and fellow former minister Walter

Padley joined Roy Jenkins, Jack Diamond, Shirley Williams and Tom Bradley in the defeated minority when the NEC voted to call for Labour MPs to oppose Heath's attempt to join the EEC. Of the six, only he and Padley, neither of whom were close to Jenkins socially, did not later join the SDP.

A keen pro-European, he nevertheless did not want to risk splitting the Party over the EEC and on 29 March 1972 he joined the NEC majority in backing a referendum. He was far closer to Callaghan than to middle-class socialist intellectuals either of the right like Crosland (whom he resented as an overlord at the Department of the Environment) or of the left like Barbara Castle and Dick Crossman, for whom he was 'a bore'. On 26 March 1969 he joined Callaghan on the NEC in voting down Barbara Castle's *In Place of Strife* and during the 1970s her diaries note with a certain relish Mulley 'bleating pathetically' over his relative failure to protect the education budget as compared to her DHSS budget.

Born on 3 July 1918 in Leamington Spa, where his father, W. J. Mulley, was a local labourer, he attended the Church of England School, Leamington, followed by Warwick School, joining Labour in 1936. Leaving school after the loss of his father's job, the evening classes he attended whilst working as a clerk secured him a scholarship to Ruskin College, Oxford, in 1939. Joining the Worcestershire Regiment at the outbreak of war, Mulley used his time as a POW in Germany 1940–45 to teach himself economics, gaining a BSc from London University. His essay, *The Economics of a Prison Camp*, describing the operation of a currency system based on cigarettes, won him an adult scholarship to Christ Church, Oxford, in 1945.

Unsuccessfully contesting Sutton Coldfield at the 1945 general election, he graduated with a First in PPE in 1947. After a year at Nuffield he took up an economics fellowship at St Catherine's College, Cambridge, remaining there until elected MP for Sheffield Park in 1950, a constituency he continued to represent until his deselection by the hard left at the 1983 election. In his spare time he read Law, and in 1954 was called to the Bar at the Inner Temple.

As a backbencher, he had long shown interest in defence issues, publishing *The Politics of Western Defence* in 1962 and serving on the Council of the Institute for Strategic Studies 1961–64. A delegate to the Council of Europe and the WEU (1958–61), he was from 1979 until 1983 the WEU Assembly President. Shadow Air Minister 1960–64, on Labour's election victory in 1964 he joined the Privy Council and was appointed Minister for the Army and Deputy Defence Secretary. Reshuffled to the post of Aviation Minister in December 1965 he inherited the burden of Concorde, a project begun under the Conservatives which he would have liked to have cancelled had it not already been so far progressed.

Appointed Minister of State for Disarmament at the Foreign Office in January 1967, he was 'a skilled negotiator', according to the memoirs of his chief, Michael Stewart. His priorities, and in particular his attempts to secure a complete nuclear test ban, were 'unexpectedly progressive' even by Barbara Castle's unsympathetic standards, as she duly noted in her diary. In October 1969 he was appointed Transport Minister outside the Cabinet, a post he held until Labour's defeat in 1970 and continued to shadow in opposition. Re-appointed Transport Minister in 1974, Wilson promoted him to Cabinet as Education Secretary in succession to Reg Prentice on 9 June 1975.

With the growing economic difficulties which were to culminate in the so-called IMF crisis in late 1976, Mulley spent most of his time battling to minimise cuts to the education budget. He tried in vain to secure from his civil servants a workable scheme to remove charitable status from private schools. It was at a meeting with Mulley on 21 May 1976 that Jim Callaghan spelt out his Prime Ministerial priorities for tackling education standards and poor teaching as later encapsulated in the Ruskin speech. 'Fred rather blanched' at this, according to Callaghan's biographer Kenneth Morgan and in consequence he was appointed Defence Secretary in the reshuffle of September 1976.

Together with Callaghan, Healey and Owen, Mulley was a member of the government's secret Nuclear Defence Policy Group which supervised the Chevaline upgrade of the Polaris nuclear deterrent and considered its replacement with Trident and the deployment of US cruise missiles from British bases. He was a firm advocate of a 3 per cent NATO-wide increase in defence spending, and of the, ultimately unsuccessful, British Nimrod airborne early warning system over its US rival.

Created Lord Mulley of Manor Park in Sheffield in 1984, he remained a loyal Labour backbencher until his death on 15 March 1995. He served from 1988 until 1991 as Deputy Chair of the Sheffield Development Corporation He married Joan Philips in 1948, with whom he had two daughters.

Greg Rosen

Harold Wilson

Lord Wilson of Rievaulx

born 11 March 1916, *died* 24 May 1995

Lord Wilson of Rievaulx, as he came improbably to be called, will not go down in the history books as one of Britain's greatest Prime Ministers. But, increasingly, he will be seen as a far bigger political figure than contemporary sceptics have allowed, far more representative of that uniquely ambivalent mood of Britain in the 1960s and a far more rounded and caring, if unfulfilled, person.

It is my view that he was a remarkable Prime Minister and, indeed, a quite remarkable man. Cynics had a field day ridiculing him at the time of his decline. Perhaps that was inevitable given his irresistible tendency to behave like the master of the Big Trick in the circus ring of politics – for whom there is nothing so humiliating as to have it demonstrated, often by fellow tricksters, that the Big Trick hasn't worked.

James Harold Wilson happened to be Prime Minister leading a left-wing party at a time when the mores of post-war political and economic change in Britain (and elsewhere) were just beginning to be perceived. Arguably it was the period of the greatest social and industrial change this century, even if the people – let alone the Wilson governments – were never fully aware of the nature of that change. Social relationships across the entire class spectrum were being transformed. What with the Pill, television, fashion, life style, pleasure and leisure, there was a deepening uncertainty in the 1960s about what it all meant and where it was all leading. Harold Wilson's 'burning with the white heat of technology,' and other famous phrases, sought to grapple with the era while never quite understanding what was happening to him or his government in a changing Britain and a dramatically changing world. He was blamed for things he never properly understood were happening.

In that sense the Wilson of the 1960s was a victim far more than a hapless architect. He lacked the deep conviction of Thatcher or de Gaulle and he never possessed the philosophical and inspirational qualities of Aneurin Bevan – who, had he lived beyond 1960, would probably have been Labour's Prime Minister. Wilson often drifted. There was no compass, no weight of ideological baggage.

But Denis Healey is wrong in his assessment of Wilson as a man who had 'neither political principle' nor 'sense of direction.' Wilson did have both – embedded not in ideology but in his intuitive sense of decency and his powerful drive to try and spread that decency among his fellow citizens.

There was another curious aspect to Harold Wilson – a strange modesty. Sometimes one had the impression that he never quite believed that he had arrived at the top of the greasy pole. Just before he was due to go to the palace in 1964 after narrowly winning that memorable election, I interviewed him for the *Daily Herald*. We sat alone in Labour Party headquarters at Transport House and I asked him how he felt. 'I still can't believe it,' he responded. 'Just think, here I am, the lad from behind those lace curtains in the Huddersfield house you saw – here I am about to go to see the Queen and become Prime Minister. I still can't believe it.' The cynics will dismiss that as an act. I am convinced it was genuine, vintage Wilson.

Not that those lace curtains concealed a working class home of poverty and deprivation. He came from a lower middle class family. His father, James Herbert, whom Harold later had pride in bringing to Labour Party conferences, was an industrial chemist who worked for ICI. But in the slump after the First World War Herbert Wilson was made redundant. It devastated the family and shaped Harold Wilson's political mind for all time. He later confessed: 'Unemployment more than anything else made me politically conscious.' At Milnsbridge New Street Council School he won a county scholarship to Royds Hall Secondary School in Huddersfield. But when Herbert found a job as a chief chemist on the Wirral, Harold was transferred to Wirral Grammar School – from where he won a history scholarship to Jesus College, Oxford. He was on his way.

One is tempted to say that he was the typical grammar school boy up at Oxford in the pre-war 1930s – almost working class, certainly lower middle class no particular privileges in his background, unless you regard the nonconformist social and moral discipline as a privilege. Yet he wasn't typical. Unlike Denis Healey, from a roughly similar background in Yorkshire, Wilson did not dive headlong into Oxford politics or literary life. He was a swot. He spent his time almost exclusively on his studies – and did brilliantly. He won the Webb Medley economics prize as well as the Gladstone history prize. He gained an outstanding first class honours degree in PPE and was elected to a junior research fellowship at University College, where he helped the master, Sir William Beveridge, in a study of unemployment and the trade cycle which had a clear influence on the great Beveridge Report.

Nor was Wilson a political lefty: his views were radical – but much more akin to the liberalism of Lloyd George than, say, the socialism of Stafford Cripps (Wilson's later hero) or even Clem Attlee. He regularly attended the Oxford Liberal Club in the mid-thirties and was hardly known at all to the band of student socialists like Healey or young socialist dons like Dick Crossman.

But shortly before the war Wilson joined the Oxford Labour Club – largely, it is said, under the influence of G. D. H. Cole, economics fellow at University College and guru of Oxford socialism in the inter-war years. There was another important influence developing – in the summer of 1938 Wilson become engaged to Gladys Mary Baldwin and they were married on New Year's Day 1940.

It was then that he began seriously to consider a political career, though he was still deeply attached to the academic lifestyle. When he registered for war service he was directed, as a specialist, to do government department work and this eventually led, through the War Cabinet secretariat, to Wilson's appointment as director of economics and statistics at the Ministry of Fuel and Power. It was a critical turning point in his developing political awareness. Soon he came under the gaze of the redoubtable Hugh Dalton, in charge at the Ministry of Economic Warfare. Dalton chose Wilson to be secretary of an inquiry into the coal mining industry which resulted in a book on the nationalisation of coal. *New Deal For Coal* became a minor political classic which provided the launch pad for Wilson's leap into a parliamentary candidature. In the 1945 election he won Ormskirk, close by the Wirral, by a large majority and remained there till 1950 when re-distribution took him to the nearby Merseyside seat of Huyton, where he remained until his retirement in June 1983.

His rise to cabinet office was exceptionally rapid. He was quickly appointed to a junior post in the Attlee administration. His feet had scarcely touched the back benches before he was made Parliamentary Secretary of the Ministry of Works and two years later, in March 1947, he was promoted to Secretary for Overseas Trade. By October he was in the Cabinet as President of the Board of Trade – at 31 one of the youngest cabinet ministers of all time – succeeding Sir Stafford Cripps who became the government's economic overlord.

Wilson fell under Cripps's spell and continued to carry out many of the policies that Cripps had already laid down – especially the intensive post-war export drive. It was while at the Board of Trade that he first established a contact with the Soviet trade mission and with Stalin's shrewd and experienced trade minister, Anastas Mikoyan. Wilson's time at the Board of Trade is perhaps best remembered for his 'Bonfire of Controls' – when between November 1948 and February 1949 he removed hundreds of controls covering consumer goods, industrial equipment and the purchase of foreign supplies. Wilson's bonfire delighted the press and the public – but not many of his backbench MPs, particularly those on the left who regarded it as a clear sign that Wilson was really a right-winger at heart.

The real test of Wilson's political courage – or opportunism if one now reads his motives that way – came when he joined Aneurin Bevan in resigning from the government in protest against the NHS charges in Hugh Gaitskell's 1951 budget. Gaitskell, a new Chancellor, was faced with the commitment to a huge re-armament programme (the outbreak of the Korean war) which Bevan opposed as fundamentally mistaken and because it meant the erosion of other spending plans, notably on the NHS. But Gaitskell was as stubborn as Wilson was flexible and, though no natural supporter of Nye Bevan, Wilson followed Bevan's resignation a day later, along with another minister, John Freeman.

For a time Wilson went along with the Bevanites, participating in *Tribune* brains trust meetings throughout the country and campaigning on a broad left wing platform. He was co-author of a famous Tribune pamphlet, *One Way Only*, a socialist argument against revisionist policies. Generally he identified himself with the anti-Gaitskell camp which split the whole Labour party after the 1951 election defeat. Yet there was never a great deal of trust for Wilson among the proven Bevanites – and always some doubt in the mind of Nye himself, a doubt which became entrenched when Wilson took Bevan's place in the Shadow Cabinet in 1954 after Nye walked out over another policy rift. That gulf of distrust between Wilson and the left was never effectively healed.

Increasingly Wilson seemed to be grooming himself for a senior role in the the Labour leadership. When Gaitskell became leader in 1955 Wilson canvassed and voted for Gaitskell – not for Bevan. In the late 1950s Wilson became a very effective Shadow Chancellor. He was also chair of an internal inquiry into organisation which produced a damning report on the party's cob-webbed methods and called for an end to the 'penny farthing' party machine. The legendary Morgan Phillips, party secretary, never forgave Wilson for that report.

Yet the 'Walter Mitty' label which was to become the trade mark of Harold Wilson's personality in his premiership years was already being woven. He hovered between moderate left and moderate right throughout the late 1950s and into the 1960s. In 1960, the year Gaitskell was defeated over nuclear disarmament, Wilson actually challenged Gaitskell's leadership – but was heavily defeated, 166 votes to 81. It was Wilson's bid to try to re-build a bridge with the left in the party, though it was regarded by the left as pure opportunism. The result of it all, ironically, was that he became Shadow Foreign Secretary.

Then came Gaitskell's sudden death. It found the Labour Party completely unprepared and the contestants had little time to develop their individual platforms. George Brown, James Callaghan and Harold Wilson went into the first ballot of MPs which eliminated Callaghan, who polled 41 to Wilson's 115 and Brown's 88. In the run-off Wilson beat Brown by 144 to 103 – largely with the help of the old Bevanite left.

So in February 1963 the little man from Huddersfield took over the Labour Party and immediately began preparations for the general election that had to take place in 1964. At the Scarborough Labour conference of 1963 Wilson produced his famous speech on the 'white heat of technology' – from material provided for him by several committees in which Richard Crossman and Professor P. M. S. Blackett played a crucial role. And in the period between that conference and the election of October 1964 Wilson made six major speeches outlining the 'socialist alternative' to 13 years of Tory rule and mismanagement. It was an unusually effective preparation in the country as a whole while, in Parliament, Wilson dominated the House against the gentle but inadequate Alec Douglas-Home.

The surprise was to come: most pundits believed Wilson would secure a substantial majority in the October 1964 election: yet Labour won by a mere five seats, soon reduced still further by deaths.

In the first hundred days of that first Wilson Government there was genuine political excitement. The inheritance was a crippling one in economic terms. There were fearful problems with the balance of payments, the strength of sterling and the entire condition of the domestic economy. Lord Cromer, Governor of the Bank of England, told the Prime Minister that there would have to be severe cuts in government spending and fundamental changes in Labour's election promises. That was an outright and direct challenge to Wilson from the City establishment – within weeks of the election. Wilson's response was equally forthright. He told the Governor that his challenge was a threat to the government mandate and to democracy itself.

Wilson told Cromer that if forced he would 'go back to the electorate for a mandate giving me full power to handle the crisis'. Perhaps gamblers' talk, but also Wilson at his most audacious and courageous. He knew he must go to the country again before long. The counterattack worked. Cromer retreated though the City never forgot.

In fact none of the four Wilson Governments was free from economic crises in one form or another. The 1966 election victory gave him a majority of 97, but by July the Government was plunged into its worst crisis of all: a seamen's strike exacerbated an already tense financial situation. Inflation at home led to a run on the pound and a severe strain on reserves. Devaluation was discussed and advocated by George Brown – but rejected by Wilson. Rumours spread about a cabinet crisis and a possible putsch against Wilson. The Government scrambled through – far from the harmonious band their majority had promised.

What should have been the beginning of Wilson's most productive period as Prime Minister began in crisis and rarely moved away from that pitch. George Brown's National Plan was dumped. There were endless problems with the trades unions over incomes policy, culminating in Barbara Castle's White Paper on reform of industrial relations, *In Place of Strife*, which was undermined by union resistance and backbench MPs, as well as cabinet divisions, where James Callaghan led the opposition. The retreat from *In Place of Strife* in summer 1969 contributed directly to the defeat of the Wilson government at the 1970 general election. Wilson's retreat in 1969 was seen by the press and public as capitulation to trade union power – which in many senses it was, though the issue was more complex than that.

On the overseas front there were few successes. Wilson's endless attempts to reach an accommodation with Ian Smith's Rhodesia ended in fudged deals culminating in UDI (Unilateral Declaration of Independence). Over Vietnam, Lyndon Johnson put increasing pressure on Wilson to provide a British contingent – which he resisted. But he also had to maintain the posture, which was costly window dressing, of a significant British defence presence east of Suez. The devaluation of the pound in 1967 virtually destroyed what was left of the economic strategy. In November sterling fell to $2.40 and a badly shaken Prime Minister made an inept television address to the nation, arguing that the 'pound in your pocket' was unaffected – an extraordinary reversal of the euphoric days of 1964–1966.

Most people, including Wilson, believed Labour would win the 1970 election. The polls were consistently in Labour's favour. The economy was showing distinct signs of improvement and Roy Jenkins's standing as Chancellor was regarded as a significant strength. Edward Heath was not rated as a dangerous challenger but turned a large Labour majority into an easily workable Tory one. Inside Wilson's Downing Street entourage there was a last-minute panic and much disagreement, especially between Marcia Williams (Lady Falkender) and other members of Wilson's 'kitchen cabinet'. These disagreements and personal animosities were to return and haunt the Wilson government of 1974.

In opposition the spark seemed to have been snuffed out of Wilson. It took him a long time to regain his confidence after the 1970 defeat. Yet he did so with, once again, unusual skill – holding the Labour Party together and avoiding serious splits over the Common Market and defence policy. He was still a master at exploiting the theme of Labour unity and finding the compromise formulas. Indeed, it was during that period that Wilson picked up the theme of the 'Social Contract' – chiefly from Jack Jones, the Transport Union leader and Professor Tommy Balogh (Lord Balogh) – which provided the main platform when Labour returned to office in 1974. The Heath Government blundered into a miners' strike after the oil crisis of 1973 and by the winter of 1973–74 appeared to offer no clearer solution to the 'trade union problem' than the Wilson Governments of the 1960s. The February 1974 election was an extraordinary political event. The Heath Government in effect abandoned ship. Wilson, to my own close knowledge at the time, did not expect to win. It was not so much an election victory for him as a defeat for Heath. No one had an overall majority though Labour was the largest group. For several days the formation of a new Labour government remained in doubt as Heath sought a deal with the Liberals. Only when that failed did the Queen call on Wilson to form his third administration – a minority Labour government.

Immediately the Prime Minister turned to settling the miners' strike and the follow-through industrial problems. He appointed Michael Foot as Employment Secretary to orchestrate the Social Contract. It was a period of intense activity, a touch reminiscent of October 1964, albeit with the climate profoundly different. Former cabinet ministers from the 1960s met in depressed mood, privately of course, to discuss what they regarded as the grim prospect of another Wilson administration. Men like Roy Jenkins – appointed unwillingly to the Home Office in 1974 – had already lost all confidence in Wilson's leadership and were actually looking for a defeat in the 1974 election. It was an unstable government – quite apart from whether a group of MI5 officers was busily trying still further to de-stabilise it. Yet in the few months between March and October 1974, when Wilson won his fourth term, the 'interim' government did actually perform rather well. Its very existence hinged on support from the Liberals, and the gamble that Scottish and Welsh Nationalists would not vote with the Tories. Healey's first budget was very tough, making no attempt to disguise the grave economic situation. Wilson began the process of trying to 're-negotiate' the terms of Britain's EEC membership. Michael Foot started to re-draw the Heath Government's industrial relations legislation. And the National Enterprise Board was established to help link the state and private industry in a re-development programme, while Wilson and Tony Benn fought their own ideological battle in the Cabinet about the degree of state intervention.

If the conspiracy theory of Wilsonia is to be believed, then it was about this time that, according to Peter Wright's book *Spycatcher*, a group of MI5 'dissidents' began to 'work' on the government. Wilson himself, albeit later, as well as Lady Falkender, became persuaded that there was 'something in it.' At any rate those months between the two 1974 elections were certainly the time when Wilson pencilled a ring around the date of his resignation – to come shortly after his 60th birthday in March 1976. The great disappointment for him was the result of the second 1974 election. He hoped for a reasonable, if not large, working majority. In the event he secured a fragile overall majority of only three. He had achieved something no previous Prime Minister had done this century: led four administrations, equalling the record of one of his old heroes, Gladstone. He had also kept the Labour Party in one piece. Yet, somehow, real success evaded him.

Wilson began his final period as Prime Minister with an outward display of boldness. He helped Giscard d'Estaing, the French president, launch the concept of annual economic summit meetings in the aftermath of the Arab-Israeli war and the huge increase in oil prices. The Wilson government managed another rescue operation to save sterling ,which Wilson described as 'the most hectic and harrowing month (December 1975) I experienced in nearly eight years as Prime Minister.'

He brilliantly trumped Tony Benn's demand for a referendum on the Common Market by holding one, certainly an act, tactically, of political genius well in the tradition of Wilson. Domestic inflation, after its peak of 27 per cent early in 1974, was beginning to fall; the Social Contract, despite all the strains, was actually working and Wilson pushed strongly for a new impetus to be given to regional policies in Scotland, Wales and the North. Quite remarkable for a man who was already tired, unwell and surrounded by personal uncertainties.

He resigned on 16 March 1976 – five days after his 60th birthday. I happened to be working for him at the time (though I had no idea of what was impending) and I knew how tired and ill he was. Some observers of that scene, like Len Murray (Lord Murray) the former TUC general secretary, still believe he could (and should) have continued. But I doubt it. He had had enough.

He was not driven out by MI5 plots, real or imagined; there were no hidden mysteries about scandals, sexual or otherwise; it was not because Marcia Williams, Joe Haines and Bernard Donoughue were squabbling in an ante-room (though they were). His doctor – the late Joe Stone – had already detected problems which, later, became diagnosed as cancer of the colon. He was taking brandy to comfort the difficult afternoons and evenings. What I witnessed, first hand, was the reality of a tired man trapped by his own deep sense of uncertainty which always lurked below the self-confident surface.

Yet after all criticism has been thrown at him, and the sneers and scepticism reduced to routine clichés, Harold Wilson, in my view, remains a remarkable man and a remarkable Prime Minister. He alone – other than Attlee in 1945 – was capable of making Labour the 'natural party of government' and maintaining a unity within such a disparate and warring coalition of ideas and ambitions. He failed to rise to greatness because he failed in the critical period after the victory of 1966.

The final tragic years in which the jewel of his extraordinary memory became increasingly destroyed by terrible illness robbed him – and probably the nation – of an opportunity to demonstrate a matured wisdom that, undoubtedly, was there.

Geoffrey Goodman

James Hacker

Lord Hacker of Islington KG, Hon. D. Phil

born 18 June 1927, *died* 4 November 1995

James (Jim) Hacker was perhaps not the most naturally gifted of Britain's Prime Ministers, but few even of his opponents denied the force of his personal charm or his sense of what the voting public wanted. Like many of his contemporaries in the party, a long period in opposition had sharpened his appetite for power without perhaps providing him with the necessary training for exercising it effectively.

His appointment as Minister for Administrative Affairs was no more than he could have expected as a reward for his loyal support for his leader in opposition, and he took up the reins of office with a number of excellent intentions. His policy initiatives showed his sensitivity to popular feeling, and indeed he was in some ways a pioneer of reforms which were implemented by others long after he had left office.

He was an early advocate of open government, of National Health reform and of an integrated transport system, and his political memoirs also show his interest in other still active issues such as cutting government waste and increasing representation of women in the higher ranks of the civil service.

It is still something of a mystery why none of these ever actually reached the statute book during his tenure of office. His critics have attributed this to his inability or reluctance to think measures through and examine their implications, before announcing them. Others attribute this failure to spending too long on the opposition front bench, where success is measured by an ability to formulate attractive sounding ideas and encapsulate them in catchy phrases (at which he was expert), without ever having to draft legislation and take it through Parliament. It is certainly true that his professional career in political research, university lecturing and journalism had never required him to engage with the relatively tedious and unglamorous task of motivating staff, controlling budgets or running even the smallest of departments, nor with the acceptance of managerial responsibility for anything.

But this was true of many of his cabinet colleagues who nevertheless produced solid and successful legislation. What makes this especially surprising is that throughout his spell at the department he had as his Permanent Secretary the legendary Sir Humphrey Appleby, one of the safest pairs of hands in the history of the civil service. Moreover, his Private Secretary was the brilliant young high-flyer Bernard Woolley, later to become Cabinet Secretary himself. With such an expert team behind him, Hacker's inability to register any significant legislative achievement (except for a small liberalisation of data protection rules) can certainly not be attributed to any lack of firmness or skill in his administrative support.

Hacker's career took a dramatic change of direction after two years at the Department of Administrative Affairs. The Prime Minister suddenly resigned, for reasons which have never been adequately explained. It was a particularly startling resignation, since his natural successor, the Home Secretary, had only two days previously had to resign over a drunken driving incident on the way home after recording a Christmas 'Don't drink and drive' broadcast. As party chairman, Hacker had an important role in organising the succession, which was assumed to lie between the Chancellor of the Exchequer and the Foreign Secretary. It is still not fully understood why both of them decided to withdraw from the contest; even Hacker's most fervent supporters do not suggest that it was because they both recognised his superior strength of character and intellectual abilities.

Nevertheless, their bitter rivalry made their withdrawal a great relief to the party, and started a search for a less divisive leader. Even so, it was a considerable surprise even to the closest political observers when Hacker's name finally went forward unopposed.

Not the least of Hacker's pleasures on entering Number 10 must have been his reunion with his old Permanent Secretary Sir Humphrey

Appleby. Sir Humphrey had been appointed Cabinet Secretary only a few days before the resignation of the Prime Minister and was waiting there to welcome his successor. Since Hacker brought with him Bernard Woolley, his departmental private secretary, the old team was now reunited at an eminence they can scarcely have foreseen when they first met on the steps of the Department for Administrative Affairs that Monday morning after the general election.

A change of Prime Minister always provokes expectations of a renaissance or a reformation, and Hacker was anxious to make his mark on events as early as possible. He selected defence as the area where radical reorganisation could produce spectacular savings, and an improvement in efficiency at the same time. His proposal to sell off most of the expensive defence buildings and real estate in London and South East England and relocate their staff to high-unemployment areas in the North could indeed have had considerable economic impact – and political impact too, since many of the designated high-unemployment areas turned out to be in marginal constituencies. Unfortunately, the senior officers in the armed forces were able to demonstrate that although they strongly approved of the policy, it would not in fact be practicable in their particular establishments. The unspoken objection that it would put their wives out of shopping range of Harrods and Harvey Nichols was, of course, no more than a light-hearted political canard.

In the same way, his proposal to cancel a major part of Britain's nuclear weapons programme and use the money to reintroduce National Service was welcomed by many people outside the defence establishment. But here too the general staff were able to demonstrate that his scheme, while eminently commendable in theory, could not be made to work in practice.

After this, Hacker appeared to run out of steam, and the rest of his premiership was spent largely in responding to events rather than seizing them and shaping them. The reformer in him had a brief revival when he investigated the possibility of abolishing the Department of

Education, but although the proposals were judged by many educational experts to be both imaginative and feasible, they followed his other proposed reforms into the sand. The subsequent election defeat, though seen by his party as a tragedy, can with hindsight be judged, at least in his case, as a merciful release.

Hacker's premiership will not go down in history as a spectacular success or a dismal failure. Most probably it will be relegated to that brief chapter occupied by Rosebery, Bonar Law, Douglas Home, and Callaghan: too brief to be memorable and characterised, if at all, by what occurred during it than by what it achieved. This is perhaps a pity, even an injustice. Hacker was a decent, likeable man, with some commendable reforming intentions. He had the misfortune of not being able to impose his schemes on those who would have to implement them, despite the sterling support of powerful officials like Sir Humphrey Appleby and Bernard Woolley. He was always open to advice and ideas, but seemed to be puzzled, if not paralysed, when they conflicted. In his favour it can be said that he provided a focus for unity in the party at the time when it was sorely needed; his weakness was that he saw his chief, and as time went on, his only duty as being to secure his re-election. When he failed in this there was little if anything left to mark his tenure of a premiership which, if the truth be told, brought more distinction to him than he brought to the office which he briefly occupied.

Antony Jay and Jonathan Lynn

Philip Piratin

born 15 May 1907, *died* 10 December 1995

The massive defeat of Winston Churchill in 1945 caused shockwaves throughout the world. President Truman, who was about to authorise the detonation of the first atom bomb, was shown a picture of Prime Minister elect Clement Attlee as he claimed personal victory at his count in Stepney; behind Attlee's left shoulder stood the smiling Phil Piratin, the newly elected Communist MP for Mile End. J. Edgar Hoover was certainly concerned, but neither need have worried, the Stepney experience had taught the new British Prime Minister a lot about what he was to term 'Communist hypocrites'.

Phil Piratin was born in 1907 in Stepney, the son of an immigrant trader; he was educated at Davenant School in the East End and originally wanted to become an architect. In the event he entered the fur trade and also served in the Merchant Navy. He was increasingly concerned about the rise of fascism and anti-Semitism as personified by Sir Oswald Mosley and also the acute social problems caused by landlords extorting punitive rents from tenants. In 1934 he attended the infamous Mosley rally at Olympia and joined the Communist Party that evening. His activities in support of tenants bought his organisational skills to the fore and he was a founder of the Stepney Tenants Defence League, where he mobilised groups of women to oppose evictions and eventually to picket the homes of some of the more notorious landlords, a number of whom (in particular Messrs Craps and Gold) were themselves Jews. His involvement did much to forestall latent anti-Semitism from amongst the wider community.

In October 1936 he was a key figure in the siege of Cable Street where over 100,000 people were mobilised to prevent Mosley marching through the East End. He became sufficiently well known that in 1937 he won the Spitalfields East ward, where he had many relatives, on Stepney Borough Council, becoming a one-man opposition and giving him a platform on housing issues.

During the war he tried to rejoin the Merchant Navy, but was refused on the personal instruction of Herbert Morrison. This did not stop his activities as an air raid warden or his campaigning in the East End, which bore the brunt of the bombing during the Battle of Britain. Air raid protection for civilians in the East End was woefully inadequate and there were immense problems associated with the largest public shelter, known as the Tilbury, where thousands gathered each night with almost no sanitation. Phil Piratin soon noted that there was excellent provision in the West End with the Savoy Hotel advertising its facilities – for a price. He led a march of East Enders to the Savoy and demand admission at no cost – fortunately the all-clear sounded before the situation got out of hand – but the Government noted the situation and paid more attention to the East End, much of it, such as the Royal visits, cosmetic, but attention nevertheless.

The end of the war and the return to party politics saw an immediate general election and the Piratin machine moved into full gear in the Mile End constituency. Bombing had seen the electorate fall to just 16,000 and Piratin had calculated how many votes were required to win. He and his campaign team went out to get the vote and he beat the outgoing Labour MP, Dan Frankel, by 1,214 votes to join Willy Gallagher in a Communist Party of two. This was a considerable surprise as observers had assumed that the most likely Communist victory would be in Rhondda East where General Secretary Harry Pollitt stood and lost by 972 votes.

The 1945 local elections saw 10 Communists elected to Stepney Council (Westminster Council also had Communists returned from Covent Garden Ward) and they would have been 15 had they contested all three seats in each of the five wards in which they secured seats.

In the Commons Piratin made his maiden speech on the day following the State Opening and unsurprisingly concentrated on housing, calling for the requisition of empty homes in wealthy areas for use by the poor and powers to be devolved from Government to boroughs such as Stepney to enable them to increase their own housing provision. Of particular interest to the modern observer in the CND era, was his reference to the dropping of the atomic bomb when he described the Churchill's first speech as Opposition leader the previous day as 'atomically energised'.

He was extremely active in Parliament over the next four sessions, regularly speaking on a wide range of issues from the Government side of the House (to the annoyance of the Labour whips), although housing (he once called for the requisition of the London home of the Duchess of Bedford) and industrial issues initially dominated. As the Parliament went on he became a vociferous opponent of NATO and questioned ministers on the Cold War.

In 1946 his organisation delivered the two Mile End seats on the LCC to the Communists despite Labour fielding Elsie Janner, whose husband was both a Labour MP and the Party adviser on rental policy. This was his high point locally as Clement Attlee ensured that there would be a fightback to contain this threat in Stepney.

1949 was the vital year for this. Redistribution had seen Stepney reduced to a single constituency for both Parliament and the LCC and in the LCC elections Labour romped home comfortably. In the Borough Council elections of the same year Philip Piratin lost his council seat by 42 votes, although the Communists won three of the 20 wards in Stepney.

Later in the year there was an industrial dispute in the docks. Attlee ordered the printing of 30,000 copies of a speech by Bob Mellish MP attacking Communist influence within the Union and had these distributed to dockers. In a speech in July 1949 Piratin, who was defending the strikers found himself attacked from all sides in the Commons. Attlee also had a number of hard left and Communist sympathising Labour MPs effectively driven from the Parliamentary Party and subsequently Parliament.

In the general election of February 1950, Labour scraped home with an overall majority of just six in Stepney Phil Piratin came in third, behind the Conservative candidate who was 27,237 votes behind Labour. He was never to hold public office again. Hoping to stand again in 1951 he was bankrupted after being sued by the Chief Superintendent of Hackney Police, whom he described a fascist.

He was later to become a successful bookseller, although he spent two years as circulation manager of the *Daily Worker*. He was very different from the established Communist figures of Willy Gallagher and Harry Pollitt, his campaigning skills and community activity indicating that he was something of a loose cannon in the tightly knit world of

Communism. He was to eventually leave the Party in 1968 following the Soviet invasion of Czechoslolovakia. In 1978 he published a memoir entitled *Our Flag Stays Red* which is written with a sense of humour not often associated with more orthodox Communists.

He was to live until his eighty-eigth year, eventually passing away in 1995.

I met him once, whilst canvassing for the Conservative Party in Willesden. He was interested at being recognised and proved a charming raconteur. His description of the grinding poverty and high infant mortality in the Stepney of his youth showed how his politics developed. He was an obvious patriot and was far less dangerous than the public school Cambridge educated group who were active at the same time.

Peter Golds

Harold Perkins

born 1 May 1936, *died* 23 February 1996

Harry Perkins who died yesterday will always be regarded as Labour's most colourful Prime Minister, loved and loathed in equal measure.

To his friends and admirers, who extended well beyond the confines of the Labour Party, he was the first British Prime Minister ever to challenge Britain's satellite status in relation to America and to confront head on the mighty vested interests at the heart of the British Establishment.

To his enemies he was a dangerous, irresponsible extremist who threatened the established order in a way that no other Labour Prime Minister had ever done. The manner in which he was brought down remains to this day a source of bitter controversy and the precise events surrounding his departure from Downing Street remain shrouded in mystery.

All those who knew him, friend and foe alike, agree that he was a modest, unassuming decent man of unbending principle. Indeed it was his unwillingness to compromise in the face overwhelming odds that ultimately led to his downfall.

Harold Albert Perkins was born on 1 May 1936, the only child of Albert and Florence Perkins of Parkside, Sheffield. At the age of 15 he followed his father into the Sheffield steel company, Firth Brown, and almost immediately became active in the steelworkers' union where he soon won the respect of his peers. At the age of 20 he was offered a scholarship to Ruskin College, Oxford, where he obtained a first class degree in economics.

Soon after returning to Firth Brown he was elected union convenor for the entire plant and in 1963 was selected as the Labour candidate for a by-election for the safe Labour seat of Sheffield Parkside, the constituency in which he had been born and bred and where his mother still lived.

In Parliament he made a name for himself as a scourge of Tory ministers, and sometimes of the Labour front bench. He soon became a darling of the Labour conference and before long was elected to the constituency section of the party's National Executive Committee where he quickly established himself as the leader of the Left.

His appointment to government was a surprise, not least to Perkins himself. He had earlier spurned an offer of a humble under-secretary-ship, preferring to build his base on the backbenches. However, in the dying days of the Callaghan government, desperate to appease unions which were growing increasingly militant, Perkins was offered the newly created post of Secretary of State for the Public Sector.

His acceptance upset some of his allies, who took the view that he should not be sullying his hands with the messy business of government in a regime that was all but doomed. The experience did, however, provide Perkins with a chance to demonstrate that he was capable of much more than just opposition. In a little over 12 months he became one of the most significant figures in a government which was by now assailed by problems on all fronts. He also endeared himself to the rank and file – though not to his ministerial colleagues – by refusing a ministerial car, preferring to travel to work each day on a Number 3 bus.

In retrospect, however, it is possible to see that it was during his early days in government that the seeds of his eventual downfall were sown. It was then that he began his clandestine affair with Molly Spence, who later married Michael Jarvis, managing director of British Insulated Industries, the company to which Perkins had awarded the contract for a new generation of nuclear reactors, including the one at Windermere which in due course came back to haunt him.

His surprise election as Labour leader came at a time when the fortunes of the party were at their lowest ebb. At first he was dismissed as a stop-gap by most commentators and many on the Right initially welcomed his rise on the grounds that it would render Labour unelectable.

It rapidly became clear, however, that this was a huge miscalculation. An economic down-turn made worse by a mixture of extraordinary incompetence and the Tory government's support for a series of disastrous foreign adventures on the coat-tails of the Americans were cleverly exploited by Perkins and resulted in Labour's 1989 election triumph. His manifesto, probably the most radical that any political party has ever put before the British electorate, included the removal of the American bases, public ownership of finance, abolition of the House of Lords and reform of media ownership. By all normal rules he ought to have been annihilated, but instead he was elected by a landslide.

Those who thought that once in office Perkins would quietly forget about some of his more controversial election promises were rapidly proved wrong. Within weeks he presented the Americans with a timetable for the removal of their bases and his first Queen's Speech contained proposals for limiting newspaper ownership to one daily and one Sunday per proprietor and an absolute ban on cross-media ownership.

The Establishment was apoplectic. None of the usual methods – flattery, seduction, abuse, even a run on sterling – seemed to work with Perkins. For a while it didn't work with the public either. It wasn't until strikes by the electricians union blacked out the country that his luck began to run out.

What finally did for him, however, was the accident at the Windermere nuclear power plant which he had authorised years earlier, as Secretary of State for the Public Sector, in the teeth of bitter local opposition. Even then he might have survived but for the revelation that, at the time he had awarded the contract to British Insulated, he had been having an affair with a woman who later became the wife of the managing director.

No impropriety was ever proved, indeed none was ever really alleged. Even Perkins' worst enemies readily conceded that he was a man of unimpeachable integrity. Perhaps that is why he went so quickly. The precise sequence of events surrounding his departure from office remains a mystery and Perkins himself never gave his version of events. All that is known is that he was whisked away to the Royal Free Hospital where he was kept in seclusion, even from his closest colleagues. His resignation was announced in a curt statement which simply said he was suffering from exhaustion. Later, he was taken to Chequers where he remained in seclusion for the best part of a year. Those who saw him said he was a broken man.

The manner in which Perkins' bitterest enemy, Lawrence Wainwright, was appointed to succeed him triggered the greatest constitutional crisis since the Abdication. The Labour Party chose Jock Steeples, the former Leader of the House and a close ally of Perkins, but the King – in a decision upheld by the Law Lords – invited Wainwright to form a government.

With Wainwright's election the Establishment breathed a sigh of relief. The Labour government limped on unhappily, but the party remained irretrievably split and, come the election, Labour was duly massacred, ushering in the long period of Tory rule that as yet shows no sign of coming to an end.

As for Perkins, he eventually reappeared at Westminster where he sat out the remaining three years of the Labour government in virtual silence before retiring into obscurity. He was rumoured to be suffering from senility, but those who knew him said this was nonsense. There were also reports that in retirement he was writing memoirs which would describe in detail the extraordinary events surrounding his downfall. A few days before his death, however, the manuscript was reported stolen.

The history of the Labour movement is littered with celebrations of glorious failures and Harry Perkins will almost certainly go down as the most glorious of all. His place in Labour mythology is assured.

Chris Mullin

Geoffrey Finsberg

born 13 June 1926, *died* 8 October 1996

Half his former Hampstead and Highgate constituents would not have recognised the mellowed Lord (Geoffrey) Finsberg who died of a heart attack yesterday in Stockholm. He died at 70 a happy and relaxed man, unlike the combative and abrasive MP who had served the constituency from 1970 until 1992.

Part of his happiness was personal. After the death of his first wife, Pamela, with whom he lived two streets from me, he married an old friend, Yvonne Sarch. When I encountered them in a local Tesco not long ago, they seemed very happy.

Part of his happiness was his enjoyment as an activist within the Western European Union and Council of Europe, after he was sacked as a Minister by Mrs Thatcher in 1983. He found appreciation there, becoming President of the Parliamentary Assembly of the Council of Europe, 1991–92. As he told fellow peers, after he was elevated to the Lords in 1992, he found that organisation a wonderful vantage point from which to observe the historic changes in central and eastern Europe. Overseas he was able to display the charm he limited to friends and fellow Tories at home.

Anyone living in the constituency during his 22–year-reign was conscious that this marginal seat boasted of an MP who enjoyed above all dismissing, insulting or pulverising almost any constituent who disagreed with him or was critical of any Conservative action. This was not a secret, because anybody similarly critical of such actions in the columns of the local *Ham and High* weekly could be sure of a letter from Geoffrey Finsberg shooting them down in print. The late Sir Keith Joseph, who shared his politics and his religion, once referred to Finsberg as a 'one-man battering ram'.

His combativeness was mainly due to his growing up as part of the old London Tory apparat, honed to belligerence in holding beachheads against the prewar Morrisonian Labour Party. He was born in Hampstead in 1926, the son of Monte(fiore) Finsberg, who had won an MC but was then a meat salesman, before becoming a Handley Page aircraft inspector. Young Geoffrery attended Warwick House School in Hampstead and then the City of London School. He did his National Service in the 'Bevin Boys' in the manpowerstarved coalmines, an arduous experience for a feline young man.

It was in the midst of this that he joined the Young Conservatives at 20, in 1946. Within three years he was elected to Hampstead Borough Council, defeating Tony Greenwood, the well known son of a famous father. By 1954 he was National Chairman of the Young Conservatives, and fought his first Parliamentary seat, Islington East the next year. But he seemed destined to remain a local government leader when he became Camden's Tory Opposition Leader in 1965.

Local Tories were stunned when Henry Brooke, the controversial and much-criticised Home Secretary, was ousted from his Hampstead seat by Labour's Ben Whitaker in 1966, the then high tide of Labour supoort. The contest was on for a fighter to retake this beachhead. The heir apparent, Sir Neil Sheilds, was unexciting. Geoffrey Pattie seemed too mild. It came down to two Jewish bachelors'. Leon Brittan and Geoffrey Finsberg. Finsberg won under the slogan, 'If being a bachelor is good enough for our Leader [Edward Heath], it's good enough for me!'. He campaigned on a hard-Right programme, promising to cure the 'plague' of strikes, sell arms to South Africa and restore capital punishment for killers of policemen. He retook the seat by 474 votes in the election which brough Heath to power in 1970. He supported Heath on entry to Europe but was unhappy about his coldness toward Israel. He was elected to the Executive of the 1922 Committee.

Things improved when Mrs Thatcher became Leader: he was named Spokesman for London and party Vice Chairman for London in 1975. When she won power in 1979 he became Parliamentary Secretary for Environment and, in 1981, he replaced Sir George Young at Health when Mrs Thatcher sacked him over his anti-tobacco crusade. But she dropped him as a Minister in 1983, apparently for being too inflexible and inclined to kick the shins of civil servants. When he was knighted for his services, the *Ham and High* wrote that 'it would be nice for a change if we could be nice to Geoffrey Finsberg' but he had made this impossible by refusing to talk to constituents unhappy about the abolition of the ILEA, which he had long advocated.

Andrew Roth

Margaret 'Peggy' Herbison

born 12 March 1907, *died* 29 December 1996

'The miner's little sister' was an improbable, but true, description of the tiny, church-going spinster, who rose to become one of Harold Wilson's ministers, and whose reputation lives on in the Lanarkshire mining villages she so dominated in the post-war years. Winning the seat that had been held by the glamorous Jennie Lee, wife of Aneurin Bevan, Peggy could not have been more different.

A gentle but determined rebel, she resigned from the Wilson Government, but not before she had successfully secured the merger of her Ministry of Pensions and National Insurance with the National Assistance Board, creating a new Ministry of Social Security. Many claim to know why she resigned, but she herself, as a determined loyalist, would not allow her name to be used to attack a Labour government. In August 1966, Dick Crossman noted in his diary that she 'can't let herself be associated any more with an attitude of which she disapproves; but on the other hand she can't let herself oppose her colleagues because she does not want to be accused of disloyalty.' She stuck to that until her death in December 1996.

In the mid eighties, unaware that one day I would be her successor in Parliament, I asked if she would allow me to make a TV documentary about her. She was not averse to the idea, but I was told that under no circumstances would she talk about that resignation, or attack the Party in any way that could be used 30 years later to damage Labour's election campaign.

In 1994, following the death of her protégé John Smith, I was to inherit the seat she won in 1945. She spoke in my by-election to a packed audience, many there to hear 'Peggy', totally uninterested in me and a young man called Blair. Then 84, she spoke for almost an hour without notes, holding her audience spellbound, and leaving the rest of us to scrabble for something left to say. Some claim she was known to all as Peggy; not true. It was drilled into me, and most of my generation, by parents who idolised her, that to us it was 'Miss Herbison'.

Born on 12 March 1907 in Shotts, a fiercely independent mining community that was to be her home for the rest of her life, Margaret McCrorie Herbison attended the local Dykehead School and Bellshill Academy, going on to Glasgow University where she graduated with an MA, as well as chairing the university branch of the Labour Party. Her father, and two of her brothers, one of whom was an Olympic boxer, were miners.

She taught English and history in Allan Glen's School in Glasgow and worked as a tutor for the National Council of Labour colleges, travelling every day from her parents' home in Shotts. She told me that when the local miners came to ask her to stand, she sent them away to find a man, but they stood their ground and she was swept to victory.

First elected to the NEC Women's Section in 1948, she served for some 20 years until her retirement from politics, becoming Chair of the Party in 1956–57. Appointed Joint Parliamentary Under Secretary of State for Scotland under Hector McNeil in 1950, she was the first woman Scottish Office Minister and the only woman to make party political broadcasts in the 1950 and 1951 elections.

In opposition she was runner-up in the Shadow Cabinet elections of November 1951 with 84 votes to the 91 of Tony Greenwood who came twelfth, beating Hector McNeil, Patrick Gordon Walker and George Brown, but Attlee did not promote her beyond her status as a shadow junior Scottish Office Minister.

Gaitskill moved Peggy to Education in February 1956; her passion for the subject gave her a searing contempt for Margaret Thatcher. She returned to the Scottish Front Bench in 1959, moving at her own request to become Shadow Pensions Minister in 1962, although she continued to speak on Scottish Affairs in the Commons. She became a Privy Counsellor in 1964.

Fearless as a Minister in her battles with the Treasury, her ability to get her own way was limited by her Cabinet overlord, Douglas Houghton, who represented both her Ministry and Kenneth Robinson's Ministry of Health in the Cabinet, although he ran neither.

Her ideas were far sighted: it could be said she was the visionary behind the Minimum Income Guarantee. She supported wage-related benefits and wanted to increase family allowances, paying for it by increasing taxes on the more affluent. The Chancellor of the time, Jim Callaghan, feared the consequences of such a clawback, and advocated means testing. In July 1967, Peggy Herbison walked away from her ministerial career.

Looking to the long term and her retirement from Parliament, she took under her wing the brilliant young advocate John Smith: she was to outlive him. Passionate to the end about children, she would sit in her neat, sheltered house in Shotts and wait for the schoolchildren coming to see her on their way home.

The only real recognition of Margaret Herbison as a ground-breaking politician of national standing came when she served as the first Lord High Commissioner of the General Assembly of the Church of Scotland in 1970–71. The post, functioning as the Queen's representative in Scotland, replete with Ladies in Waiting and the mandatory title 'Your Grace', is the ultimate gathering of the Scottish Establishment. Always dignified, behatted, a church member of real Christian dedication, Peggy would have none of the flummery. She turned the traditional garden party over to the young people of Scotland.

Behind the staid image was a politician of principle and passion, earning criticism when she visited the United States and could not bite her tongue about the evils of segregated schooling. She loved the States but despaired of some of their politics, although she encouraged her niece, Karen Whitefield, who now represents the Airdrie & Shotts constituency that grew out of North Lanarkshire in the Scottish Parliament, to work as an intern on Capitol Hill.

A chain smoker who discovered training shoes in her latter years, she was much more fun than the picture painted of her by her contemporaries would suggest. She did not live to see the Labour Government, dying on 29 December 1996, but she would have approved of 'Education, education, education'.

Helen Liddell

James Goold

Lord Goold of Waterfoot

born 28 May 1934, *died* 27 July 1997

Lord Goold, the 63–year-old Lord Lieutenant of Renfrewshire and former Scottish Conservative Party chairman who has died of lung cancer, was the epitome of party loyalty. At a Chequers meeting nine years ago he asked Mrs Thatcher if he could leave his post after overhauling the Scottish party in the wake of its disastrous showing in 1987, when they lost 11 of their 21 Scottish seats. Because nobody else suitable in the business community could be found quickly to captain the sinking ship, he soldiered on until 1989, when he handed over to Michael Forsyth.

A super-loyal Thatcherite, he more than any other fuelled the poll tax band-wagon in 1984, by persuading Mrs Thatcher to scrap rates in favour of the poll tax. He was thought to be uncommunicative and ruthless in his control of the Scottish Tories on Mrs Thatcher's behalf. In August 1987 he unilaterally disbanded the Scottish Conservative Candidates Association, whose 106 members included many of the Scottish Tories' internal policy critics. Since his round face was topped by a bald head, Andrew Marr, then on the *Scotsman*, asked in 1989 whether he would greet Mrs Thatcher at the Scottish Tory conference at Perth displaying 'the words 'Ten More Years' tattooed on his pate'. When others tried to get rid of her in November 1990, he urged her 'to stay and fight'.

Throughout the home rule travails, this senior accountant businessman stuck to his exhortations that devolution or independence would be disasters for Scotland and the Union. In the Lords and in Scotland, he proclaimed that opportunities for Scotland under the Single European Market would turn to ashes if the UK were broken up. In his last major anti-devolution speech in the Lords in July 1996, he claimed that a 3p bigger income tax in Scotland would mean that 'a person working in Dumfries would be forced to pay 12.5% more in income tax than someone doing the same job a few miles away in Carlisle.'

Asked in 1989 whether he thought Scots were incapable of running their own affairs, he said, with the assurance of a top accountant-businessman: 'No absolutely not. We are part of the UK and our whole economy is tied up with that. If you had a situation where taxation was higher than in other parts of the UK, people would stop investing in Scotland and there would be an exodus of business to other parts of the same landmass. If you ask any group of businessmen, you will find that is the case'. He warned that an independent Scotland would mean higher taxes, rising unemployment, falling investment and lower house prices. Since he was the Chairman of a large Glasgow building firm, this was considered to be within his expertise.

James Duncan Goold was typical of the Scottish businessmen who are the shrinking backbone of Unionism and Conservatism north of the Border. Born 28 May 1934, he was educated at Belmont House and Glasgow Academy. Qualifying as a Chartered Accountant in 1958, he then did a two-year stint with a firm of accountants in New Zealand and then a further year with Price Waterhouse in Australia. He came home to be company secretary to the large Glasgow building firm of Mactaggart and Mickel. The millionaire Mactaggart partner was an aspirant Tory candidate who fathered the present Labour MP for Slough.

James Goold rose in the business community. By 1971 he was President of the Scottish Building Contractors Association, by 1977 President of the Scottish Building Employers Federation, followed by the chairmanship of the CBI Scotland '81–83. In 1984, he became a Director of American Trust PLC and in 1986 of Edinburgh Oil and Gas PLC.

His Conservative political career ran in parallel. He was President of the Conservate Association in Eastwood, Scotland's safest seat 1978–95. In 1981 he became Treasurer of the Scottish Conservatives, becoming Chairman in 1983; he was knighted in 1983 and became a life peer in 1987.

He asked to be released from his post as Chairman after the disastrous 1987 results for the Tories in Scotland, but Mrs Thatcher only agreed in 1989, when she replaced him with Michael Forsyth.

She continued to respect his judgement. When moderate Scottish Secretary Malcolm Rifkind was locked in fierce combat with his insubordinate Thatcherite subordinate Michael Forsyth, she asked Lord Goold's opinion. He said Forsyth could continue to have a major role in any Scottish campaign.

His support for abrasiveness was also on show in his clash, as Chairman, with the players in the Royal Scottish Orchestra. This convulsed the entire Scottish cultural community in 1991.

His wife of 33 years, Lady Sheena, who was on the Glasgow Health Board for 11 years, died in 1992. Two sons and a daughter survive.

Andrew Roth

Denis Howell

born 4 September 1923, *died* 18 April 1998

Denis Herbert Howell was the quintessential Brummie. His autobiography was entitled *Made in Birmingham,* and he was hugely proud of being a Freeman of the Second City.

He was born in Handsworth – to be precise in Lozells – 'the back-yard of Birmingham' in 1923. His father was a factory foreman who was sacked for taking part in the 1926 General Strike. Dennis was educated at Handsworth Grammar School, but left at 15 to become an office boy. Active in the clerical workers union from his early working days he eventually became President of APEX, after the CWU merged and expanded. He joined the Labour Party in 1942, and it remained in his blood ever after. He lost his job after taking three weeks leave to help the Party in the

1945 general election. In 1946 he was first elected to Birmingham City Council; four years later becoming Secretary of the Labour Group.

He fought and lost the Kings Norton Division in 1951, and was elected for All Saints in 1955. This was a marginal seat, made worse by boundary changes, and he lost it by 20 votes in 1959. During his first stint in Parliament, and in those highly factional days, he had become strongly associated with the right wing , and after losing his seat he retained close connections with the national political scene through being the organiser of the Campaign for Democratic Socialism, following on from the 'Victory for Sanity Group'.

He came back into Parliament at a by-election in 1961 for the safe seat of Small Heath, which he represented with great distinction for the next 31 years.

He had always been interested in sport and was already famous for being the only MP who was simultaneously a Football Association referee, when Harold Wilson appointed him as Minister of Sport – Britain's first Minister of Sport – after the Labour victory of 1964. The post was then, strictly, Joint Parliamentary Under-Secretary of State and the Department of Education and Science. In 1965 he set up and became first chairman of the Sports Council, aimed at promoting sport and improving facilities. In 1966 Britain hosted, and England won the World Cup. Short of actually scoring the winner himself Denis could not have had a happier ministerial career.

But he was to achieve greater fame a decade later when – still Minister of Sport, though now at the Department of the Environment – he also had responsibility for water resources. There was a terrible drought in 1976 and Jim Callaghan, in an uncharacteristic gimmick, designated Denis the 'Minister for Drought'. He introduced some emergency legislation rationing water usage and at the precise moment that the Bill had its Second Reading in the House of Lords the heavens opened and the mother-and-father of a thunderstorm swept the country and torrential rains fell for most of a month. He managed the same feat of coincidence when visiting Uzbekistan some time later. It had not rained for three years, but his arrival was met by a serious downpour, and the delighted population of Tashkent named him 'the Rainmaker'.

It is however, his contribution to sport in this country for which is his lasting and endurable memorial. Roy Hattersley wrote, 'almost 20 years after he gave up the job, one of his successors said that the British sporting community was divided into two groups – those who think that Denis Howell was the best Minister of Sport we ever had, and those who think he still has the job.' It took the arrival of Tony Banks to finally dispel the latter myth.

Denis Howell retired from the Commons in 1992 and was created a Life Peer.

Alan Haworth

Cub Alport

Lord Alport of Colchester

born 22 March 1912, *died* 28 October 1998

The death at 86 of Baron 'Cub' Alport, for 22 years a Deputy Speaker of the Lords, will be seen by most as the passing of one of the last of the distinguished generation of Conservative 'One Nation' ex-officers who reached the Commons in 1950, including names like Powell, Maudling and Macleod, with Sir Edward Heath as the last survivor. Cuthbert Alport served as the Tory MP for Colchester 1950–61 before being kicked upstairs to the Lords. In the Lords he attained the distinction of becoming the only Tory peer ever to have the Whip withdrawn, in his case for his 1984 attack on Mrs Thatcher for destroying her own party and dividing the country.

His longtime political opponent, the late Fenner Brockway, once described Alport as 'ill-tempered, snobbish, patronising and unhelpful.'

But to a handful of their close friends in the Lords his passing a year after her death will mark the end of a discreet and touching cross-party romance between 'Cub' and the late Baroness (Pat) Llewellyn-Davies, the first woman Labour Chief Whip in the Lords. Their spouses had both died and Pat spent her last lingering months of suffering from ME lovingly cared for by him at his Colchester home, with a final holiday together in the West Indies. Apart from his long adoration of lovely Pat, they were linked by their joint fascination with Africa, which long dominated his life, especially in the late '50s and early '60s, when he was Under Secretary and then Minister of State in the Commonwealth Relations Office and later High Commissioner in the Central African Federation.

Unlike Pat, Cub Alport was a typical Conservative from the professional classes. He was born 22 March 1912 in Johannesburg, South Africa, the son of Cairo-based Professor Arthur Alport MD FRCP (a onetime colleague of Alexander Fleming) and Janet McCall, who came from Dumfriesshire.

He was educated at Haileybury and Pembroke College, Cambridge, where he took an MA in History and Law, became Vice President of the Cambridge Union Conservative Association and President of the Cambridge Union in 1935. He then lectured at the Conservatives' Bonar Law College in Ashridge and wrote his first book, *Kingdoms in Partnership*. In 1937, at 25, he became Assistant Secretary of the Conservative Education Department. He also qualified as a Barrister at Middle Temple.

Just 27 when war broke out, he was called up in the Artists Rifles, which he had joined at 22 as a Territorial. He commanded a company in the Royal Welsh Fusiliers, served in the War Office, was sent to Staff College. He was dispatched to East Africa where he commanded a company of the King's African Rifles, ending the war as a Lieutenant Colonel in the Territorials.

Back in Britain in 1945 he married Rachel Bingham, by whom he was to have a son and two daughters. He was named Director of the new

Conservative Political Centre, the re-education department of the crushingly-defeated Conservative Party, and therefore one of 'Rab's Boys'. This lasted until he was elected for Colchester in the Tories' comeback election of February 1950. With his background, it was natural that he should be on the 1954 Parliamentary delegation to East Africa to study the Mau Mau uprising. He decided Britain needed a Colonial Service Army manned by Africans but officered by Britons able to speak local languages.

In 1955 Sir Anthony Eden curiously promoted him to Assistant Postmaster General, probably to silence him. When Harold Macmillan replaced Sir Anthony after his Suez fiasco, he made him first Under-Secretary at the Commonwealth Relations Office and then Minister of State there.

As an enlightened imperialst. he conducted a two-front war: against the encrusted unenlightened in his own party who opposed even his moderate reform proposals like settling African farmers in Kenya's 'White Highlands' and against left-wing Labour's Fenner Brockway and John Dugdale – supported behind the scenes by Labour candidate Pat Llewellyn-Davies – who wanted to speed African liberation.

In 1961, at Harold Macmillan's urging, he accepted a peerage to enable him to serve as British High Commissioner in the doomed Federation of Nyasaland and Rhodesia. In 1967 he was considered enlightened enough for a Tory by Harold Wilson to be dispatched to Rhodesia to try to mediate the conflict with insurgent Ian Smith. He was reviled both by Smith's white settlers and by fellow Tories, whom he had not consulted on his mission. In 1971 he attacked Edward Heath for supplying arms to South Africa. With his cool sympathy for Africans, he had little in common for the many right wing Tory peers who enthused about Apartheid South Africa. After he warned in 1984 that Margaret Thatcher's policies would destroy the Conservative Party and divide the country, the then Tory Chief Whip, Lord Denham, deprived him of the Tory Whip. He then sat as an Independent Conservative.

He continued to debate a wide range of issues. With his father's medical background and his intimate friendship with ME-stricken

Baroness Llewellyn-Davies, it was natural that one of his last joint ventures with her was to bring to the fore a discussion of euthanasia. In 1993 he introduced a Bill dealing with the termination of medical treatment, pressing for a Select Committee on euthanasia. The next year this Select Committee presented a brilliant report, to which Pat made her last major contribution in the Lords.

Andrew Roth

John Golding

born 9 March 1931, *died* 20 January 1999

John Golding, the former Labour minister and MP for Newcastle under Lyme, who has died aged 67 from complications after a heart operation, was a tireless soldier of Labour's trade union right-wing. He possessed a natural political nous, authority and energy that belied his short, but stout stature. For him or against him, he was the best friend you could have, or the worst enemy. If you found yourself on the wrong side, his sharp, impish sense of humour would always liven up the room.

He and his wife Llin made a formidable political team, instinctively 'old Labour' in their support for the working class, pensioners, the unemployed and the rights of ordinary people to be represented by trades unions.

In more than 40 years of active politics, including 17 years as an MP, Golding would admit he made more enemies than friends. Often, as when he led the Labour moderates' fight against Militant in the late 1970s and early 1980s, the blood feud would come down to politics, pure and simple. Golding was uncompromising in his hostility towards dreamers and schemers on the left, including Tony Benn and Eric Heffer, whom he believed offered nothing for everyday folk.

At that time, when organising the trade union-led fightback for 'common sense', he was justifiably known as the most influential man in the Labour movement. A master of every political trick in the book, he was bloody-minded enough to copy the left's tactics and use them to the moderates' advantage. In the Commons tea-room, MPs under threat but innocent in the finer arts of the rough-house such as Robert Kilroy Silk would frequently ask Golding how to get themselves organised.

'I'm fed up of this f'...in' idiot. I'm going,' Eric Heffer once shouted at a home policy meeting of Labour's national executive, after Golding stalled another left quick-fix by giving the meeting a two-hour long insight into ordinary, working-class views on every subject under the sun. Alas, in a scene worthy of Basil Fawlty, Eric walked straight into one broom cupboard, then another, before slamming his papers down and shouting 'Oh f... it, I'm stopping after all.'

'And these were people who thought they could run the country,' Golding remarked in the political memoirs he was near completing before suddenly falling ill at Christmas. The memoirs, strongly encouraged by Llin, are a testament to the trade-union brothers, many from the West Midlands, including John Spellar, now a defence minister, and Roger Godsiff, MP for Birmingham Sparkbrook who carried the torch during Labour's darkest hours before Militant was finally routed and the party began its tortuous climb back to respectability under Neil Kinnock, John Smith and Tony Blair.

Occasionally, the hostility to Golding was purely personal. It often fell to John to step where others feared to tread. In 1983, during Labour's leadership election in the wake of a disastrous general election defeat and the resignation of Michael Foot as party leader, union tacticians calculated that Roy Hattersley simply did not command enough votes to defeat Kinnock. Hattersley would have to bite his ambition and be content with the deputy leadership instead.

'Do you mean to say that I am going to have to play second fiddle to a red-haired Welsh windbag?' Hattersley exclaimed, when Golding was deputed to deliver the black spot. 'Yes, if you put it like that, you are going to have to play second fiddle to a red-haired, Welsh windbag,' came the uncompromising reply. Hattersley's undying enmity cost Golding a place in the Shadow Cabinet. If he was bitter at the time, the scars never showed. In politics, his attitude was that you win some, and you lose some. 'I got Benn, then they got me,' he said after losing to the left the position he always kept as political officer in the Post Office Engineering Union (POEU). That victory over Benn and the recapture of Labour's feuding NEC in 1982 after 'five years hard labour', as he put it was undoubtedly the high point of this strand of Golding's career. Using the moderate and soft left's narrow majority on the NEC, as Foot abstained, he ruthlessly removed Benn and his acolytes from all their positions of power.

To many, with Golding playing a key role in determining the 1983 manifesto, it remained a mystery why Labour fought the election on what became known as 'the longest suicide note in history'. The answer, if Golding was asked, was straightforward: he had already decided that because of all the feuding, Foot as leader and the Falklands to boot, Labour had already lost the election. He was cunning enough to allow the left enough policy rope to hang themselves, so the Bennites could never again blame the right as they had done after Jim Callaghan's defeat in 1979.

While the annals of Labour history will undoubtedly record Golding as one of the right's best ever 'fixers' a label he took pride in, there was much more than that to his political career. Well versed at an early age in politics and philosophy, he reserved a healthy disregard for ideologists with their heads in the clouds.

He went to Chester Grammar School before studying, eventually, at Keele University and the London School of Economics. He had begun his working life in the Civil Service in London as an 'office boy' at 16, as he described it, then as a clerical officer at the Ministry of National Insurance, and it was as a researcher with the Post Office Engineering Union that he returned to Newcastle to stand in a 1969 by-election.

It was then, too, that Golding first met his future wife, Llin, a hospital radiographer, Labour activist and the daughter of a former Labour MP, who was given the task of driving the young candidate during the election campaign. Both were already married, with separate families of their own, but 11 years later they were to tie the knot together a second time round.

After winning the Newcastle by-election, Golding quickly joined the Wilson Government, first as Parliamentary Private Secretary to Eric Varley, then Minister for Technology, then as a whip. As Minister for Employment from 1976, he was intensely proud of Labour's efforts to cushion the blows of unemployment and short-time working, despite the best efforts of the left to undermine the Callaghan Government in the party and the unions.

To a born street-fighter, after 1979 (an election tainted by the tragic death of his eldest son), opposition under Margaret Thatcher came as second nature. Golding still holds the record for the longest-ever Commons speech 11 hours and 15 minutes speaking to one small amendment which successfully delayed the privatisation of British Telecom until after the 1983 election. It was a tactic, as one of the outstanding parliamentarians of his day, that he would use repeatedly to great effect. These days rules have changed, so Golding's record is unlikely to be broken, but delay was then often the only effective tactic against a massive government majority.

Golding was certainly not though one of those pompous MPs who enjoy the sound of their own voice. Indeed, he showed an almost childlike pride in his award by the *Guardian* in the 1980s as the Commons' worst-dressed MP.

In 1986, aged 55, Golding gave up the Newcastle seat after becoming general secretary of the newly-merged National Communications Union, following another vicious battle with the left. There, he had to summon all his negotiating skills in deft handling of strikes and disputes with British Telecom at the height of Thatcher's onslaught against the unions. To the end, he remained active in local politics, both in support of Llin and Newcastle's Labour borough council.

Politics aside, Golding's great passions were fishing, horse-racing and, latterly, Spanish. Weekend after weekend, he would throw himself waist deep into the rivers of mid-Wales or well-stocked lakes of Hampshire, with the Spanish ambassador often in tow. A fair cook, his family freezer was stocked to the brim with freshly-caught salmon and trout. Asked, too, how come the pot was always full of game, he said it was because of a case he was assisting at an employment tribunal. 'The chap's good with traps,' he would say, 'I'm being paid in rabbits instead.'

Just before his death, John took a new mischievous delight in running rings yet again around civil servants in his new appointment to a Ministry of Agriculture advisory panel on the plight of British fresh-water fishing. If the Sir Humphreys of this world thought they could 'fix' any committee they liked, they got their lines snagged with Golding. They would always be caught out by the master-fixer himself.

Golding is survived by Llin and his second son, Simon. His memoirs, *Hammer of the Left* were published pothumously in 2003.

Paul Farrelly

James Hill

born 21 December 1926, **died** 16 February 1999

Amiable, thickset Sir James ('Jimmy Double Portions') Hill, for 22 years the Conservative MP for hard-fought Southampton-Test has died at 72. We last me, just before the May 1997 election, when he asked whether I thought he could hold his 585 majority against his third-time Labour opponent Alan Whitehead. Expecting a 10% pro-Labour swing, I replied, 'Not a chance!'. He accepted this, smiled resignedly behind his pebbled specs, and waddled away.

James was one of those low-profiled MPs whose emolient geniality helps give Westminister politics its clublike atmosphere. He enjoyed the economic success which came from raising 1,500 Large White pigs on his 100–acre

Gunsfield Farm near Romsey in Hampshire. In London he had his flat in the Park Lane Hotel. There and elsewhere he indulged his gargantuan appetite.

A shrewd, pragmatic, commensensical man who served as chairman of Commons committees and on the prestigious Procedures Committee, he was a gut-Rightwinger, an enthusiastic backer of Margaret Thatcher and Norman Tebbit, but not easy to categorise. He liked the Council of Europe and Western European Union, on which he served, but hated the Common Agricultural Policy, for its squeeze on pigs. Although right wing, he favoured allowing gay sex at 16 and figured on the blacklist of anti-hunting MPs targetted by *The Field* before the 1997 election.

Above all, he was a local crusader against vandals, pub thugs, kerb-crawlers and prostitutes who infested the less salubrious parts of his seat, divided between middle-class residential areas and large council estates. He sometimes showed a tinge of politicised class war against Labour-controlled Southampton City Council.

His own origins were modest. He was born in Southampton in December 1926, the son of a merchant navy officer. He attended the Regent's Park Secondary School in Southampton, the North Wales Naval Training College and University College, Southampton.

After acquiring Pilot's, Radio Officer's and Navigator's licenses, at 21 he began working as aircrew for BOAC, mainly on Solent flying boats. He also did a three-year stint with Aden Airways.

His marriage to a vivacious Tory, Ruby Susan Ralph, in 1958, helped persuade him to stay ashore. From 1960 he became a partner in Waller and King, local estate agents. then a director of Clanfield House Developments and Second Clanfield Properties. In 1964 be became a partner in a Hampshire piggery.

His political career began on Southampton City Council in 1966. He then showed his winning ways by ousting Labour's Bob Mitchell from marginal Southampton-Test in 1970, but lost it in October 1974, by 530 votes. Still in the European Parliament, he campaigned vigorously to stay in the EEC in the 1975 referendum, addressing 70 meetings. He retook the Test seat in 1979, holding it with shrinking majorities until 1997.

While supporting Mrs Thatcher 'through thick and thin', he had his own line of reforms he thought made sense. He introduced two Bills to enable publicans to bar known thugs. He sought to license sex shops as a first step toward licensing bordellos. He campaigned against tyre-clampers. He fought the privatisation of the local Royal Ordnance Survey. He backed exemption from optical charges for the parially-sighted. All were pursued amiably. He was knighted in 1996. But his Parliamentary career was finished in May 1997 by a 10.5% swing against him, giving Labour's Alan Whitehead a majority of 13,684.

He leaves his wife, who earned her CBE as Chairwoman of the European Union of Women, and their two sons and three daughters.

Andrew Roth

David Eccles

Viscount Eccles

born 18 September 1904, *died* 25 February 1999

David Eccles is best remembered for his act of self-immolation in July 1962. Unlike others in Macmillan's 'Night of the Long Knives', he was offered another post. 'It's the Exchequer or nothing', he told the Prime Minister and was promptly added to the list of those to go. Although later to claim that he had intended to stand down before the next election, he complained bitterly that he had been 'sacked with less notice than a housemaid' and his animus against Macmillan was fuelled when he was elevated to the Lords as a mere Baron. Alec Douglas-Home typically put matters straight in 1964 by conferring the Viscountcy more appropriate to Cabinet ministers of Eccles's standing.

In many ways Eccles was his own worst enemy. Macmillan thought him 'very vain . . . frightfully bumptious' and he certainly had a high opinion of his own intelligence and his ability to manage a department. That this view was largely justified did not make it any more acceptable to his colleagues. He was nicknamed 'smarty boots' and the unkind reference was to more than his sartorial elegance. Antony Part was right nevertheless to think that 'his chances of rising further would have been enhanced if he had gone to a less good tailor!' He could be contemptuous of colleagues, whom he thought less intelligent, and was more than a little abrasive when dealing with political opponents. There was a nicer side. He refused to be interviewed by the biographer of one colleague because he knew that he would run him down and did not wish to upset his wife. Although capable of making racy and sometimes idiosyncratic speeches, his style was more often pedestrian, the content much less so. As a former colleague noted, his 'brilliant and unorthodox mind compels one to forgive his flat and lethargic voice – I should never omit him from any Cabinet of mine.'

He deserves to be remembered as the architect of the postwar expansion in further education and the first minister to regard educational expenditure as an economic investment. His appointment of an economist, Geoffrey Crowther, as Chairman of the Central Advisory Council opened up education to a wider constituency and the report which Eccles commissioned on education between 15 and 18 repaid the compliment by making an economic case for raising the school leaving age. He was ever an enthusiast for an expansion of higher education. He could be sharply political also. Under pressure earlier to reduce the school leaving age, he wrote: 'If we, who mainly send our children to boarding schools, encouraged early leaving from the country's secondary schools we should present the Opposition with a first class election issue.' His officials paid tribute to his genuine commitment to opportunity and to parental choice and Edward Boyle, who worked with him in Education, spoke warmly of his 'creative imagination'. He saw the increasing importance of education to the modern world and while he was there, Education looked set to become a major department.

David McAdam Eccles came from an upper middle class Harley Street background, the son of a distinguished surgeon and strong Presbyterian. Educated at Winchester, a great generator of intellectual arrogance, and New College, he imbibed his knowledge of liberal economics from Lionel Robbins. While at Oxford he demonstrated a 'barrow boy's instinct' for trading, combining a love of antiquarian books with an ability to secure a good price for them. From there he went into the City, rather to his father's dismay, and made a good deal of money. Much of it he invested in books, paintings and sculpture. He gave generously to charity. In 1928, he married Sybil, lovely daughter of the King's physician, Lord Dawson of Penn, to whom he was ever afterwards constant, if not always faithful. They had three children, John, Simon and Polly.

One of his business activities, chairmanship of a Spanish railway, led to his wartime employment as Economic Adviser to the British Ambassadors in the Iberian peninsula. There he laid out bribes to good effect to keep both the Franco and Salazar regimes out of the war. His correspondence with Sybil (published after her death in 1977 as *By Safe Hand*) reveals how well he played his hand. However searing letters from Sybil suggesting disenchantment with their marriage hastened his return to England in 1942, where they fell in love all over again and lived thereafter in total domestic felicity. A brief spell at the Ministry of Production ended because he happened to be with Churchill in 1943 when the latter learnt of the death of the MP for Chippenham in a plane crash. 'Why don't you stand?' Churchill asked. Eccles did and he held the seat until he went to the Lords in 1962.

In Opposition he became one of Butler's circle (although their relationship was strained when in 1950, he claimed 'the intellectual leadership' of his party). He was one of the group who drafted the Industrial Charter in 1947 and was active also on the European scene as a key member of the European League for Economic Cooperation. He served as a Conservative delegate to the initial meeting of the Council for Europe.

Just before the 1951 election, characteristically indiscreet, he called for cuts in the social services and waited vainly for the expected call to head an economic department. Instead he went to the Ministry of Works. The King's ill fortune was his good fortune. He stage-managed the Coronation in 1953 with all the skills of a great impresario. Although haunted ever after by the use Randolph Churchill made of his remark (taken out of context) that the Queen had been 'a perfect leading lady', he was knighted by her and was an obvious candidate for promotion when Churchill reshuffled his government in October 1954.

At Education he put his faith in Grammar Schools and the development of science. Defending selection, however, meant that he would have to strengthen the Modern schools. They were to become 'magnets' by developing their own specialisms. There were to be extended courses, more vocational courses and links with the Grammar and Technical schools and with further education. The latter was a new avenue of opportunity and with Eden's backing, he not only secured major funding for the sector for the first time since the war, but produced a rationalised structure offering an alternative pathway into higher education. Rescuing the Percy Report from eleven years obscurity, he created a hierarchy of colleges peaking in the new Colleges of Advanced Technology. He was tough and largely successful with the Treasury, winning a major clash with Butler when the latter sought to slow his programme for replacing the all age schools. However, his final battle against the block grant system of local government finance was lost, although not until he had left the Ministry for the economic department he had long craved.

At the Board of Trade, curiously, he seemed less at home, although he showed himself a vigorous promoter of British exports. The detailed negotiations to embed the EEC into a wider free trade area were in other hands, although when they broke down, it fell to Eccles to denounce the French veto and press unsuccessfully for mutual tariff reductions. He was less than enthusiastic about EFTA – describing it as 'marrying the engineer's daughter when the managing director's is no longer available'. He was responsible for the Distribution of Industry Act 1958, which marked a partial shift back to regional policy.

Returning to Education in 1959, he ensured that all those with two A-levels would receive a local authority award to go to University, created the CSE examination and, despite divisions amongst his own advisers, took the first faltering steps 'to make the Ministry's voice heard rather more often and no doubt more controversially' in what he memorably called 'the secret garden of the curriculum'. In February 1962, in the teeth of bitter resistance from the local authorities and the NUT, he established the Curriculum Study Group. His successors replaced it with the Schools Council. However, he clashed with his colleagues when he refused to make cuts in the education budget and was one of those who rebelled against the detail, if not the thrust of Lloyd's budget in 1962. Macmillan suspected that he was engaged in some deep-laid plot and was trying to engineer a good issue on which to resign. That was pure paranoia.

After his sacking, Eccles returned to business, becoming a director of Cortaulds and chairman of West Cumberland Silk Mills Ltd. He became a trustee of the British Museum in 1963 and chaired the trustees from 1968 until unexpectedly recalled to government in 1970 as Paymaster General with responsibility for the Arts. His relationships in that field were soured by the government's determination to impose museum charges. That should not obscure some very real achievements, particularly in relation to craftsmanship. He was later to become President of the World Crafts Council.

He left Heath's Government in December 1973 to become the first Chairman of the British Library, a body, which, sensibly, he had separated from the British Museum. He served a five year term. He was appointed a Companion of Honour in 1984 and in the same year married a fellow member of the Roxburghe Club, bibliophile and Johnson expert, Mrs Donald Hyde.

He had completed a thoughtful book on *Life and Politics at Siena* in the early summer of 1966. It was a moral diagnosis of Britain's problems. Identifying a growing moral vacuum to which none of the parties appeared to have an answer, he argued that Britain faced a choice between a move towards technocracy, which he thought not only wrong but unworkable, and the religious solution which he favoured but for which the times were not propitious. A later book, *Halfway to Faith*, records the uncertainties of his own search for God. It is dedicated to his father, who had an 'unshaken belief in a Creator. And to my mother who showed me that the knowledge and love of God would be very difficult, and probably impossible to attain.' In his own life, a hankering for monastic seclusion was always subordinate to his desire for the arena, but his ambition always was for the public good.

His eldest son, John, succeeds him.

John Barnes

'Screaming' Lord Sutch

born 10 November 1940, *died* 27 June 1999

Screaming Lord Sutch, who has committed suicide aged 58, was an outsider, shaped by postwar poverty, who achieved celebrity in the early 1960s, and fame in the Thatcher era as founder and frontman of the Official Monster Raving Loony party. When his mother was asked about her son and his exploits, she explained that it was, after all, just an act, indeed that his whole life was just an act.

Sutch ran for Parliament 39 times, first as the National Teenage Party candidate in the 1963 Stratford-on-Avon by-election that followed the Profumo scandal. The narrowly victorious Conservative, Angus Maude, treated him, Sutch recalled, like 'vermin from another planet'. In the 1966 general election he fought Prime Minister Harold Wilson in Huyton and picked up 585 votes. Four years later, he ran in Westminster as the Young Ideas Party candidate, and in 1974 for the Go To Blazes party in Stafford and Stone.

But it was in the next decade, with the flowering of Thatcherism, that Sutch first ran as an OMRLP candidate. The contest was Bermondsey, the Labour candidate Peter Tatchell, and the victor the Liberal Simon Hughes. Sutch advocated a statue to Tommy Steele – 'the Bermondsey bombshell and the only decent thing to come out of the place' – and attracted 97 votes.

Soon after, at the Darlington by-election, the local paper reported that more people were in the toilets at Sutch's (pre-election) victory party than attended the Social Democratic Party's rally. Sutch won 374 votes. In the 1983 election 11 candidates ran for the OMRLP, with Sutch 'against Margaret Thatcher – a nasty experience, as Denis can testify'. The following year it was Chesterfield and Tony Benn.

Thus did a decade unfold where, whatever the national crisis, whatever the earnest fatuities of the victorious by-election candidate, there on the edge of the screen would be Sutch, or a sidekick, a Shakespearean antick for the TV age. It was a great joke, but the viewer could never be absolutely certain that Sutch was in on it.

Sutch was born in north London. His father, a war reserve policeman, was killed in an accident when his son was 10 months old. His mother – to whom he was devoted – was a fan of Dickens; she christened him David after David Copperfield. For most of the next 15 years they shared a flat and poverty in what he called a dead-end street in Kilburn, while she worked as a cleaner and shop assistant. Entertainment was Saturday morning pictures and the Metropolitan Music Hall, Edgware Road. In 1956, after David had left school, they moved to south Harrow, where he became a window cleaner.

It was the birth of British rock music; a time when the young and desperate could pursue a new escape route. What he called his 'wild man of Borneo look' got Sutch a spot singing at the Two I's coffee bar in Soho. His style evolved, or lurched, out of that slurry of music hall (he was a Max Miller fan), horror movies, Grand Guignol, pulp comics, slapstick and transatlantic pop. Thus did the black American rhythm & blues singer Screaming Jay Hawkins provide a name, and the basis of an act.

In 1961 he was spotted by the curious and doomed independent record producer Joe Meek. 'I was doing the horror,' Sutch once told me, 'screaming and yelling. I had 18 inches of hair and I was running around in buffalo horns and my auntie's leopardskin coat. The scout said "You've got a different approach. You want to make a record?"' Sutch made records, and recorded with a clutch of (later) distinguished British rock musicians. The early subject matter focused on disembowelment and graveyards – on one occasion Meek posed Sutch, as Jack the Ripper, in Whitechapel at night. Both men, observed Sutch, were intrigued by horror films. But he had no real hits. Indeed, by 1963 his career had been swamped by the Mersey boom.

It was then that he went to Stratford, campaigning for commercial radio, votes at 18, abolition of dog licences and his share of the spotlight, with the mix of native wit and puerility that marked his aimless – or dadaist – media courtship. The live act around Europe, and playing small halls and pubs, provided an income.

His last political hurrah was in the 1995 Littleborough and Saddleworth by-election (the OMRLP didn't have the money to run in the last European elections). But more than finances, it was perhaps the times that had finally run out. His autobiography, *Life As Sutch*, written with Peter Chippindale, was published in 1991.

Sutch is survived by his partner Yvonne Elwood, and his son Tristan, from his relationship with Thann Quantrill. The death of his mother, in 1997 on the eve of the last general election, greatly affected him.

Nigel Fountain

Robert Rhodes James

born 10 April 1933, *died* 20 May 1999

Sir Robert Rhodes James, who has died at 66, was Conservative MP for Cambridge 1976–92 and before that Clerk of the Commons 1955–64. He buttressed these activities as a prolific and wideranging historian and biographer. He wrote on Gallipoli, the Czechoslovak crisis and British politics. His biographies included Rosebery, Randolph and Winston Churchill, 'Chips' Channon and, most controversially, Sir Anthony Eden. In this last, specialists thought him too much under the influence of Sir Anthony's widow, leaving out Sir Anthony's mental health breakdown which led to his surprise resignation in December 1956.

Dark, tall and thin, alternating a lop-sided grin and a troubled look, he never lost the superior manner commonly displayed by Clerks of the Commons. He could be a congenial companior to those he counted as his intellectual near-equals. But he detested his 'noisy, shallow, self-important, opportunist' MP colleagues.

It was his superior manner which made an unfortunate accident into a source of mirth. Aroused from sleep by a ringing 'phone in the middle of the night, he tripped over a table and smashed his nose on the wash basin, only to find it was a wrong number. Everyone thereafter enjoyed insisting his wife, Angela, had clocked him one.

Robert was a sprig of the old Anglo-Indian establishment. He was born in India in 1933, the son of Lt. Col. W.R. James, who spent 40 years there. Young Robert himself began his education in private schools there, returning to attend Sedbergh and then Worcester College, Oxford. His first job, as a 22–year-old in 1955, was as an Assistant Clerk of the House of Commons, a highly-paid post which goes only to top young graduates. Within four years he had published his well-reviewed *Lord Randolph Churchill*, followed by his *Rosebery*, then by *Gallipoli*. He reached a much wider audience in 1967 by editing *Chips: The Diaries of*

Sir Henry Channon, an earlier, bitchily homosexual equivalent of the later Alan Clark sensation. Enoch Powell tagged him a 'compulsive author'.

By 1961 he had become a Senior Clerk at the Commons, near the top of Westminster's own civil service. There was some surprise that this erudite scholar and civil servant should himself want to engage in the rough and tumble of politics. He was undoubtedly a Tory, having supported Sir Anthony's Suez invasion at 23. He could not resist becoming the first postwar Commons Clerk to become an MP. In 1976 he was selected to follow in Cambridge the retiring David Lane as the Conservative candidate. He trebled Lane's majority in the December 1976 by-election.

He hit the political ground running. Two months later he urged the Callaghan Government to 'cut the throat' of its devolution Bill. He described himself as 'on the liberal wing of the Conservative Party' generally but 'a hardliner on defence and private enterprise'. He was strongly anti-Communist and anti-Left, calling the USSR 'deliberately aggressive' and attacked 'followers of darkness on the Left'.

He was at his best on colonial and immigration matters. He was the only Tory MP apart from Ted Heath to attack Mrs Thatcher for her January 1978 remarks about being 'swamped' by coloured immigrants. He urged a 'return to the bi-partisan approach' on Rhodesia. He was against 'abortion on demand' but supportive of David Steel's Abortion Act, especially if modified.

Although his Cambridge seat was thought to be 'ripe for picking' by the SDP after the loss of 10,000 voters in a strong Tory ward, he proved this wrong in the 1983 election.

He was disappointed that his high intelligence and deep knowledge of politics was not appreciated by fellow Tories. He only reached the PPS level at the FCO 1979–82. He failed when he contested the 1922 Committee in 1984. He never expected anything from Margaret Thatcher, but was miffed when John Major ignored his talents. In his cups in Annie's Bar' he alluded to the subtitle of his Churchill book, *A Study in Failure*.

If not with office, his talents were recognized. John Major recommended him for a knighthood in 1991. He had visiting professorships at several US universities and was a Fellow of All Souls.

He leaves his wife of 43 years and four daughters.

Andrew Roth

Alf Robens

Lord Robens of Woldingham

born 18 December 1910, *died* 27 June 1999

Lord Robens of Woldingham – 'Alf' Robens – who has died aged 88, was the classic Mr Might-Have-Been Man. He might easily have become leader of the Labour Party and, in 1964, Prime Minister instead of Harold Wilson. Instead, he had a remarkable and successful, not to say lucrative, career as an industrialist.

It was a prime example of rags-to-riches; the elementary schoolboy from a poor Manchester home, very working class, starting as a messenger boy in the local Co-op, doing a stint as an umbrella salesman, and then becoming a full-time official of the shop workers' union, USDAW, in 1935. No one could have had a better Old Labour pedigree.

That very background seemed to help Robens develop a forceful, thrusting, ambitious self-confidence a contemporary once described to me in glowing terms. 'We always recognised something special in Alf even as a young union official. If he met someone new, he would always make a note of their personal details in his notebook; the names of their wives, children, etc, in case he met them again. He had that kind of organised mind even as a young official.'

Robens was medically unfit for war service, and that gave him the opportunity to enter politics, on Manchester City Council from 1941 to 1945, when he became Labour MP for Wansbeck (Northumberland). That constituency disappeared in 1950 and Robens became MP for neighbouring Blyth, where he remained until he became chairman of the National Coal Board (NCB) at the end of 1960.

In the 15 years he sat in Parliament he had a number of junior ministerial roles; at Transport, then at the old Ministry of Fuel and Power, where he served with Hugh Gaitskell, until in April 1951 he was promoted into the Attlee Cabinet as Minister of Labour to succeed Aneurin Bevan. It was only a brief spell – the Attlee Government fell in October 1951 – yet Robens made his mark with considerable diplomatic skill in handling a period of tense industrial relations.

In the years that followed Robens was always associated with the Gaitskell camp against the Bevanite rebel lion on the left. He was close to Gaitskell personally and politically. Yet he shrewdly never closed the door on his contacts with the left, and in the mid-1950s – when the clash between Bevan and Gaitskell was at its height – Robens, in the Shadow Cabinet, voted against withdrawing the party whip from Bevan. He was in a minority of nine votes to four.

Then came the great turning point in Robens's career – the 1959 general election with Labour defeated by a huge swing to Harold Macmillan's Tories. Robens was despondent at the prospect of a long period in opposition; he was approaching 50, and although Shadow Foreign Secretary, the defeat had a profound effect on his outlook. Macmillan brilliantly timed his invitation to Robens to become NCB chairman.

Robens was taken aback. He suggested to the Prime Minister that, given the state of NCB finances, it would be next to impossible ever to make a genuine profit. 'Don't worry, dear boy,' Macmillan replied. 'Just blur the edges, just blur the edges.' So Robens took over Britain's coal industry in October 1960 for his *Ten-Year Stint* (the title of his own 1972 book).

It was his 10 years at the NCB that have left their imprint on the nation, the industry (even allowing for its virtual disappearance), and on his reputation. No nationalised industry has experienced as much trauma as coal; perhaps no other industry in the country, publicly or privately owned, has so much dramatic luggage in its history bag. No wonder Macmillan advised 'blurring the edges'.

When Robens took over at Hobart House, the NCB's London headquarters, there were 698 pits employing 583,000 miners. Ten years later, when Robens left, there were 292 pits employing only 283,000.

What Robens inherited was not merely an industry, it was a social and political culture. And though the industry had been nationalised for more than 13 years, it was still living through a good deal of its bitter inheritance; unofficial strikes were still the norm. Much of the trouble was due to the endless disputes about the chaotic system of piece-rate payments endemic to the old wages' practices under private ownership. Then there was the market situation in which coal was steadily being priced out by oil.

Robens tackled all these battlefronts with energy and courage. He established a punishing schedule of pit visits – roughly one pit visit a fortnight – which he maintained throughout his 10 years. He reckoned to have visited 350 pits in that period. He persuaded the Macmillan Government to provide the industry with a measure of protection by tax concessions and import restrictions. In particular, he succeeded in holding on to the coal industry's key customer – the power stations – and received government help to do so.

He also had a remarkable stroke of luck from the National Union of Mineworkers. Shortly before he took over, the NUM had elected a new general secretary, Will Paynter, leader of the South Wales miners and a veteran communist of Spanish civil war vintage.

Quite quickly – and unexpectedly – Robens and Paynter established a working alliance, and eventually a mutual trust, which without doubt laid the basis for a reformed and revitalised – if smaller – coal industry. It was only with the help of Paynter that the NCB succeeded in introducing a more rational and equitable pay structure, which, in turn, significantly reduced the number of disputes.

Paynter came under constant criticism from his CP comrades, but he stuck to his guns, convinced that the only way to save the coal industry – and sustain it within the public sector – was to help modernise and, however reluctantly, accept the closure of exhausted collieries. There is little doubt that the Robens-Paynter alliance saved the industry until the combination of Margaret Thatcher and Arthur Scargill finally closed the shop.

While Paynter was persuading the NUM to face realities, Robens was in constant session with ministers and civil servants, lobbying for the industry's salvation. Curiously, he found it easier to do this under Macmillan's (and later Home's) Tory government than with Harold Wilson's Labour administration. He was perpetually, at war with Whitehall during the Wilson period, and became convinced that if senior civil servants in the Treasury and Department of Energy had their way most of the coal industry would disappear. He was right.

Perhaps the outstanding feature of Robens's fight to sustain a smaller coal industry was his moderate success in persuading governments of both parties to adopt what he called 'a social policy' to cushion the pit closures he was compelled to make. He demanded that national and local government combine to ensure that new industries and investment moved into the declining coalfields. This, too, brought him into regular conflict with Whitehall and a succession of Labour ministers, many of whom he despised.

When the Aberfan disaster came on 21 October 1966, killing 116 children and 28 adults after colliery waste slid down a mountain to engulf Pantglas School, the knives were out for Robens's scalp. His immediate behaviour did not help. Instead of going direct to Aberfan, he kept an appointment to be installed as Chancellor of Surrey University. He only went to Aberfan the following day – a grave error of judgement for which he was never forgiven.

His critics wanted his resignation, and when the Aberfan tribunal of inquiry reported in July 1967, the demands became more widespread. The tribunal report found the coal board culpable of neglect and, by definition, responsible for the Aberfan tragedy. Robens offered his resignation in a letter to the then Minister of Power, Richard Marsh. In September, Wilson and Marsh rejected Robens's offer though several Cabinet Ministers argued strongly that he should go.

Robens himself believed that the tribunal report was seriously flawed and unfair to the coal board. Yet he was ready to quit. What, in the end, was particularly significant was the decision of the NUM to urge him to stay on.

Without doubt the Aberfan disaster played an important part in Robens's ultimate decision not to accept a third five-year term as coal board chairman. It was certainly offered when Edward Heath's Conservatives won the 1970 election. Perhaps an inner intuition warned him about the dangerous, even disastrous, years ahead, though the industry did enjoy a modest recovery in the early 1970s.

Robens had been a supreme chairman – virtually an emperor of this once great nationalised industry, which he liked to run at times like a feudal kingdom. A member of his board still argues that 'there was simply noone like him in either public or private sectors of industry; at his peak he reigned like a king.'

From then on all seemed a little like anti-climax. He was still recognised as 'the voice of industrial common sense' on television and radio; he became chairman of Vickers Ltd, and of Johnson Matthey Ltd, as well as a director of Trust House Forte and a string of others. He had earlier been a director of the Bank of England, and Times Newspapers Ltd, and was an original member of the National Economic Development Council from 1962. He sat on the royal commission on trade unions and employers (1965–68), where he advocated tough new legislation to curb unofficial strikes and secondary picketing.

He held honorary degrees at numerous universities and he was a governor – one-time chairman of governors – at Guy's Hospital, where a Robens' Suite is named in his honour. Almost to the end, his advice was still sought.

Alf Robens was one of those remarkable products from the legendary generation of Labour and trade union talent, largely untutored, who scaled the heights, loved the glamour and successes, yet did not forget their roots.

He is survived by Lady Eva Robens and a son, Alfred.

Geoffrey Goodman

William Whitelaw

Viscount Whitelaw of Penrith

born June 28 1918, *died* June 30 1999

When he first became an MP in 1955 Willie Whitelaw was difficult to distinguish from the many country gentlemen on the Conservative benches. Twenty-eight years later, when he was elevated to the House of Lords, he was one of the best-known of British politicians, admired by colleagues and opponents alike. In part, he was distinctive because he represented a class which was disappearing from public life. But to a much greater extent he owed his reputation to personal qualities which would have made him an outstanding figure at any time.

In the last decade of his career Whitelaw embodied a number of contradictions. An orthodox member of the Establishment, he cooper-ated with a radical Prime Minister who left few of Britain's traditional institutions intact. An exemplary symbol of 'One Nation' Conservatism, he registered only muffled protests when unemployment soared over three million. He was a consummate professional with the ambience of a bumbling amateur, capable of acting ruthlessly even against personal friends when the interests of his party were at stake. Journalists loved him because he could be wildly indiscreet; but senior colleagues knew that they could always trust him with the most important confidences. His public image was so emollient that his detractors called him 'Woolly

Willie'; but his temper, under suitable provocation, was postively Vesuvian.

In fact to an unusual degree Whitelaw's contradictions were not in himself, but in his circumstances. He entered politics out of a sense of public duty, and if that impulse had been weaker he would have stepped away when the profession had been transformed by 'career politicians' who only worked on behalf of their party and country when this coincided with their own advancement. In what he considered to be happier times, serving as Chief Whip to Alec Douglas-Home and Edward Heath, Willie seemed as straightforward as anyone at Westminster. His creed in those days was very simple: he would offer complete loyalty to a party leader who broadly shared his own outlook. His problem was that by 1975, when the leadership was taken by a very different personality, he had become a prisoner of his own success as a totem of party unity. If he had refused Mrs Thatcher's offer of the Deputy Leadership after she had beaten him in the leadership election of that year, he would have plunged the party into civil war.

Whitelaw was born in Edinburgh. He was brought up by his mother; he barely remembered his father, who was killed by pneumonia after surviving the First World War. Although his grandfather played a secondary role, Willie closely resembled him. He had briefly served as an MP, and a distinguished career in the railways had enabled him to add to the landed property in Scotland which he had inherited.

Young Willie was groomed for the comfortable life of a squire. His grandfather was opposed to any idea that he might go in for politics, because his own experience had left him disillusioned. But Willie began to thwart his grandfather's intentions at an earlier age. Although he never pretended to be an intellectual, he was bright enough to win a place at Winchester. Subsequently he reverted to the game plan by spending most of his time at Cambridge playing golf. He inherited the family properties on his grandfather's death in 1946, while Willie was still in the army. He had won the Military Cross in a battle which took place within days of the Normandy landings, and his ability to inspire confidence in his colleagues had been widely recognised. In 1943 he had married Celia Sprott, who had a similar background to his own and shared his commitment to public service. After seeing further action in Palestine after the end of hostilities in Europe, he decided to leave the army and returned to Britain with nothing to cloud his prospects.

Willie entered Parliament at the third attempt, having been persuaded to contest the safe Labour seat of East Dumbartonshire in 1950 and 1951. In 1955 he switched his sights to Penrith and the Border, which no Conservative could lose and also offered the perfect rural milieu for one of Willie's tastes and temperament. In the Commons he was initially taken at face value – as affable, reliable, but limited in intellect and ambition. He was promoted to the Whips' Office in 1959, and three years later became a junior minister in what was then the Ministry of Labour (later Employment). This might have been the pinnacle of his career had he been no more than he seemed; but in both roles his diligence and good nature attracted favourable notice on all sides of the House.

When the Conservatives lost power in 1964 Douglas-Home made Willie his Chief Whip. In the following year Home's position as leader became untenable, and despite their close friendship Willie did not shirk the responsibility of breaking the news. Home's successor, Heath, was a very different character. But if Willie was sometimes exasperated by his refusal to court easy popularity, he fully appreciated Heath's intellect and efficiency. The partnership was vital to the survival of the party through the difficult opposition years, which were marked by deep divisions over Rhodesia and the furore over Enoch Powell's sacking in 1968.

When the Conservatives won the 1970 general election Willie became Leader of the House of Commons. He, rather than Home, was Heath's right-hand man, a constant source of emotional support and sound tactical advice. However, these qualities meant that he was the ideal candidate to deal with the problem of Northern Ireland after the imposition of Direct Rule in March 1972. Twenty months in the province at the height of the 'Troubles' was a serious trial to Willie, although he had produced what seemed like a workable solution by the time of his departure. Heath recalled him in December 1973 as Secretary of State for Employment, amidst the most dangerous industrial disruption of the whole post-war period. Willie was exhausted, and felt that he lacked clear guidance from Downing Street in his negotiations with the miners. But in any case it was a hopeless situation, which propelled the Conservatives out of office in February 1974.

A year later Heath lost his leadership. Entering the second leadership ballot as the candidate of the 'old guard' against Mrs Thatcher, Willie was badly beaten. Later he maintained that he had never wanted the position, but that was not precisely true. Rather, his undoubted qualities as a unifier and decision-maker were better suited to government than to opposition – and certainly not to the circumstances of 1975.

Although he was urged to play hard to get, he readily offered his loyalty to Mrs Thatcher after his defeat. This decision shaped the rest of his career. He knew that other 'One Nation' Conservatives would look to him for some resistance to Mrs Thatcher's radicalism. However, he felt that the party had made its decision; and although he shared Heath's distaste for monetarist theory he was no less convinced than Mrs Thatcher of the need for some radical changes in the post-war settle-ment. He used his influence far too sparingly for the taste of the 'wets', some of whom came to despise him.

From the Conservative victory of 1979 to his enforced retirement after a mini-stroke at the end of 1987, Willie served as Home Secretary, then as Leader of the House of Lords after the award of an hereditary peerage in 1983. As Home Secretary he had to deal with a series of terrorist outrages, inner-city rioting, and an uninvited intrusion into Buckingham Palace. Although he was subjected to almost continuous sniping from both left and right, he had every reason to be proud of his record. If his achievements were essentially negative – for example, in withstanding raucous demands from every level of his party for repres-sive measures after the riots – they were considerable nonetheless, considering the climate of the time. If he could not persuade this govern-ment to be tough on the causes of crime, at least he recognised its social roots and was always as fair as he was firm in dealing with its symptoms.

Life was much easier in the Lords, where Willie quickly quelled suspicions that he would act as a stooge for the Conservative majority in the Other House. He thought that the peers should be allowed to defeat the government now and again – but not too often, in case Mrs Thatcher's radicalism was visited on the Upper Chamber. These tactics chimed in with his natural inclination, for patient persuasion rather than confrontation if this could be avoided. This preference also marked his conduct in key government committees, where his tactical skills won the admiration of unlikely friends and allies like Norman Tebbit and Nigel Lawson.

Willie was ill for much of his last decade, and the strife within his party grieved him. His death prompted a flood of warm tributes, but if he was far from forgotten he was barely relevant. He was remembered best for his 'Willie-isms' – remarks which sounded nonsensical but which contained a nugget of wisdom. Perhaps the best of these was delivered at his first press conference in Northern Ireland, as he tried to wrestle with age-old hatreds: 'I always feel it is wrong to prejudge the past'. But Mrs Thatcher herself proved an inadvertent master of the genre when she said that 'Every Prime Minister needs a Willie'. The double-entendre ensured that the remark became a political cliché, but it was perfectly true. Every leader needs a dependable, shrewd, warm-hearted deputy. In this respect Willie Whitelaw set a standard which can never be surpassed.

Mark Garnett

Lord Orr-Ewing

born 10 February 1912, *died* 19 August 1999

The Lords had their own way of paying tribute to Lord Orr-Ewing, who has died at 87. after 20 years in the Commons 1950–70, and 28 in the Lords, from 1971. In 1985 he was allowed to pose the first question on the first day the Lords was televised. This was their Lordships' way of celebrating that, as a 22-year-old graduate apprentice at EMI in 1934, he had been part of a team of three which built the first production television set. 'Early in 1937 my mother bought one with her winnings of £2,016 since she was the only winning ticket on the Tote double.'

A tall, slender, well-muscled man, he was long the Lords' leading man in tennis, cricket and skiing. In 1989 he wrote *Lords and Commons Cricket 1850–1988*. As founder of the Lords and Commons Ski Club, he took part in its annual race against Swiss Parliamentarians for four decades. 'I won it in 1965,' he admitted, adding modestly in 1991, 'there is a very generous handicap for those over 70 and because of that I have managed to win the Seniors' Race on several occasions. Sadly, the day before this year's race I fell badly and dislocated my shoulder.'

This paragon of sporting virtues nevertheless had his critics. Although Lord Orr-Ewing never hid his (partial) enthusiasm for his *Alma Mater*, the BBC – for which he worked as TV Outside Broadcasts Manager from 1946 to 1948 – he has been described by the amiable Lord [Joel] Barnett, onetime BBC Deputy Chairman, as the leader of the anti-BBC 'Mafia'. This was the Labour peer's summary of Orr-Ewing's unending pressure on the BBC – along with Lord [Woodrow] Wyatt and Tory Rightwinger Dr Julian Lewis – to observe 'due impartiality', which meant curbing criticisms of Conservatives by such 'Leftists' as the *Today* programme. His idea of impartiality was illustrated by his claim that he had 'often' heard humanists deliver their atheist messages in the *Today* morning religious slot. He was also one of the band who forced through the commitment to 'predominantly Christian' religious education in schools in 1990.

Lord Orr-Ewing was a typical prewar style right-wing Conservative. He bemoaned the passing of the old days. 'As recently as 1963 the MP James Ramsden was offered promotion to Secretary of State for War and only accepted on condition that he could hunt his own pack for two days a week. This was readily accepted by Harold Macmillan but I doubt whether there has been any Prime Minister since who would show the same understanding and tolerance.'

He gave up his marginal seat of Hendon North in 1970 when he realised that he would never reach the Cabinet under Edward Heath. He had been PPS to Sir Walter Monckton, the notable Employment Secretary from 1951 to 1955 without Sir Walter's conciliatory attitude toward trade unions ever rubbing off on him. With seven wartime years in the RAFVR – becoming SHAEF's Chief Radar Officer (Air) – he was more at home as Under Secretary for Air 1955–57. He progressed to Parliamentary and Financial Secretary to the Admiralty in 1959, and then served as Civil Lord of the Admiralty 1959–63. He had considerable Commons responsibility because the First Lord of the Admiralty, Peter Carrington, was in the Lords. 'I was lucky enough to have two consider- able personalities as First Sea Lord: Lord Mountbatten and [Admiral] Casper John, son of the painter.'

'Whilst Civil Lord I only had one difference of opinion with the Board of Admiralty, when I recorded my objections over their plan to build three 55,000-ton aircraft carriers. I took the view that it would be better to build ships of half the size, as the French and Dutch were doing and develop the unique Harrier jump jet which we would be able to sell to our allies.'

During the first Wilson administration of 1964–70, he made up for the low salaries he had earned as a junior Minister. Luckily for him he was a qualified electrical engineer, with an MA in Physics from Trinity College, Oxford. He became Chairman of two public engineering companies, Ultra Electronics and Clayton Dewandre Holdings, and Chairman of the Electronic Engineering Association. He also became a Lloyd's name. This did not impede his becoming an officer of the 1922 Committee and Vice Chairman to the Conservative MPs' Defence Committee 1966–70.

He continued his interest in defence in the Lords, insisting – as the man who had made the 'Polaris' agreement in 1962 – on the need for continuing the 'Trident' deterrent. But he made much bigger waves as a union-basher, leading the right wing pack against moderate Jim Prior, then Employment Secretary to try to ban secondary strikes in 1980. He also made a lot of noise about the non-secret that the World Peace Council was a Soviet-financed Communist front, evoking the unfair charge that he was a belated 'McCarthyite'. Although a non-smoker himself, he was a fierce opponent of all limits on tobacco companies, one of which was a client of lobbyists who employed him. In 1994 he was active in trying to reverse the Commons vote to reduce the age of consent for homosexuals from 21 to 18.

His assiduity in attendance and in debates and in serving on Lords committees won admiration even from those who strongly opposed his very right wing views. His preoccupation with politics well into his eighties was possibly hereditary, if not directly. 'My father was a sugar broker and my parents were not at all political. I was bitten by the political bug [at 19] during the 1931 general election campaign when I canvassed in Bermondsey for my aunt, Norah Runge, who was standing as the National Conservative against Ben Smith. He had a 30,000 majority and she won after a recount, much to the surprise of her family and friends. When I entered the Commons I discovered that before 1930, six generations of Orr-Ewings had served in Parliament. It must have had something to do with genes, because only two were father and son.'

Andrew Roth

Alan Clark

13 April 1928 – 5 September 1999

A memory of Alan Clark, who has died aged 71, is of a lean figure standing just below the government side gangway in the Commons, legs apart, arms folded, head tilted back, asking a question – so very often a question disagreeable to his party, the Conservatives. And until 1983, and appointment to a junior post in employment, Clark was seen as pure backbencher

– eccentric, clever, no doubt, but not imaginable in office. He was rude, outrageous, on certain issues very right wing. Even under Margaret Thatcher he would surely be one of those weird ultras, loyal to her but offensive to good taste, like the Quasimodoish intriguer, George Gardiner.

In fact, Clark would hold office until 1992 – at Employment, Trade and Defence, where he wrote amusingly about thoughts on the mortality of his superior, Tom King. King was involved in a minor car crash and slightly injured. 'No hope of it being serious?' Clark's wife, Jane, commented, the sort of thing cheerfully said in the Clark circle.

Such indulgence, in what Clark himself would have called 'the farouche', was part of a wider contempt for political correctness before the phrase was invented. Not many people can say, as he did in 1971, that Ugandan Asians should be told, 'You cannot come here because you are not white', and live. But Clark, who also objected to a ban on a National Front march as the 'insatiable hunger of the extreme left', not only lived, but was widely liked, and with the publication of the most candid diaries since Creevey, became something of a national treasure. For a man of 67, who had left Parliament at short notice four years earlier, to win the plum seat of Kensington and Chelsea in 1997 is pretty eloquent.

But then Clark himself was eloquent – literate, astringent and insolent. His manner, languorous and throwaway, and his accent, ostentatious old upper-class, both suggested a gent chippily entertained by the resentful rest of us. With Clark residing in what was once delightfully described as 'the 14th-century Norman Saltwood Castle', and given to musing about long bonds, there was plenty to resent. 'Last year I spent £11,000 replacing the lead on just one roof. What's the point? The Aubuisson can really take no more punishment.'

Clark, who served briefly in the Household Cavalry (Training Regiment) as a teenager, and in the Royal Auxilary Air Force in the early 1950s, was called to the Bar in 1955. Despite an education at Eton and Christ Church, Oxford, he was new money. His father might be Sir Kenneth of *Civilisation*, who knew the last thing about Mantegna and instructed us on such subjects for BBC television, but the ancestors were trade – Paisley cotton-thread spinners, upon whose factories the whole beautiful edifice rested.

He came to the Commons first in the February election of 1974, as MP for Plymouth Sutton, and remained there until that short-notice resignation in 1992. He had come to politics after writing history of distinction. A prize pupil of Hugh Trevor-Roper and Basil Liddell-Hart, and fascinated by war, he wrote *The Fall Of Crete* (1963) and *Barbarossa; The Russo-German Conflict 1941–45* (1965), both classics. But the paradox of Clark's scholarship, and also the paradox of his political life, was contained in his first book, *The Donkeys* (1961), a savage assault on the British military caste of the First World War, the 'red-faced majors at the base'.

Orthodox military historians hated it. Joan Littlewood, of the Theatre Royal, Stratford East, loved it and created *Oh! What A Lovely War*, a smash hit, left-wing, anti-war pierrot show with death and military stupidity in the main roles, a musical in which blind, gassed men, their hands on each other's shoulders, paraded round the stage to a melancholy music-hall tune. But Clark, multi-millionaire, lordly Tory, mindful of racial distinction, who gloried in being rich and clever, was not flattered by Littlewood's adaptation. In him, English nationalism of the sort which dislikes Europe and the United States in roughly equal proportions, combined with serious feeling for the poor bloody infantry, military and civil.

Calling Clark right wing is to beg questions. He disliked spotty working-class youths, and yet had a sincere impulse for poor people, and rather liked bloody-minded left wingers. His regard for Margaret Thatcher had nothing to do with her Manchester school economics, still less her lurking dislike of workers. She was asserting the country, fighting in the Falklands, being gutsy in ways startling but agreeable to a notable non-feminist. She also offended prim liberals, and, as Clark cheerfully told diary and friends, had given him one job and might give him another.

But the devotion didn't entirely stick. He came to see Thatcher as a class warrior with a stack of resentment, petty bourgeois in fact.

Money and intelligence gave Clark a freedom denied even to the very gifted, aspiring politician, never mind the common toad of the committee corridor. He ached to be a cabinet minister for the vanity and panache of it, and to kick all sorts of bottoms. But nothing would make him trim, amend, dilute, tack or muffle the glorious freedom with which he actually enjoyed politics. As Minister of State at Defence, his greatest contempt was for military politicians. He once ran through the prerequisites – school fees, allowances, cars, drivers and other moneysworths – he thought a certain kind of briefcase soldier really cared about.

The diary relates this about a naval high-up keen on nuclear storage: 'I got the little admiral round. People tried not to tell me his name, just referred to him as IFS (everyone, or thing, here is denoted by their acronym; all part of a conspiracy to befuddle incomers). I told him that nuclear power was essential to the security of this country in two fields and two only: warheads and maritime propulsion. If we were to retain public support, or at least assent, for these, we must lean over backwards in assuaging their environmental concerns.

'What he was proposing to do (nuclear waste near an infants' school) wasn't just bad PR, it amounted to wilful sabotage. He bounced about in his chair crossly; conveyed he thought I was half red-spy, half do-gooder academic. Card marked.'

Another notion of the quality – and the perverseness – comes with 'I might give up drink for Lent. A good start in Arabia next week, as I always enjoy refusing an ambassador, they're so loathsomely arch when they produce the whisky bottle. 'I expect you'd welcome some of this, eh? Ho-ho', and the orange juice at these meetings is the best in the world.'

It is for that diary that Clark will be remembered. Published in 1993 – the year after his first resignation from the Commons, allegedly to make way at Plymouth Sutton for a non-appearing David Owen – it was the political equivalent of posthumous memoirs. Another unexpurgated volume, 'Jane's pension fund', as he called it, exists in glorious expectation. 'They will,' wrote the late Robert Rhodes James, 'send a wave of terror around the House of Commons.'

Or in Sarajevo in 1986; revisiting the location of the assassination by the Serbian nationalist Gavril Princip of Franz Ferdinand in 1914, and on that certain street corner: 'This is where 'the old coachman', gaga Czech chauffeur, had taken a wrong turning (or did he do it on purpose?) . . . nearby was the little Princip museum showing the youth to be exactly as I would expect. Tiresome, ego, mare-eyed, consumptive-looking. Something between 70s CND and Baader-Meinhof.'

In 1986 there was a rumour of resignation by the (hated) Michael Heseltine. 'I don't believe it, but Michael always has this slightly scatty side. It is the only even half-endearing trait he possesses.'

Clark was a romantic – hence the nationalism. There was always an anterior glance towards an age more golden (or better gilded) – just read his account of the memorial service for Harold Macmillan and its invocation of antique soldiery.

He was a free spirit, yet he could be gratuitously spiteful. The freedom included plenty of role-playing and attitude-striking. He was a genuinely loving husband to Jane, with whom he had eloped, yet sexually he hovered between clipboard operator and bore. The race and class remarks could bring out the snivelling lower-middle class in most of us.

But he was different, and the diaries, for all the media concentration on sex, are about politics as it is – chummy, acquisitive, antagonistic, funny, full of not quite consummated hatreds and swings of mood. And their author, in his damn-you-all way, was not a representative minister of state.

He married Jane in 1958. She and his two sons survive him.

Edward Pearce

Edmund Dell

born 15 August 1921, *died* 28 October 1999

Edmund Dell, who has died at 78, was a high-flying practical intellectual who served as Birkenhead's Labour MP from 1964–79 and became

James Callaghan's Secretary of State for Trade 1976–78. He later joined the Social Democratic party and the Liberal Democrats.

After Parliament came a City career as chairman of Guinness Peat and Channel 4 and as a director of Shell Trading. An enduring legacy is his 1996 volume, *The Chancellors: A History Of Chancellors Of The Exchequer 1945–90*.

Self-effacing with a deep voice and a quiet, dry style, Dell liked civilised discussion. The *Economist* tipped him as in the running to take over as Chancellor in 1978 from his embattled friend Denis Healey. Unlike Healey, Dell had made few enemies.

Dell was born in London, the son of a Jewish manufacturer. After elementary school and Owens School he went on to Queen's College, Oxford, as a scholar. Like Healey, he was a Communist at Oxford. (At a cabinet economic committee on 1 March 1977, Callaghan said: 'Right, once and for all, all those who were in the Communist Party, please hold up your hands'. Healey and Dell held up their hands.)

Before graduating with first class honours in modern history in 1947, Dell served from 1941 to 1945 in the Rifle Corps and the Royal Artillery, emerging as a first lieutenant. Post-graduation he lectured in modern history at Queen's, but he then decided to work for ICI as an overseas sales manager in their Manchester-based operation. He specialised in Latin American trade for 14 years.

In 1953 he was elected to Manchester City Council and served for seven years, persuading the council to become the first such body to invest its superannuation funds in equities. He was also involved with Joel Barnett and Robert Sheldon in a left wing coffee shop venture, which subsequently failed. He also failed to win Middleton and Prestwich as the Labour candidate in 1955.

Finding ICI unwilling to give him a sabbatical for a study on developing countries, Dell became a Manchester University Simon research fellow in 1963, writing a Fabian pamphlet, *Brazil: The Dilemma Of Reform*. Then in 1964 he won Birkenhead, arriving in the Commons with Barnett and Sheldon.

In a joint letter to *The Times* he joined with them in pushing the new Labour Prime Minister to withdraw from 'East of Suez', which was wasting £500m-worth of military expenditure.

In 1965 Dell became Parliamentary Private Secretary to his friend Jack Diamond. He then became Parliamentary Secretary for Technology under Tony Benn in 1966 and Under Secretary in Economic Affairs under Peter Shore in 1967. In 1968 he was promoted to Minister of State for trade. Switched to employment in 1969, he wound up a Privy Counsellor in 1970, at 49, but still an unknown, despite praise from colleagues and civil servants.

But he was known for hating to mislead the public. Dell was popular in the Treasury as one of the first converts to a Labour-industry partnership and for curbs on expenditure – it led him to oppose the Chrysler deal pushed by Harold Lever.

A pro-European from the 1960s, he voted with Edward Heath's Conservative Government in 1971–72 to enter the EEC. Rejecting Wilson's offer of an opposition front bench post he served instead as chairman of the prestigious Public Accounts Committee. He also wrote his well-reviewed, little-read, *Political Responsibility And Industry*. Its undogmatic approach to trade, particularly with the Middle East, led to attacks on him in Jewish weeklies, which knew about his Jewish background from the Zionist activities of his father.

When Wilson returned to office in 1974, Dell became Paymaster General, number two in the Treasury to Denis Healey. In 1976 he was promoted to Secretary of State for Trade, after Callaghan became Prime Minister, although Dell had supported Healey to succeed Wilson. There he determined to maximise trade, in the Middle East and elsewhere, to reduce Britain's crippling debts. He had a quietly brutal way of delivering home truths, giving his Scottish colleagues a devastating analysis of the economic dangers of separating Scotland's economy from that of the rest of Britain on the temporary basis of its oil.

In 1978 he quit his Birkenhead seat, after difficulties with left wingers. Nominally he was leaving to become a merchant banker, concealing his dissatisfaction – as a pro-EEC social democrat – with Labour. In 1981 the 'Gang of Four' formed the SDP and he was one of the 100 supporters of the Council for Social Democracy whose names appeared in the *Guardian*. He joined the SDP's finance committee, had a place on its industrial working party and became a trustee. Although he was ambivalent about the SDP-Liberal merger, in January 1988 he led the three SDP negotiators working on the scheme and became a Liberal Democrat trustee. As Hendon's delegate to their 1988 conference, he argued against its federalists, insisting that EC countries faced the threat of becoming a 'centralised protectionist lump'. The Liberal Democrats should champion the principle of devolving power to ordinary people, not endorse the gradual transfer of decision-making to Brussels.

After 1979, his political attitudes were subordinated to his chairmanship and post as chief executive of the Guinness Peat merchant banking group. That only lasted three years because Lord Kissin, its founding chairman, did not approve of Dell's policies. Then came seven years as founding chairman of Channel 4 and he also spent 13 years as a director of Shell Transport and Trading. In 1991–2 he was president of the London Chamber of Commerce and Industry. He worked on the Hansard Society's commission on the financing of politics and chaired the Prison Reform Trust 1988–93. All of his activities produced sober analytical reports, factual letters to the press and solemn, well-researched tomes like *A Hard Pounding: Politics And Economy 1974–76*.

He is survived by his wife of 36 years, Susan (Gottschalk).

Andrew Roth

Sir William van Straubenzee

born 27 January 1924, *died* 2 November 1999

Puckish Sir William van Straubenzee, who has died aged 75, was the Tory MP for Wokingham 1959–87 and Ted Heath's junior minister in education and Northern Ireland. As a 'One Nation wet', he hit his glass ceiling when Margaret Thatcher became party leader in 1975.

Thereafter, apart from his stint as second church estates commissioner (1979–87), representing the Church of England in the Commons, he became leader of her backbench opponents, the 'Lollards', named after his grace-and-favour apartment in Lollards Tower in Lambeth Palace.

A bachelor out of Trollope rather than Dickens, he was exquisitely dressed and mannered, with a thumbs-in-the-waistcoat style of oratory. Extremely polite to those on his side, he could be bitchy to his enemies. Apart from Thatcher, these included John Gummer and Lord Cranborne on church matters, racialists, Ulster Unionists and individual heads of crusading organisations.

The descendant of eight generations of military men, van Straubenzee was disadvantaged among Tories by his foreign-sounding name, inherited from a Dutch ancestor who came across in 1745 to help the Young Pretender and married a rich Yorkshire lass.

He himself was born in London, the son of a much-decorated brigadier. At Westminster School, he was briefly a socialist, thanks to the persuasive powers of a classmate, one Anthony Wedgwood Benn. He reverted to family type when he went from Westminster into the Royal Artillery, becoming a major by 22. After the war he qualified as a solicitor and busied himself rebuilding the Young Conservatives, becoming London chairman in 1949 and chairman of the national advisory committee by 1951. He narrowly lost marginal Clapham in 1955, but was then selected for safe Wokingham in time for the 1959 election. In his campaign he urged a royal commission to reform the unions and 'the reintroduction of the birch' for 'a certain type of thug'. Once in the House he was soon made Private Parliamentary Secretary to the elegant 'One Nation' education secretary, Sir David Eccles. His own initiatives varied. In one outburst he attacked 'unsavoury' Americans coming to Britain to avoid the Vietnam draft. But, more seriously, he pushed prayer book reform legislation for the Church of England.

Named Under-Secretary for further and higher education when Ted Heath became Prime Minister in 1970, he soon clashed with his boss, Margaret Thatcher, then Secretary of State for Education, when he blocked her effort to cut off funds for university student unions.

To avoid further clashes, he was promoted to Minister of State in Northern Ireland. There he came to loathe the Ulster Unionists. When Heath tried to do a deal with them in 1974, he interjected: 'I would rather see the Conservative Party in opposition for 15 years than depend on the votes or support of men such as this!'

His 'wet' views got him in trouble in other ways. With the Tories in opposition, in 1974 he became spokesman on education, but was soon removed because he was too pro-comprehensives. He was demoted to assistant opposition spokesman on defence.

His chance for political advancement ended when Thatcher became Tory leader in 1975. He became a backbench critic of the Tories' increasingly right wing policies. He said it was 'dishonest' to advocate school vouchers without disclosing its adverse impact on 'sink schools'. He attacked Tory racialists, threatening one constituent with her inclusion in his 'Register of Racialists'.

His brand of 'One Nation' Tories organised themselves in the 'Lollards Group' to fight inner-party elections against the Thatcherites. In 1979 he defeated right winger William Shelton to become chairman of the Tory MPs' education committee. He was also elected to the executive of the 1922 Committee.

In his last near-impotent eight years in the Commons, apart from church issues (like opposing Lord Cranborne's attempt to keep the old Book of Common Prayer), he concentrated on defending 'One Nation'

Tory virtues. He opposed student loans and Sir Keith Joseph's education cuts. He backed Jim Prior's Ulster initiatives against Tory harassment.

By 1984 he decided it was pointless to fight the next election. He retired from political life but carried on with his involvement in the Church of England.

Andrew Roth

Bernard Braine

Lord Braine of Castle Point

born 24 June 1914, *died* 5 January 2000

Lord Braine, who has died at 85, never reached his full potential, despite a very full political life. In 1987 he became Father of the House of Commons before standing down in 1992 to enter the Lords. He was much bemedalled, particularly by the Poles, for his attacks on Stalin's butchery of Polish officers at Katyn.

He was honoured by being made Deputy Lieutenant of Essex for his 42 years devoted to the boundary-changing seats of Billericay, Southeast Essex and Castle Point. The intensity of his devotion was shown in his record-breaking 195-minute filibuster which killed the 3rd Reading of the British Railways Bill, which would have allowed rail connections to carry threatening oil and chemicals to and from vulnerable Canvey Island.

This filibuster led the *Daily Express* to ask Kathleen, his wife of 39 years, how chatty he was at home. She said she had hardly had a substantial conversation during his 25 years as an MP. 'He comes home from Westminster on Saturdays. He always has a long list of constituents to see in the agent's office during the morning. He then has a scrappy lunch, spends the afternoon at bazaars and garden parties, has an hour with the motor mower and that is about it. I almost have to make an appointment to speak to him.'

In a talk on the problem of being an MP's wife Kathleen told how she went to London to attend an official luncheon. Bernard then sent her out shopping while he signed letters. When she returned, heavily laden, she could not find his office because he had moved it without telling her. 'I had a dreadful journey home by train in the rush hour carrying a huge parcel'. 'In bounced my husband, sporting a red carnation, complaining about waiting 20 minutes for me before driving home. And, to cap it all, he told me he had just been made President of the local Marriage Guidance Council. I nearly threw the settee at him'.

These disclosures were not the first time his family let him down. The wife of one of his three sons was arrested for stealing money from a shop till, explaining that Sir Bernard's son only allowed her £15 a month for food for the two of them and Sir Bernard's grandchild. 'I have asked him for more money, but he only shouts at me.'

Braine's intense activity at Westminster is party explainable by his unhappy home life, partly by his frustrated career. His crucial mistake was to show his enthusiasm for the African Commonwealth before his pro-European contemporary, Edward Heath, became Prime Minister and blocked him from further ministerial office. Braine hid his disappointment by crusades against abortion, alcoholism, video nasties, Maplin and Stansted airports, war criminals, murderers of Polish officers and, above all, against those who planted potentially explosive methane, oil refineries and chemical stores on Canvey Island, 'the most dangerous island in the British Empire'. This could convey the impression of a bustling, publicity-mad busybody.

His disappointments were all the greater because, with Heath and others, Braine was part of the famous 'Class of 1950' of Tory MPs who entered the Commons after wartime successes as officers. Like Heath, Braine came from a modest home: his father was a minor civil servant, a Fabian. He too was a grammar school boy, in his case Hendon County.

Unlike Heath, who made it to Balliol, Braine became a clerk in the Inland Revenue.

Like Heath, he became an active young Tory, in the minority pro-Churchill anti-appeasement wing. He fought Mosley's anti-Semites in East London. After a barnstorming speech demanding a voice for young Tories, by 1938, at 24 he became National Vice Chairman of the Junior Imperial League (or 'Junior Imps'), the prewar Young Conservatives.

He joined up as a private on the first day of the war. Commissioned in the North Staffordshire Regiment in 1940, he served in West Africa, absorbing his first knowledge of the continent. After Staff College at Camberley, he was on the Staff in the final push into Northwest Europe 1944–45. He took time out to fight hopeless Leyton East in the 1945 election, before a post on the staff of Admiral Lord Mountbatten as a Lieutenant Colonel and Deputy Director of Civil Affairs.

He returned in 1946 to become a Tory party apparatchik: Education Officer for the belt of suburbs arcing around north London. With his pamphlet, 'Tory Democracy' and by signing Peter Thorneycroft's 1947 'Design for Freedom' he aligned himself with the progressive New Tories' who disowned Baldwin and Chamberlain.

Lucky to find a winnable seat, Billericay, he entered the Commons in 1950 with other Tory ex-officers like Heath, Powell, Maudling and Macleod, all intent on getting rid of the Labour Government. He derided it as run by people 'who could not be trusted to run a coffee stall intelligently'.

Braine's early reputation was ambivalent, his progressive brain warring with his right wing gut. He often sounded like a gut-Right backstreeter, urging Government to 'thrash the thug and slash crime'. He also voiced a 'mounting suspicion that Communist and pro-Russian sympathies exist in the vital activities of the state'.

Simultaneously he showed his enthusiasm for an evolving African Commonwealth. He became Deputy Chairman of the Empire Economic Unon and an officer of the Tory MPs' Commonwealth Affairs Committee. He became PPS to Alan Lennox-Boyd, like him a Commonwealth enthusiast. By 1954 he was welcoming the Commonwealth 'as a family of sovereign nations, the circle of which is gradually widening...' By 1955 he wanted to abolish the Colonial Office 'which no longer has any relevance to the times in which we live'.

But the Suez invasion of 1956 hit his Right wing Tory gut. He attacked Tony Benn, then still a moderate Labour MP, as a 'treacherous defeatist' and 'Nasser's little lackey' for opposing Eden's last imperial spasm.

None of this schizophrenia affected his enthusiasm for defending his constituency, by 1955 redrawn as South East Essex and, after 1983, Castle Point. This included low-lying Canvey Island, damaged by the 1953 flood, and later threatened by the construction of potentially explosive chemical storages and oil refineries.

His ambivalence continued to haunt him. Nobody doubted that this prewar battler against Mosley's fascists was an opponent of racial discrimination. In 1957 he agreed that modern economic developments ran counter to Apartheid. But when Fenner Brockway tried to make racial discrimination illegal, Braine first talked it out and then had it counted out.

In 1958 he suggested a union of the British Commonwealth and the French Union to develop a 'third interest' rivalling the American and Russian empires. He also showed prescience in warning that 'storm clouds are gathering over the Horn of Africa... in the Somalilands a situation is boiling up which could lead to ignominious defeat for the West and easy victory for the Egyptians and their Soviet backers.' But when the crisis in Cyprus matured, he urged the arming of all British civilians there.

Harold Macmillan rewarded his loyal partisanship by giving him his first ministerial chance as Pensions Under Secretary in 1960. He could not post him to more suitable Commonwealth Relations where the waspish Iain Macleod did not appreciate Braine's occasional flashes of imperial orthodoxy. But in 1961, when Cuthbert Alport went off to become High Commissioner for Central Africa, Braine replaced him, serving under Duncan Sandys. After Macmillan's post-Orpington 1962 reshuffle, better known as the 'July massacre', Braine became Parliamentary Secretary for Health under Enoch Powell, who envied him his backslapping bonhommie.

Braine's four-year ministerial experience came to an abrupt end with Labour's 1964 victory and Heath's 1965 succession to the Tory leadership. Braine voted for pro-Commonwealth Maudling rather than for pro-European Heath in the July 1965 vote for the succession to Sir Alec Douglas-Home. When Maudling was made Heath's Commonwealth spokesman, he named Braine as his deputy. Braine may have suffered from his tendency to shoot from the hip in opposing Wilson Government policies. Braine strongly objected to sanctions after Ian Smith proclaimed the independence of Rhodesia's white minority.

His great disappointment came after Heath unexpectedly won the June 1970 election and found no ministerial job for Braine. Naming him Deputy Chairman of the Commonwealth Parliamentary Association, with its automatic knighthood after two years, was poor consolation. Braine immersed himself in battles from the backbenches. He fought the idea of having London's third airport at Foulness and against a second oil refinery on Canvey Island.He tried to make himself more attractive to Heath, proclaiming in October 1971 that 'the rejection of the European opportunity would be unforgiveable'. But the 1972–73 immigration scares caused by the crisis for Uganda Asians, just as entry for EEC nationals was easing, showed where Braine's heart lay. In the tightening of immigration rules against the Commonwealth, he became the 'leader of the Old Commonwealth loyalists' (*Sunday Times*) who insisted on special rights for 'patrials', descendents of British emigrants. He also surfaced as the voice of wastedumpers. A Director since 1965 of Purle Brothers Holdings, industrial waste disposers, he complained against local authorities which did not provide sites for safe dumping.

The defeat of the Heath Government in March 1974 did not alter his status as much as if he had been a minister. He was re-elected to the Executive of the backbench Tories' 1922 Committee. His volcanic eruptions began again after the Flixborough disaster, when Labour' new

Environment Secretary, Tony Crosland, told him the same explosive chemical was stored on Canvey Island.

From 1975 on, Sir Bernard became one of the most high-profile anti-abortionists, backing every effort to curb the 1967 Abortion Act, which he had resisted when enacted. In 1978, he narrowly secured leave to introduce his own Bill to cut the 28-week maximum to 20 weeks and to allow nurses to opt out if they had objections to abortion.

As Chairman of the National Council on Alcoholism, he was the chief strategist against Ken Clarke's 1976 effort to bring in Continental-style drinking by easing pub licensing hours and allowing children into family rooms in pubs. He talked the Bill out. In his new guise of defender of public morality, he also complained against a plan to make a pornographic film on the life of Jesus Christ.

Sometimes his aggressive and unctuous style invited deflation. When he complained to the Scottish Secretary about a three-week delay in a reply to his complaint about the incarceration of a constituent in a psychiatric hospital, the delay was explained by Braine's having posted the letter to the patient himself. 'Not quite the Braine of Britain, is he?' joked the Sunday Express.

Long before the 1982 Argentinian invasion of the Falklands, he was the islands' fiercest defender, roaring that 'we should never even have discussed sovereignty with them in the first place'. In his last decade in the Commons, when Mrs Thatcher promoted him a Privy Councillor, he touched all his usual bases. He opposed Stanstead Airport, voted against Sunday Trading, was the only Tory to vote against liberalising pub licensing laws. He tried to secure a free vote to secure random breath testing. He sponsored a horrific, stomach-churning film on late abortions. As Consultant to the Police Superintendents Association, he opposed all suggestions that the police were racists. In 1991 he strongly backed the revived Bill to prosecute suspected war criminals. His last act in the Commons in 1992 was to vote for a Bill banning hunting with hounds.

At the farewell for retiring MPs, the Speaker, Sir Bernard Weatherill, told of his first encounter in 1950 with Braine. After establishing they were the only two Bernards in the House, Weatherill showed him a motion he was tabling, soliciting Braine's support. Braine borrowed the motion. Returning after some time, he told Weatherill he had secured some publicity. Weatherill sought the story in the next day's newspapers. 'And do you know, 'he recalled, 'I was not the Bernard who was mentioned.'

Andrew Roth

Michael Colvin

born 27 September 1932, **died** 24 February 2000

Michael Colvin, the 67-year-old Conservative MP for Romsey who died with his heiress wife in a fire at Tangley House, would have made a presentable US-type presidential candidate. With handsome acquiline features and wavy white hair, the son of a naval captain, married into the Cayzer shipping fortune, he had the background to pursue his political ambitions. And the cushion of a 1000 acre farming estate to fall back on. He was a friend of the Prince of Wales, but a sharp critic of the late Princess Diana. He was a leader of the post-Hungerford and post-Dunblane gun lobby' and of the pro-hunting field sports lobby. He was also a somewhat secretive former lobbyist for Apartheid South Africa and a friend of other lobbyists like Ian Greer, Neil Hamilton and Derek Laud. But he was not monochromatic. He was liberal on abortion. And he would have preferred the whites he backed in southern Africa to be more reformist.

Above all, he was a defence and aviation specialist, serving actively until his last month on the Defence Select Committee, which he chaired 1995–97. On Tuesday, a day or so before he died, he made the longest,

25-minute speech in the Commons Defence debate. His swansong deplored the forces' manpower shortage, a result of the MoD's losing battles with the Treasury.

Michael came by such interests naturally. He was born in London in 1932, the son of Captain Ivan Beale Colvin RN and Joy (Arbuthnot). His family had a political background: a great-great uncle had successfully introduced a Bill to ban bear-baiting.

His education was suited to the military wing of the Tory squirearchy. He attended West Downs prep school at Winchester, Eton, the Royal Military Academy at Sandhurst. At 18 he went into the Grenadier Guards, serving in Berlin, Suez and Cyprus, emerging as a Captain at 24. His economic future was assured when, at 24 in 1956, he married Nichola Cayzer, the daughter of Baron Cayzer, top man in the British and Commonwealth shipping company. Initially, he worked for four years as an advertising man with J. Walter Thompson, then for fourteen years as a Director of Accrep Ltd, a property investment firm.

A decade or so ago the family funds had swollen adequately for him and his wife to become Lloyd's names and to buy the 1,000 acre Tangley Estate near Andover, run from Tangley House. He also became briefly the owner of The Cricketers' Arms, to save it for the village. To qualify himself as a big farmer, he studied at the Royal Agricultural College at Cirencester.

Initially, his political ambitions were satisfied in local government. He was elected to Tangley Parish Council for twelve years from 1964, to Andover Rural District Council for seven years from 1965 and to Hampshire County Council for five years from 1970.

His first Parliamentary seat was Bristol North West, which he captured from Labour in 1979, when Mrs Thatcher achieved power. He showed political ambivalence, urging a new Centre Party on the one hand but also calling for privatisation of NTIS services. He showed his commitment to the doomed right wing white forces in southern Africa by endorsing the South-African-backed anti-SWAPO regime in Namibia in 1981.

In 1983 he switched to the new, much-safer seat of Romsey and Waterside, stretching out from the Southampton suburbs. As a Cayzer son-in-law, he opposed the phasing out of tax allowances on new ship-building and urged a larger, more modern merchant marine fleet. He opposed the slicing off of BA's routes just when it was becoming successful. He favoured easier conditions for pubs. But above all, he spoke up for the whites of southern Africa, particularly after twice visiting Apartheid South Africa and Bophuthatswana as a guest of their governments, first in 1986. He was liberal enough to support reformist Dennis Worral's 1987 election campaign. But in 1988 he criticised the BBC for broadcasting its Mandela concert tribute. He visited Bophuthatswana again in 1989 and Angola as a guest of Unita, backed by the CIA and South Africa. He also welcomed the visit of F. W. de Klerk to Britain and condemned a telecast by Peter Hain and anything emanating from Anti-Apartheid.

Such views led him to become in 1991 a Consultant, at £10,000 a year – replacing Neil Hamilton – to Strategic Network International, a lobbyist front organised by pre-Mandela South African intelligence organisations, possibly unbeknown to him. Later, he became a Director, with the black Tory Derek Laud, of the Ludgate Laud lobbying organisation.

As Chairman of the Council for Country Sports from 1988, he stepped up his opposition to gun-control and to ban fox-hunting. As Captain of the Commons Shooting Club, he opposed the conversion of its shooting range into a creche.

In all things Michael Colvin was an ardent advocate of those he chose to speak for. Among his last words on Tuesday, in the midst of his Defence speech, was to complain for farmers: 'As a farmer, I am experiencing a crisis at present. I have postponed the purchase of a new combine because I cannot afford it this year.' That problem has been left in the hands of his two daughters, Amanda and Arabella.

Andrew Roth

Bernie Grant

born 17 February 1944, *died* 8 April 2000

Bernie Grant wholeheartedly engaged with radical politics throughout his life. From the bauxite mines of Guyana to Britain's Parliament, Grant carved a political path few parliamentarians dared. As one of Britain's first black parliamentary figures, Grant was an outspoken populist. He often openly challenged the party line as an advocate for ethnic minorities, women, youths, the poor and the elderly. He also fought racism and intolerance in England as well as in Europe as chairman of the Standing Conference on Race Equality in Europe (SCORE). As a result, Bernie Grant ended his life as a revered and respected politician, a dedicated constituency MP and a national and international anti-racism campaigner, who had gained the admiration of politicians across party lines for his tireless activism and commitment to issues of social importance.

Although Tony Blair counted him among his friends, describing him as a man of powerful convictions – a politician who did not hesitate to vote against his own government on behalf of his constituents – for most of his parliamentary career Grant had to cope with press vilification. It began in 1985, when riots sparked in reaction to the death of Cynthia Jarrett erupted on the Tottenham Broadwater Farm estate. Jarrett, a resident of Broadwater Farm, died suddenly following an unnecessary police raid at her home. In the ensuing protests, a policeman, Keith Blakelock, was murdered. At the time uninformed of the policeman's death, Grant, then Labour Leader of Haringey Council, in an attempt to explain what had happened, commented that the youths on the estate felt that the police had received a 'bloody good hiding'. After he was told of the murder the next day, he issued a statement condemning the horrible assault, but the damage had been done; he was misquoted and condemned across the country. During the 1980s, he was branded with alarming regularity 'Barmy Bernie of the Loony Left' by tabloids, and along with other radical members of the party, he became anathema to a Labour leadership who considered his grassroots politics anachronistic to their increasingly centre-of-left policies. He was dubbed by Conservative Home Secretary Douglas Hurd a 'high priest of racial conflict'.

It was perhaps a label that Grant may have adopted proudly. For after all, he dedicated his life to illuminating the burning issues of race and class – issues that until black representatives began to question in respect to their urban constituencies were not considered serious variables in British political life.

Bernie Grant was born the second of five children on 17 February 1944 in Georgetown, British Guyana. His parents, Eric and Lilly, descendants of African slaves, were both schoolteachers. An ardent student, Grant won a government scholarship to St Stanislaus College, a Jesuit-run secondary school.

In 1961, aged only 17, Grant left school to become a lab technician in the Guyana bauxite plants. Faced with the harsh realities of colonial inequality, Grant joined a radical youth wing and immersed himself in labour politics. These early years spent analysing economic, political and social injustice and, most significantly, racial oppression, helped mould the passion, vision and courage that would define his future politics.

In 1963 Grant moved to England with his mother Lilly and sister Rosamond, where they settled in the North London borough of Haringey. He attended Tottenham Technical College where he took his A levels. He continued his education at Edinburgh's Heriot-Watt University, studying for a mining and engineering degree, but withdrew from the course in his second year in protest at whites' only work-experience scholarships to South Africa.

Back in London he became a railway clerk, a postal employee and international telephonist and in 1978 a NUPE Area Officer. He joined the Marxist Party briefly, but left it to join the Labour Party, which he saw as the only realistic force for delivering social justice to Britain's minorities and working class.

In 1978 he became a Haringey Borough councillor, where he met Sharon Lawrence, a fellow, white councillor whom he would eventually marry. Just one year later in 1979, Margaret Thatcher was elected Prime Minister, and race relations in Britain plummeted. Grant led a campaign against the rising white-supremacist National Front during this time and though many celebrated him for his efforts, the press ironically depicted him as a dangerous extremist. Grant continued to campaign hard within the Labour Party for a stronger voice for black people. In 1985 he was elected leader of Haringey Borough Council, becoming the first black leader of a local political body in Europe.

He became Tottenham's MP in 1987, replacing the veteran incumbent Norman Atkinson. He and fellow MPs Paul Boateng and Diane Abbott were the first black MPs to enter Parliament in half a century. Grant was the most senior, the one with the most radical grassroots background and certainly the most controversial parliamentarian. On his first day in Parliament, he cut a dashing figure dressed in African robes. It was a significant gesture not missed by his supporters. As representative of one of the most vibrant and diverse multi-ethnic areas in Europe, he had aligned himself with a transatlantic tradition of black freedom political figures firmly rooted in anti-colonial, anti-racist, radical democratic politics, who were nonetheless dedicated to working within existing political structures.

Bernie Grant worked tirelessly for his constituents. During periods of racial tension and stressful economic times, he was a champion for black youth and the black community. He was often the solitary voice in authority translating the frustrations and desires of his urban community to the rest of the country as well as to the party. He was also an effective bridge between a frustrated black community and the local police. When in 1993, Joy Garner died after an encounter with the police, Bernie Grant moved quickly to prevent another Broadwater Farm. This time round, entrusted with leadership by his community, he provided absolutely crucial political leadership and effectively defused rising tensions.

As controversial as he may have been perceived by wider society, Grant had enormous respect among black Britons. He attracted international friends and allies in South African Nelson Mandela and American Democrat Reverend Jesse Jackson. He campaigned for anti-apartheid and reparations for the descendants of slavery. He was a supporter of revolutionary governments, feminist causes, black studies and an inclusive school curriculum. But although he inhabited a politically left-of-centre terrain, he held several convictions to which natural allies took exception. He was, for instance, a monarchist, believing that the monarchy bound Britain to the Commonwealth. He supported Harriet Harman's decision to educate her children at an opt-out grammar school. While he sent his own children to local schools, he pointed out that middle-class parents could afford to take a principled stand over the furture of their children's education. Their postcodes were a guaranteed passport to quality state schools where their children could be sure of getting over five GCSEs grade A to C and then three 'A' levels.

Increasing illness overshadowed the final years of Bernie Grant's political career. He continued to work as an MP in spite of heart trouble, kidney failure and failing eyesight. In October 1998, he had a triple bypass after a history of ill health caused by diabetcs and phlebitis, a circulatory disease.

Grant continued to return to the House of Commons, even though he was clearly ill. He advised the Prime Minister and the Home Secretary Jack Straw on race relations and foreign affairs and was valued by central government as a serious politician and an authentic voice of his constituents. Indeed, until his sudden death on 8 April 2000, Grant continued to campaign for an increase in black and Asian Labour Parliamentary candidates.

It was Grant's striving to understand the realities and needs of his constituents that forever ensure him the respect and unswerving affection that large segments of Tottenham still feel for him. It was his determined pursuit of justice for the underdog that made Bernie Grant a national and international leader for those who needed a voice, who needed someone to articulate wordless aspirations and misunderstood frustrations. It was Grant's alternative agenda – his hope rooted in a pragmatic, radical and economically just Britain – that his supporters continue to work towards today. He is succeeded by three children and his wife Sharon, who became not only his partner in life, but also his political ally in working toward a vision of an inclusive and truly representative politics.

David Lammy

Sir Giles Shaw

born 16 November 1931, *died* 12 April 2000

Tiny, genial Sir Giles Shaw, the Conservative MP for Pudsey from 1974 to 1997, who has died of a stroke aged 68, was probably the most popular man of his time in the Commons. This might have been put beyond question in 1992, when many on all sides wanted him as Speaker, but the Tory cabinet insisted on backing his senior, Peter Brooke. Consequently, 74 Tory MPs, led by John Biffen, voted for Betty Boothroyd as the first woman speaker.

Sir Giles's popularity derived both from his warm, witty, affable personality and his role as a consensus-seeker, in the best tradition of one-nation Toryism. It was certainly his lack of right wing zealotry and europhobia that led to his otherwise inexplicable sacking by Mrs Thatcher in 1987, with the consolation of a knighthood. He had played the game as a loyal Tory, restricting his deviations to backing joining the ERM, and opposing capital punishment and curbs on abortion.

Because everyone agreed he had proved himself a shrewd and highly skilled minister in five departments, it was thought remarkable that he did not seem to bear a grudge for his unfair dismissal, when he should have been promoted to the Cabinet. Fellow Tory MPs showed their admiration by electing him treasurer of the 1922 Committee the following year.

Born in York, Shaw was the son of a qualified motor engineer in fiercely partisan Yorkshire. It was probably education which broadened Giles's viewpoint beyond that of his party and Commons colleague, the Yorkshire Thatcherite Marcus Fox. He went to Sedbergh School and St John's College, Cambridge, joining its Conservative association and becoming president of the Cambridge union. On returning to York, he became an executive of the confectionery firm Rowntree Mackintosh, rising to advertising manager, then marketing director. After fighting hopeless Hull West in 1966, he defeated Keith Hampson for selection for safe Pudsey, in the Leeds suburbs, after Joe Hiley retired.

Arriving in Parliament in March 1974, when Labour under Harold Wilson unexpectedly returned to power, Shaw did not have a chance to show his abilities until Mrs Thatcher made him Parliamentary Under-Secretary for Industry in Northern Ireland in 1979. He helped slim down Harland and Wolff, but was over-optimistic about De Lorean's car scam.

In 1981, he followed Marcus Fox as Under-Secretary for Environment. He stuck to the Thatcherite line, abolishing the Noise Advisory Council, resisting better access for the disabled to public buildings and insisting that dumping sewage at sea was acceptable. He also disclosed that licensed brothels and sex shops were under consideration. But he did make chimes on ice cream vans a nuisance, and resisted the privatisation of the Ordnance Survey.

His brief stint as Energy Under-Secretary included the beginning of the miners' strike and his stunt of swimming off the coast at Sellafield to demonstrate the safety of nearby bathing waters. He was promoted to Minister of State at the Home Office in 1984, taking over from Douglas Hurd the Police and Criminal Justice Bill, whose stop-and-search provision he defended. He refused to rule out advertising on the BBC, and reduced the levy on ITV companies. But he resisted pressure to birch football hooligans.

After replacing Peter Morrison as Minister for Industry in 1986, Shaw showed an aversion to intervention. He was one of three ministers at the Department of Trade and Industry who opposed its Secretary of State,

Paul Channon, when he wanted to protect Pilkington from takeover. He also refused to guarantee a long term steelmaking future for Ravenscraig, and relaxed the ban on alcoholic drink in directors' boxes.

Sacked in the wake of Mrs Thatcher's third victory in 1987, he urged flexibility on the poll tax and opposed the freezing of child benefit. He was a member of the 1922 Committee delegation in 1989 that urged Mrs Thatcher to moderate her stance.

In 1990, Shaw became a director of British Steel and Yorkshire Water – after strongly supporting privatisation as 'the natural way to improve the water supply'. The Friends of Water group that he led campaigned for immunity from prosecution for polluting water and freedom to meet the costs of new pollution standards from higher charges.

The 1992 refusal of the Cabinet to back him for Speaker took the shine off Parliament for him. He was appointed to the prestigious liaison committee in 1992, and the privileges and intelligence and security committees in 1994. But he announced he would not stand again and retired at the 1997 general election.

Shaw leaves his wife of 38 years, Dione, and their son and two daughters.

Andrew Roth

Sir Robin Day

born 24 October 1923, **died** 6 August 2000

Sir Robin Day, who has died aged 76, was the most outstanding television journalist of his generation. He transformed the television interview, changed the relationship between politicians and television, and strove to assert balance and rationality into the medium's treatment of current affairs.

Day was the youngest of four children. His father, a Lloyd George Liberal, was on the administrative staff of the Post Office. Robin was educated at Bembridge School, had an uneventful war in the Royal Artillery, became a captain, and went on to St Edmund Hall, Oxford, in 1947 at the age of 24, to read law. He made his mark as a memorable president of the Oxford Union.

After two years at the Bar, he decided that the prospect of success was too distant. He spent one year with the British Information Services in the United States, was briefly employed, on a temporary basis, by BBC Radio and, in 1955, joined Independent Television News, at its launch, as one of its new breed of newscasters.

ITN made him. It gave him, by his own account, his happiest four years in television – though he was not an instant success. It was originally felt that he was too unsympathetic and harsh in manner, but this view changed as he developed an entirely new style of interviewing.

In the pre-Day era, television interviews were almost always respectful, generally dull and stiff, often insipid. Day asked the direct question pointed like a dagger at the jugular. The turning point in his career was an interview with Sir Kenneth Clark, then chairman of Independent Television, at a time when proposals were mooted to cut ITN's airtime and money. Day asked him questions about the station's future which dumbfounded colleagues and critics by their directness. It was unprecedented that the person in ultimate charge should be questioned about his responsibilities by one of his own employees – and the impact was dramatic.

There followed a number of historic interviews which established Day's reputation: with Egypt's President Nasser after the 1956 Suez crisis, when Day sought to pin him down on whether he accepted the existence of the state of Israel; with ex-President Truman – 'Mr President, do you regret having authorised the dropping of the atomic bomb?'; and, notably, with Prime Minister Harold Macmillan in 1958, in what the *Daily Express* called 'the most vigorous cross-examination a Prime Minister has been subjected to in public'.

This interview turned Macmillan into a television personality, and was probably the first time that television became a serious part of the political process. Day also made Parliament come alive with his unscripted reports of the heated debates during the Suez debacle.

In 1959, Day moved to the BBC and *Panorama*, then the most prestigious current affairs programme. The corporation never really made the best use of his talents, except at elections and, eventually, on *Question Time*, between 1979 and 1989. The fashion turned against 'talking heads' and 'government by debate', with which he, above all others, was identified. He was gradually sidelined, as a chairman figure who simply opened and closed programmes. He described his pre-*Question Time* period as '10 years in the wilderness'. There was even a spell of nearly two years when he did not appear at all.

In the early-1970s, Day became more deeply involved in radio, where he proved an innovator with *It's Your Line*, from 1970 to 1976. This was a national phone-in programme that enabled ordinary people, for the first time, to put questions directly to the Prime Minister and other politicians (it later spawned *Election Call*).

He also presented *The World At One*, from 1979 to 1987, but never felt that radio was his metier. He was not at his best reading from a script, and it is significant that, in his memoirs, he dismisses his eight-year contribution to the programme with a single sentence.

General elections, however, were the time when all the grand inquisitor's talents as cross-examiner came on full display, when the televsion public saw 'the scowling, frowning, glowering' Robin Day 'with those cruel glasses' (Frankie Howerd's description), as well as the relieving shafts of humour.

His most satisfying role in television came with *Question Time*. At last, he was given his own show, with an audience – which he had long asked for – albeit late at night, as a temporary, six month 'filler' and mainly as a way of giving him something to do. Its success in becoming, under his chairmanship, the most popular and effective current affairs programme on television reveals a great deal about his talents.

Why did Robin Day become a national institution, one of the most immediately recognised people in the land, outshining in reputation and respect other television stars whose shows commanded far larger audience figures, and, as he much resented, far higher salaries?

It was because he had a unique combination of qualities. He was a very big personality in the true sense, with immense authority. He was extraordinarily witty. A collection of good Day jokes would fill a minor anthology. *Question Time* also brought out his charm and showmanship. He was inordinately proud of his music-hall gifts, and would insist on showing visitors to his flat videos of his appearances on the *Morecambe And Wise* Christmas shows and (especially) his Flanagan and Allen rendering of 'Underneath The Arches' on the Des O'Connor show, in which he outstarred and outsang O'Connor. But, above all, he was one of the most well-informed, widely read and serious political figures in public life.

Day imbibed politics almost with his mother's milk. His father brought him up to revere parliament and great parliamentarians. As a nine-year-old, he was taken to hear Churchill speak, in the rain. Respect for Parliament and the traditional institutions of British life, such as the monarchy and the legal profession, was at the heart of his philosophy all his life.

It might be said that his interests were somewhat conventional and narrow. He was almost fixated by Parliament, and seemed to think that if someone had made a great parliamentary speech, they had won a great battle, when, in fact, it was events outside Parliament that were transforming British politics. His world was one of party politics and current events, rather than long-term trends. He was not particularly interested in industrial affairs or economics, or developments in European countries.

Gradually, his private views became more and more conservative, at times rather narrowly nationalist, although he did not allow his personal prejudices to show in public or influence his professional performances. But, within the boundaries of his particular interests, he applied his formidable powers of argument and his extensive knowledge to devastating effect, in private as well as public.

He believed passionately in 'government by debate' and in the need for television to balance pictures of current events with reasoned analysis. Otherwise, the powerful visual impact of television would distort and trivialise. He was equally dedicated to the principle that the interviewer had a duty to be well-informed.

Many observers commented on his careful preparation; few realised just how assiduous he was. He would read every current biography and autobiography, and nearly every government white paper. Without research assistants to supply him with background briefings, he would generally be better informed than the many Cabinet Ministers he interviewed. No wonder Prime Ministers treated him as their equal, and lesser mortals on the political scene regarded him with awe.

Day's contribution to British public life was not confined to the media. For 25 years he campaigned tirelessly, and eventually successfully, for the televising of Parliament – not in the interests of television, but of Parliament itself. He claimed that he was the first to present the detailed arguments in favour, in a Hansard Society paper in 1963.

He also played a major part in the establishment of the national lottery. When the Rothschild Commission on Gambling was set up in 1979, he wrote a letter arguing in detail for the kind of lottery we have today. Lord Rothschild wrote back questioning his arguments. Day replied refuting all criticisms; his arguments prevailed and the eventual report recommended the scheme Day had originally proposed. He followed up with endless letters to successive ministers with relevant responsibilities.

In his private life, Day had two personalities. To those who did not know him, he could, at times, appear aggressive and insensitive, seemingly interested only in those who were important because of their fame, public success or wealth. He sometimes found it difficult to talk naturally to intelligent women. He might, to some, have seemed the quintessential member of the all-male Garrick Club, one of his favourite haunts.

To those who knew him well, however, he was the most stimulating, amusing, convivial and warmest of companions. He was one of those rare people who was genuinely loved by his friends. He was prepared to take infinite pains on their behalf. He was also surprisingly modest; despite his obvious success in public life, he frequently talked of his career as a relative failure, because he had not achieved anything solid.

He regretted that he had never entered Parliament – although he ran as a Liberal at Hereford in 1959 – and contributed to the real world of politics, instead of playing a secondary role through television. He thrived on his public fame and was proud to be the first television star to be knighted, but privately seemed to feel that his achievements did not compare with those of others who had made their mark in the more traditional professions, especially the law, or by writing learned books.

In 1965, he married Katherine Ainslie, an Australian law don at St Anne's College, Oxford, and had two sons. The marriage was dissolved in 1986. One of the tragedies of his life was that his elder son never fully recovered from the effects of multiple skull fractures he sustained in a childhood fall.

Some years ago, Day had a coronary bypass, and he suffered from breathing problems that were often evident when he was on the air. He had always fought against a tendency to put on weight. As an undergraduate, he weighed 17 stone, and claimed that, in the course of his life, he had succeeded in losing more weight than any other person.

He is survived by his two sons.

Dick Taverne

Sir John Jacob Astor

born 29 August 1918, *died* 10 September 2000

The Hon. Sir John Astor, who has died at 82 after a long battle against Parkinson's, won distinction in his second and third postwar careers after being vilified in his first.

He won his 1978 knighthood for his contributions to agriculture, partly from his success on his 1,800 acre farm at Hatley Park in Bedfordshire, but especially as Chairman of the Agricultural Research Council, on Victor Rothchild's invitation.

He won even wider plaudits for his key roles in the racing world, as a successful breeder with three establishments at Newmarket and many winners. More crucially, he was a steward of the Jockey Club, on the Tote and the Horserace Betting Levy Board, widely recognised for his outspoken good sense.

But both these careers were embarked on after his vilification and rejection by the Conservative Party for having been one of the six Tory MPs to refuse to support Sir Anthony Eden's 1956 invasion of Egypt in cahoots with the French and Israelis. Like his older brother David, then editor of *The Observer*, he found it 'unnecessary and wrong', deploring also Sir Anthony's lying to President Eisenhower, Britain's senior ally.

'Jakie' Astor found himself ostracised by Tories and constantly villified by the 'Wog'-bashing Tory press, especially Lord Beaverbrook's *Express* newspapers. He discovered that the Conservative Party was 'not a party but a regiment'. He decided that it was not one to which he wanted to belong, soon announcing he would not stand for the 'family seat' of Plymouth Sutton, which had been first occupied in 1910 by his father, William Astor, and then his mother, American-born Nancy Astor, the first woman to sit in the Commons.

To be ostracised from any part of the Establishment was a rare experience for an Astor. Although the first John Jakob Astor had been an 18th century German economic migrant to the United States, he had made a fortune in the fur trade which he invested in Manhattan real estate, the basis of the ongoing Astor millions even after his descendants transferred their affections and some of their funds to Britain, where they secured a barony and a viscountcy.

Jakie was born John Jacob Astor at Cliveden in August 1918, as the youngest of the four sons of the 2nd Viscount Astor. He followed his father to Eton and New College, Oxford, where he first displayed his enthusiasm for racing. This could be afforded because, when he came of age in August 1938 he received his first million under his grandfather's will.

He joined the Life Guards, but soon transferred to the Phantom Regiment and later the Commandos and then the SAS. Although the excitement of frontline service appealed, his skills with signals equipment gave him key supporting roles. In the 1942 Commando raid on Dieppe, he was signals officer on a supporting destroyer. He ended the war a major with a military MBE, a Legion d'Honneur and a Croix de Guerre.

On demobilisation, partly to please his mother, he agreed to fight her old Plymouth Sutton seat. He failed by 924 votes in 1950 but succeeded by 710 in 1951, when Winston Churchill returned to office. Jakie showed himself to be a liberal Tory, aligned with Peter Thorneycroft and R A Butler, and was one of the first Tory MPs to oppose capital punishment. He also sought to legalise gambling and was an early pro-European.

But for postwar imperial Tories, still smarting from the loss of the Indian subcontinent, it was blatant 'treachery' not to support Eden's attempt to humiliate the upstart Colonel Nasser and his 'threat' to the Anglo-French Suez Canal. Even after Jakie announced his impending departure from the Commons, vindictive Tory pressmen clocked every vote he missed.

He married three times, first in 1944 to the late 'Chiquita' Carcano, the daughter of the Argentine Ambassador, from whom he parted in 1972. In 1976, after being cited in her husband's divorce action, he married Susan Sheppard, from whom he parted in 1985. He married Marcia de Savary in 1988. She survives him, together with a son and daughter from his first marriage.

Andrew Roth

Lord Aldington

born 25 May 1914, *died* 7 December 2000

Lord Aldington, who has died aged 86, had three distinguished careers, in the army, politics and big business, His tragedy was that for more than a decade, his life was overshadowed by being the target of obsessionals with friends in high places.

His pursuit, by Count Nikolai Tolstoy and his helpmates, was for allegedly being an accomplice to the murder, by Soviet troops and Tito's Yugoslav partisans, of Nazi-aiding Cossacks and anti-Tito Ustachi – for which Aldington had little, if any, responsibility. It was as if he was being tormented when the real targets should have been Winston Churchill and Harold Macmillan.

For seven years after Aldington won a record £1.5m damages (plus £500,000 costs) in his 1989 libel action against Tolstoy, the count avoided payment by making appeals to 15 courts in Britain and Europe, including a ruling by the European Court of Human Rights that the size of the award violated his right to freedom of expression. He did this, while continuing to live in his big house, and send his children to expensive schools, because of the support of Tory right wingers, including Aldington's own leader in the Lords, Lord Cranborne.

It began to look as though Aldington was being persecuted for having been too close to the deputy Conservative leader, R. A. 'Rab' Butler, in the early 1960s, and a friend of Edward Heath.

Until he collided with Tolstoy, Aldington could have been judged the happiest, and most decorated and appreciated, of Tory establishmentarians, with a near-perfect curriculum vitae. Born Toby Low, he was the son of Colonel Stuart Low, who died in action in 1942; he sailed through Winchester School and New College, Oxford, where he read jurisprudence, and was called to the Bar in 1939. Having joined the King's Royal Rifle Corps in 1934, he was called up immediately and served in Greece, where he won the DSO, then in Crete, the western desert and Tunisia with the Rangers. In 1943, he joined the Eighth Army staff for the Sicilian campaign (MBE) and served as a lieutenant colonel on the staff of 13 Corps in Italy. In 1944, he was appointed brigadier on the general staff of 5 Corps for the final assault from Italy on Austria.

It was these last May days in Austria, before Low returned home to stand for Parliament, that saw the messy aftermath of the Yalta agreement of February 1945, signed by Churchill, Roosevelt and Stalin. It was agreed that those Soviet citizens and Yugoslavs who had fought for the Nazis would be turned over to Soviet troops and Yugoslav partisans in exchange for British prisoners liberated by both.

There were 70,000 Cossacks and Yugoslav Ustachi in the British zone of Austria, with long and bloody trails behind them. Low was the departing chief-of-staff to Field Marshal Alexander, in charge of operations in food-short Austria. Under Macmillan's orders – as Churchill's minister resident in the Mediterranean – Alexander turned over all the ex-Soviets and ex-Yugoslavs, despite his doubts about 11,000 women and children, to a slaughter that began almost immediately.

Having left behind this carefully-shrouded event within days of its beginning, Low began his next two careers. He was elected Conservative MP for Blackpool North in June 1945, when Labour's Clement Attlee replaced Winston Churchill as Prime Minister. A year later, he began what was to be a successful business career as a director of Grindlay's Bank.

As soon as Churchill returned to power in 1951, Low became Parliamentary Secretary to the Ministry of Supply, then Minister of State at the Board of Trade, and a Privy Counsellor in 1954. Knighted in 1957, he was made chairman of the select committee on nationalised industry. Two years later, he became deputy Conservative Party chairman. In 1962, he became Lord Aldington, and was free to launch his business career untrammeled.

Almost as a one-man show, Aldington linked together all the elements of the Establishment, political and economic. In 1964, he became chairman of Grindlay's Bank, and of GEC. In 1971, he joined the BBC general advisory council, and became chairman of Sun-Alliance and the Port of London Authority. In 1972, he became co-chairman, with Jack Jones, of the joint special committee on the ports industry, cutting over-manning massively. He became chairman of Westland in 1977.

He remained always a one-nation Tory, who had supported Rab Butler rather than Harold Macmillan. As a pro-European, he was a friend and backer of Edward Heath (and was happy to praise him when I was writing Heath's biography in 1971–72). But although normally loyal, Aldington expected his critical judgement to be taken seriously. He was chairman of the Lords' select committee on overseas trade when, in 1985, it judged that Britain was not doing well enough in manufactured exports, which angered the Chancellor, Nigel Lawson. When, 15 months later, an obedient Lord Lucas of Chilworth tried to sneer at Aldington's committee findings, he stalked out of the chamber in high dudgeon, with Lord Whitelaw signalling whips to try to soothe him.

It was in the mid-1980s, when Aldington was over 70 and winding down his business career, that misdirected lightning struck. He had earlier ignored Tolstoy's books, *Victims Of Yalta* (1977) and *The Minister And The Massacres* (1986), which claimed that, back in 1945, Macmillan had wanted to please Stalin by handing over the Cossacks.

What put the fat in the fire was the intervention of another obsession-alist, the property developer Nigel Watts, who was fighting Sun-Alliance over a disputed insurance claim on his brother-in-law, who had renewed his insurance without disclosing that he was at death's door. Having read *The Minister And The Massacres*, Watts drew up a leaflet vastly exaggerating the wartime role of Aldington, who had been chairman of Sun-Alliance.

Ten thousand copies of this leaflet, somewhat toned down by Tolstoy, were circulated to politicians, the press and Aldington's friends. It was so damaging that Aldington had to sue Watts, but Tolstoy insisted on being sued as well. The Establishment, which had facilitated an inquiry by Brigadier Cowgill – which cleared Macmillan – also made it easier for Aldington to have access to the necessary files. He had only to write to the then Defence Secretary, George Younger to see the material he needed.

After the nine-week trial, and Tolstoy's years of prevarication on payment, Aldington tried to end it all by offering to accept £300,000, but Tolstoy insisted on martyrdom. He was backed by continuing support from Tory right wingers, the latest of whom was Lord (Bernard) Braine, who accused then then Foreign Secretary, Douglas Hurd, of participating in an Establishment plot against Tolstoy.

Events relating to the long-running cases punctuated Aldington's last decade. In April 1995, Watts was jailed for 18 months after repeating the libellous claim that Aldington was a war criminal in a pamphlet. At the end of the hearing, Aldington said plaintively: 'I do feel my family and I are entitled to some relief sometime.'

Of course, Toby Aldington had other interests, some local, some international. As deputy lieutenant of Kent, in March 1993 he tried to ensure that British Rail's plans for the channel tunnel kept to their promise of not splitting the community of Willesborough, near his home at Knoll Farm, Ashford. In the big debate on the Maastricht Bill in June 1993, he identified with Lord Whitelaw, and others of that generation, who believed that only a closer European Union could avoid another war.

He is survived by his wife Araminta, two daughters and a son.

Andrew Roth

Reg Prentice

Lord Prentice of Daventry

born 16 July 1923, *died* 18 January 2001

It would be easy to dismiss the turbulent political life of Reg Prentice as marginal to the history of the Labour Party: the unhappy tale of a confused maverick who earned notoriety on the left as the first Cabinet

Minister since Winston Churchill to cross the floor of the House and join the Conservatives. In fact, in several fundamental respects, Prentice's career prefigured the emergence of New Labour – albeit at many years' distance.

Prentice's sensational defection on the eve of the 1977 Tory conference was one of the first portents that Labour was about to lose all middle-class respectability – a loss it would take the party 20 years to correct. The manner of his deselection foreshadowed the vicious constituency battles with the militant left of the 1980s. And his calls for Labour moderates to 'stand up and be counted', frustrated at the time, were eventually answered: first by the splitting away of the SDP, and, second, many years later, by the victory within the party of the Blairite modernisers.

Reginald Ernest Prentice was born in Croydon, Surrey, on 16 July 1923, and was educated at Whitgift. Between 1942 and 1946 he served in the Royal Artillery, before proceeding to the London School of Economics where, like so many left wingers of his generation, he was profoundly influenced by Harold Laski. Prentice's disenchantment with the union movement would eventually drive him from the party, but it was there, as an official with the Transport and General Workers' Union after 1950, that his political roots lay. He contested three seats unsuccessfully, before capturing East Ham North in May 1957 – a constituency he continued to represent until February 1974 when he became MP for the new seat of Newham NE.

In his long and varied career as a Labour minister, Prentice displayed an ideological complexity which is too readily obscured by his final act of apostasy. Appointed Minister of State for Education in October 1964, he was, for instance, an early and passionate advocate of comprehensivisation, and a powerful inspiration to Anthony Crosland's subsequent campaign to abolish the grammar schools. Prentice also believed in root-and-branch reform of the public schools. 'But Reginald,' C. P. Snow teased him once, 'does that mean I can't send my children to Eton?' Asked on a visit to that venerable institution what he planned for its future, he replied: 'We're going to make it into a special school for the deaf'.

In 1966, Prentice was given his own department, Public Building and Works, becoming Minister for Overseas Development in August 1967. His closely-connected belief in the importance of overseas aid and fierce opposition to racism were at the heart of his politics: he was a leader of the all-party Fair Cricket Campaign, which succeeded in its battle to have the 1970 South African tour of England cancelled.

Yet for Prentice there was an all-important difference between idealism and ideology. His politics were Gaitskellite: he often cited his fallen hero's 'fight, fight and fight again' speech to the 1962 Labour conference. As the party drifted to the Left, he became more and more uncomfortable. He did well in Shadow Cabinet elections from 1971, but found himself increasingly at odds with the militant caucuses within the party. In November 1973, as Shadow Employment Secretary, he fell into open conflict with Tony Benn over whether to support strikers who broke the law. As Secretary of State for Education and Science after March 1974, he began to speak out beyond the parameters of his ministerial brief in a way which enraged his colleagues.

Prentice claimed it was his duty to confront those 'prepared to sacrifice the working people of this country on the altar of their Marxist ideology'. Michael Foot, then Employment Secretary, denounced such outbursts, with Harold Wilson's backing. But Wilson knew that Roy Jenkins would resign if he sacked Prentice and so moved him back to Overseas Development.

Meanwhile, Prentice faced a vicious battle in his constituency, where militants – the 'little gang' as he called them – launched a campaign to unseat him. Newham in east London fast became a bloody microcosm of Labour's future traumas, as Trotskyites fought with Labour moderates – including the young Julian Lewis, later to become a right wing Tory MP. In March 1975, the Newham NE executive passed a vote of no confidence in its candidate, and deselected him four months later.

At the 1976 Labour conference, Prentice bitterly denounced the NEC's endorsement of his local party's action as 'political cowardice as the price of political survival'. After abstaining in a key vote, he resigned from the Government in December 1976, before his defection the following

October, a decision he took, he said, to help stop Britain 'lurching further down the Marxist road'. The party's Chief Whip, Bob Mellish, called Prentice 'a nauseating traitor', a view shared at the time by many of his fellow Labour moderates – including Shirley Williams – who were later to jump ship themselves. The defector was found a Tory seat in Daventry in 1979, which he represented until 1987. As Margaret Thatcher's Social Security Minister, the politician who had started his career as a union official ended it by removing unemployment benefit from strikers. By the end of 1980, however, the drugs he was taking for hypertension made it difficult for him to carry on as a minister and he withdrew to the back benches in 1981, this time for good. He was knighted in 1987 and ennobled in 1992. In his last years he was president of the local Conservative Association in Michael Ancram's Devizes constituency. He died on 18 January 2001, survived by his wife and daughter.

Matthew d'Ancona

Jean Denton

Baroness Denton of Wakefield

born 29 December 1935, *died* 5 February 2001

Jean Denton had a rich and varied career, including four seasons as a highly successful racing and rally ace, before John Major brought her into the Government as a life peer in 1991. After a brief spell as a whip, she became a junior minister, first at the DTI and then at the DoE. But her most rewarding spell as a Parliamentary Under-Secretary was at the Northern Irish Office, where she remained until the Conservative defeat in May 1997.

The Conservative MP Andrew Mackay recalls that 'she was a much-loved minister in Northern Ireland, where she worked tirelessly as

Minister of Health, Agriculture and the Economy. As the first woman to serve as a minister at Stormont, her unstuffy enthusiasm was infectious.' She was high-profile, clearly understood the economic issues, and used her bulging address book in full measure as she travelled the globe in a never-ending quest to bring business to the province.

Born Jean Moss in Yorkshire in 1935, the daughter of a hospital clerk and a school cook, she was educated at Rothwell Grammar School and the London School of Economics. She joined Procter and Gamble as a marketing executive in 1959, and then, after relatively brief spells with the Economist Intelligence Unit and IPC magazines, she moved to the hotel and catering department at Surrey University in 1966.

She had married an engineering graduate from Cambridge shortly after graduating from LSE and her husband, who lectured at Imperial College, was a motor-racing enthusiast. Jean Denton took up the sport and, within 10 months of passing her driving test at the late age of 26, was driving in Formula 3. She had, she recalled later, a pang of conscience at giving up full-time work, but described her experiences in the sport as 'a kind of high-speed maternity leave'. More typically, she claimed in 1967 that she had been treated as bit of a joke when she first went racing, 'but now they know mine is one of the cars to be beaten'.

'First is first, second nowhere' was a lesson learnt on the course and later applied to her business career. She was twice ranked as Britain's woman racing champion in 1967 and 1968 and she then moved into rallying. Hers was the only sports car to complete the London-Sydney rally in 1969, and in the World Cup rally the following year, which covered 16,000 gruelling miles in Europe and South America, she was the first woman privateer home.

She was recruited as marketing director by the Huxford Group 1972–78 and was then headhunted to be marketing director of the Heron Group. After two years, she became the managing director of Herondrive, the car-leasing business, a post she held until 1985 when she became external affairs director of Austin Rover. Already a powerful advocate for women, and the first woman to serve on the executive committee of the Institute of Management, she helped found Forum UK, the British branch of the International Forum for Women, which she chaired from 1989 until 1992. At a Women in Business Conference in 1988, she told them, 'A lot of businesses are being started by women who have been working for idiots for years. They know they can do their boss's job, but they know they will never be given it.'

She left Rover to become the deputy chairman of the Black Country Development Corporation in 1987. The corporation did valuable work in regenerating the industrial areas of Walsall, Sandwell and Wolverhampton. That and her period on the Engineering Council, from 1986 to 1991, gave her an insight into the problems of small businesses. She was valued as a director with a real contribution to make and her directorships included the Ordnance Survey, British Nuclear Fuels, the London and Edinburgh Insurance Group, Triplex Lloyd and Think Green.

It was at this stage that her career in public life took off. She had been appointed to the Board of UK 2000 in 1986, to the Teachers Pay Review Body in 1989 and to the NHS Policy Board in 1990, although her interest in health matters had started more than a decade earlier.

Her common sense, warm personality and shrewd counsel, when coupled to her wide knowledge of industry, made her an ideal candidate for recruitment to the House of Lords and propelled her rapidly into a series of ministerial jobs. At the DTI she was not only responsible for small businesses, she also took on the consumer affairs portfolio. She also gave a good deal of time to encouraging industry to include more women on boards and when she went to Northern Ireland, in addition to her other responsibilities, she took on women's affairs.

But for the change of government, her ministerial record might well have included greater responsibilities. Instead she had to continue her keen interest in the province from the opposition benches in the Lords and was always appreciative of the success of her friend in the 'women's mafia', Mo Mowlam.

John Barnes

Michael Grylls

born 21 February 1934, *died* 7 February 2001

Silken, silver-haired Sir Michael ('Mickey') Grylls has died at 67. He survived for 27 years as the Conservative MP for Chertsey and then North West Surrey, and 16 years as Chairman of the Tory MPs' Trade and Industry Committee despite being the most senior and voracious of the team of five Tory MPs run by the lobbyist Ian Greer. In 1992 he was knighted, after having lied, together with Ian Greer, to the Committee on Members' Interests on the number and amounts of Greer's payments to him.

He largely succeeded in such evasions, in contrast to Neil Hamilton, who married Grylls' secretary Christine, because he avoided public notoriety and, with Greer's help, long postponed disclosing the sleazy truth. This was an old friendship. John Russell, Ian Greer's former partner in the lobbying firm Russell and Greer, broke up that partnership when he discovered that Greer was paying Grylls for trips he never took to fight double taxation in California.

Much of this was known within closed Conservative circles. When I moaned to a Tory MP-accountant serving under Grylls on the Tories' Trade and Industry Committee about my difficulty in pinning down the nature of Grylls' corruption, he snorted: 'Everyone knows Mickey Grylls is making £25–35,000 a year as chairman of our committee!'

A former employee of Ian Greer, who resigned in disgust at the Grylls-Greer collusion, explained how it worked. Whenever businessmen approached Grylls for help – even from his own constituency – he made it a condition that they hire Greer's firm to lobby for them. For this Grylls received a percentage of Greer's contracts, probably 10 per cent.

Grylls' most dramatic and open procuring for Greer came when Nicholas Ridley tried to divert £20m of international routes from BA to British Caledonian, to sustain that troubled line. Its existing lobbyist, Shandwick, run by John Gummer's brother, advised BA to approach

MPs, many of whom had been provided with free or upgraded flights. When an unhappy top BA executive approached Grylls, he insisted they switch their lobbying contract to Greer. Greer's success in organising a BA fan club among MPs was so successful that Ridley was defeated in Cabinet. The continuing BA contract contributed to Greer's peak total of £3m in contracts and Gryll's hefty percentage.

An attempted scam-documentary by Central TV in 1994 confirmed the continuing Grylls-Greer collusion. A TV team pretended to be Russo-American entrepreneurs, ready to spend $40m on buying decanted government agencies, particularly the insolvency agency. A fancy office with concealed cameras was set up in Park Lane, with a black American actor in the team pretending to be gay, to attract Greer. Grylls was approached and he referred them to Greer. Greer boasted about what he could do for these potential clients. When he also boasted about his close connections with John Major, he frightened off the top men in Central TV, who pulled the whole show. A verbatim of the Grylls-Greer claims appeared in the *Guardian* in May 1994 but John Smith's death then obscured the disclosures.

In compiling his successive entries in Parliamentary Profiles, I had had serial troubles in documenting Grylls' deviations. When we met to agree final versions, he always attempted to avoid any hint of impropriety. He tried unsuccessfully to avoid my reference to his having been found guilty of evading exchange controls in connection with his Spanish wine importing business. He tried to change my disclosure of his 'link' with Greer to one of 'friendship', trying to cut the number of entries where he backed companies for which Greer was lobbying. But he slipped up in 1994 in letting through my reference to his taking a percentage for referring business to Greer. When this was published, he frightened newsmen off referring to my disclosure by telling them he was suing me for libel. Instead, his libel lawyer told him to put his connection with Greer belatedly into the Register of Members' Interests. He did this so quietly that, a few days later, Dale Campbell-Savours persuaded the Conservative majority of its controlling committee to investigate my 'scurrilous' allegations to 'clear' Grylls' name. That was the beginning of the end, in two ways. The committee discovered more about the Greer–Grylls connection. Later, when Greer and Neil Hamilton sued the *Guardian* for £2m, with the backing of the Conservative Party and John Major, Greer's changes in accounting after I published the Grylls-Greer connection, enabled the *Guardian*'s lawyers to unravel all Greer's payments to MPs in the 'discovery' process of libel actions.

A major further disclosure of the Grylls-Greer connection occurred in March 1997, by which time Grylls had decided to retire from politics. In Sir Gordon Downey's initial disclosures, Greer admitted to having lied about Grylls' payments. There had been six or seven payments, not three. He later disclosed that he paid Grylls £10,000 annually plus a percentage of the contracts Grylls had secured for him.

Grylls, who also had other consultancies and directorships, was shrewd in investing his illicit gains. In 1994 he became the chairman of a biotechnology company, Electrophoretics, holding 300,000 shares and options on a further 211,000. By October 1995, they were worth £650,000, with the help of a government contract to develop a quick diagnostic test for BSE.

His was a strange career for one seemingly destined for military achievement. He was born in Folkestone in 1934, the son of Brigadier W. E. H. Grylls OBE and Rachel (Knapp). After St Ronan's in Hawkhurst, he passed through the Royal Naval College at Dartmouth. Because his eyes did not meet the Royal Navy's high stardard, he served briefly in the Royal Marines.

After language studies in Madrid, at 22 he went into importing Spanish wines, as chairman and managing director of the Costa Brava Wine Company, of which he owned 40 per cent. He achieved notoriety by importing sparkling white wine as 'Spanish Champagne' to the intense hostility of the lucrative French exporters of genuine champagne. He was acquitted of false trading but later found guilty of 'passing off'.

He displayed his early interest in politics by securing election to St Pancras Borough Council at 25 in 1959 and to the Greater London Council in 1967, becoming Deputy Chairman of the ILEA in 1969. He twice fought the the senior Labour figure, Michael Stewart, in Fulham, in 1964 and 1966. He made it into the Commons in 1970 by being selected as Sir Lionel Heald's successor in safe suburban Chertsey, later redrawn as North West Surrey.

He proclaimed himself a right winger anxious to liberate business, particularly small business. He urged uneconomic mines be closed more rapidly. But he showed opportunistic deviations from the beginning. He urged public funds to build the BAC-311 aircraft, knowing they would be built by his constituents in British Aerospace's plant in Weybridge. He applauded the 'fantastic' restraint of British troops in Ulster. From 1971 he was anxious to join the EEC to help solve the UK's economic problems. His pro-European attitude led him to back Michael Heseltine against Mrs Thatcher in 1986 in favouring a European consortium to help Westland in its crisis. He was one of the few right wing Tories who never voted against the Major Government on Maastricht.

Early on, as a spokesman on pharmaceuticals and secretary of the all-party pharmaceutical group, he became a spokesman for the industry. He urged a ban on BBC broadcasts causing unnecessary alarm about drug side-effects. He warned the drug companies might leave the UK if threatened by Labour's nationalisation.

By 1979–80 he secured twin backbench bases as chairman both of the Tories' Small Business Bureau and their Trade and Industry Committee. He sought immunity from having to pay redundancy pay for small businesses. He attacked the capital transfer tax as interfering with family control of businesses. He opposed the indexing of unemployment benefit. He attacked the 'disastrous' threat of manufacturers' product liability. He continually campaigned to liquidate still-nationalised companies and the National Enterprise Board, proclaiming himself well to the right of his new leader, Margaret Thatcher.

His social views were more mixed. He was a stern opponent of smoking. He introduced a bill to curb abortion 'vultures' by licensing referral agencies. 'I voted for capital punishment for acts of terrorism with reluctance and only after resolving deep personal doubts,' he said in 1974. He later broadened his support for capital punishment.

In world affairs he backed the Apartheid regime in South Africa, supporting a tour there by the UK's rugby team and Mrs Thatcher's invitation to P. W. Botha. He also supported the US intervention in Grenada and was strongly Unionist on Ulster.

He leaves his wife, Sally, the daughter of the late former MP Patricia Ford, his Everest-climbing son Edward ('Bear') and his daughter Lara Sarah.

Andrew Roth

Lord Bellwin

born 7 February 1923, *died* 11 February 2001

Short, perky Lord Bellwin, who has died aged 78, left a mystery behind him when, as Margaret Thatcher's most successful workhorse minister, he suddenly departed in 1984 after five years of unequalled hard work.

As Parliamentary Under-Secretary at the Department of the Environment from 1979–83, and then Minister of State, he put through 28 bills, including three controversial ones. He piloted the right-to-buy legislation – based on a scheme he had pioneered in Leeds – and spoke 1,000 times on the local government, planning and land bill.

Then, in September 1984, he was gone, allegedly to spend more time on his Leeds golf course. The inside story was that, as a devotee of local government, he had been angered by Thatcher's determination to get rid of the six big Labour-dominated metropolitan councils.

Heckling brought his speech – introducing a bill to abolish the following year's Greater London Council elections – to a humiliating halt in June 1984.

But he was too loyal to talk out of school. To give the lie to gossipers, he even became one of three Tory backbenchers who spoke up for the GLC's abolition. He was named to the New Towns Commission, and became a director of Taylor Woodrow. He spoke only occasionally in the Lords, once in favour of quangos, such as urban development corporations, pointing out that local authorities in London's East End had been unable to cope with their 6,000 acres of derelict docklands.

Bellwin's own political life was a demonstration that local authorities could do a great deal at low cost, if they were well run by someone like himself. He had been born Irwin Bellow in Leeds, the son of Leah and Abraham Bellow, a machine designer. In Lovell Road School, he recalled, 'the average size of classes was 44'. He went on to Leeds Grammar School and Leeds University, where he read law.

He then went into the Bellow Machine Company, a sewing-machine firm started by his father. In 1969, it was sold to Staflex International for £2.4m, with Irwin as chairman of both boards. But, after setbacks, the firm was sold to Pfaff, with Staflex itself going bust.

Irwin entered politics on a fluke: he had been elected to Leeds City Council in 1966, after a colleague urged him to do something about the rates instead of just moaning. He was council leader from 1975–79, and was drawn to Thatcher's attention after he had cut rates and sold 3,000 council houses.

When she took power in 1979, she made him a life peer and a junior minister. His unassuming personality and hard work won over Tory grandees and political opponents, but he knew he could not win an argument with the Iron Lady.

He leaves Doreen, his wife of 53 years, a son and two daughters.

Andrew Roth

John Mackay

Lord Mackay of Ardbrecknish

born 15 November 1938, *died* 21 February 2001

Spirited, engaging Lord (John) Mackay of Ardbrecknish, who has died suddenly at 62, was formerly the Tory MP for Argyll and then for Argyll and Bute, before being 'kicked upstairs' in 1991 after his 1987 defeat at the hands of the Liberal Democrats. Having been a junior Scottish minister in the Commons from 1982–87, he became a Minister of State for Social Security in the Lords under John Major from 1994–97.

When William Hague purged Lord Cranborne and his cohorts in December 1998 for their secret deal with Tony Blair, he made Lord Mackay deputy leader of the Conservative opposition in the Lords. As such, he made some of their best speeches, claiming for the Tories the role of the effective reforming party. He gave up this post last November, nominally to become chairman of the committees of the Lords, the most senior member of the House after the Lord Chancellor.

Widely popular, he did not seem to fit wholly in with the new, increasingly right wing and Europhobic regime. Only last week he took a major job outside the House. A man of modest means, he required extra employment when deprived of ministerial pay. When he lost Argyll and Bute, he became chief executive of the Scottish Conservatives from 1987–90.

Irreverent, he even dared make fun of the hereditary backwoodsmen who came out of the woodwork to make up Tory majorities in the Lords. In November 1998 he said: 'There are some people here I have never seen before and (was) wondering who they were.' According to Viscount Thurso, his witty debating style was 'rather like a well-executed Scottish reel. There is lots of style, much movement, lots of euching and at the end you find that you are back where you started!'

Mackay was the son of a policeman. He was educated at Dunoon Grammar School, as were Labour ministers George Robertson and Brian Wilson, and the late Labour leader John Smith, and at Campbeltown in Argyll. After Glasgow University, where he started a lifelong friendship with the late Donald Dewar, he became head of the mathematics department at Oban High School. After a brief flirtation with the Liberals in his early years, he sought a Westminster seat for the Tories when he contested the Western Isles and then Argyll, in the two general elections of 1974.

But it was not until five years later that he succeeded, becoming MP for Argyll in 1979 when he snatched the seat from the SNP.

In the 1980s he had a three-year stint as chairman of the Sea Fish Industry Authority.

He was a keen angler but was allergic to dogs, confessing in a debate: 'In close proximity with dogs, I become unwell,' adding, 'cats are worse and rabbits worse still.' He leaves his wife, Sheena, two sons and a daughter.

Andrew Roth

Cledwyn Hughes

Lord Cledwyn of Penrhos

born 14 September 1916, *died* 22 February 2001

Lord Cledwyn of Penrhos, who has died aged 84, was Labour leader in the House of Lords from 1982 to 1992. Earlier, as plain Cledwyn Hughes, he served as a senior figure in the Commons under three Labour leaders – as an opposition spokesman under Hugh Gaitskell, and as a cabinet Minister under both Harold Wilson and James Callaghan, most notably as Secretary of State for his beloved Wales.

Widely popular for his shrewdness and warm personality, he had an unending store of anecdotes, which were imparted with relish in the corridors of Westminster and to audiences in Wales, whether in his native Welsh language or in English.

The stories derived from his climb up the political ladder, from Anglesey County Council (1946–52) to the Commons backbenches in 1951, through his government posts as Minister of State for Commonwealth Relations, Welsh Secretary and Minister for Agriculture, to his leadership of Labour peers for the decade that ended with the 1992 general election. One of his oft-repeated classics concerned James Callaghan's retort in 1976, when Cledwyn told him the Parliamentary Labour Party had elected him leader and Prime Minister: 'And I never even went to university!'

Cledwyn's confidence – and the quality of his anecdotes – grew steadily from the time he arrived at Westminster as a small-town solicitor and the new Labour MP for Anglesey, who had just ousted Lady Megan Lloyd George, daughter of the last Liberal Prime Minister. His shy clannishness initially only allowed him to eat at the Commons Welsh table and speak, preferably in Welsh, to fellow countrymen from north Wales. More aggressive solicitor-MPs from the bigger practices of south Wales tended to ridicule his parochial timidity.

Cledwyn's feelings about north Wales were so strong that, in 1959, he and his wife Jean decided that they did not want their two children brought up as Anglo-Welsh mongrels in London's English-language culture. Jean returned to north Wales, converting Cledwyn into a train-wearied weekend husband.

His initial timidity derived partly from the large red birthmark on his face, and partly from the womb of Welsh culture – that combination of chapel and north Wales Liberalism – into which he was born in Holyhead, on the Isle of Anglesey. He was doubly embedded as the son of a respected Presbyterian minister and leader of the local Liberals, the Reverend David Hughes, himself the son of a Snowdonia quarryman.

But young Cledwyn did well at Holyhead Grammar School and went on to read law at the University of Wales at Aberystwyth, which then had only 750 students, almost all of them Welsh. He became president of the university Liberal society.

In 1937, he returned to Holyhead to be articled to a local solicitor. As local unemployment deepened, and the Czechoslovak crisis intensified, he listened to local Independent Labour Party speakers – and joined the Labour Party in 1938.

Called up in 1940, he served in the Royal Air Force Volunteer Reserve until 1945, doing administrative, legal and intelligence jobs, and was commissioned as a flight lieutenant, without being able to fly. In 1944, local Labour stalwarts urged him to stand in the impending general election against Lady Megan, but his father resisted. Cledwyn fought the 1945 election almost on his own, making 50 speeches – 45 of them in Welsh. Nonetheless, he came within 1,000 votes of victory.

Back in Holyhead after demobilisation, he opened his own legal practice. In court, he defended clients with unexpected fierceness and, by 1949, his position had improved enough for him to marry the lovely Jean Hughes, who had the same surname, the same religion and the same politics.

Cledwyn's political advance looked less hopeful. In 1946, he had been elected to Anglesey County Council, but when he challenged Lady Megan again in 1950, she beat him by 2,000 votes, largely because, although a Liberal, she had identified with Labour. In 1951, however, when Labour was receding nationally, he ousted the crown princess of the Lloyd George Liberals by 595 votes.

Cledwyn made a diffident start, unsure that he would survive beyond one term at Westminster. Initially, he left Jean behind in Holyhead with their infant daughter, Ann. In the Commons, he became a fringe Bevanite, largely because he liked Aneurin Bevan (though not his wife, Jennie Lee). In 1955, with a number of other Welsh-speaking Labour MPs, he urged devolution for Wales. The following year, they started a petition for a Welsh parliament, for which rebelliousness Cledwyn was reported to the Labour national executive by the south-Wales-dominated Welsh Council of Labour.

Thanks to his battle to bring jobs to the constituency, in 1955 he was returned by a comfortable 4,568 votes, and brought Jean, Ann and son Harri down to London. He helped to bring the Wylfa nuclear power station to Anglesey, and subsequently get an aluminium smelter project in the area. He knew unemployment forced Welsh-speaking locals to emigrate and lose their Welsh culture.

Cledwyn began his rise in 1959, when Gaitskell made him an assistant spokesman on housing and local government. When Harold Wilson led Labour to victory in 1964, he became Minister of State for Commonwealth Relations, with African troubles on his plate. In 1966, he became Secretary of State for Wales.

A firm believer in Wales as a nation entitled to its own parliament, he faced the problem that four-fifths of Welshmen lived in non-Welsh-speaking south Wales and did not share his aspirations. His two years in the job were spent in building Wales's economic base and civil service, disappointing nationalists and Welsh-language fanatics. 'Language is a thing you cannot push down people's throats,' he told those who shouted 'Traitor! traitor!' at him at the eisteddfod.

In 1968, Wilson made him Minister for Agriculture, partly to get rid of Fred Peart, who was a fanatically anti-common marketeer, partly to promote another Wilson loyalist, George Thomas (later Viscount Tonypandy) to the Cabinet, thus giving south Wales its due voice in the Welsh Office. At agriculture, Cledwyn could not compete with Peart as a trencherman. But he became a moderate pro-marketeer and a great admirer of Roy Jenkins, an uprooted South Walian – although he stopped short of following Roy into the Social Democratic Party.

As a capable administrator, Cledwyn did not enjoy Labour's period in opposition from 1970 to 1974. When the party returned to power, he became chairman of the parliamentary Labour Party 1974–79, a job well suited to his ability to nudge most people into loyalty. As Jim Callaghan's envoy to southern Africa at the end of 1978, he tried, unsuccessfully, to accelerate the handover of power in Rhodesia. In 1979, he stepped down from the Anglesey seat, and was made a life peer.

His greatest test was his decade as Labour leader in the Lords, which began by ousting a disintegrating Peart. He had 120–130 ageing peers, only two-thirds well enough to vote regularly. It was an arduous task to put up a creditable show against at least three times as many Tories, both declared and undeclared, backed by the civil service. It was a disappointment that his time was not capped by a Labour victory in 1992, which would have allowed him to reform the institution. He had the compensation, however, of handing over to another Welshman, Lord (Ivor) Richard, even if he was from south Wales.

Lord Cledwyn is survived by his wife and two children.

Andrew Roth

Cranley Onslow

Lord Onslow of Woking

born 8 June 1926, *died* 13 March 2001

The peak period of influence of Lord Onslow of Woking, who has died aged 74, was between 1984 and 1992, when, as MP Cranley Onslow, he chaired the Tory backbenchers' 1922 Committee – a discreet, uptight loyalist sandwiched between two extroverts, Edward du Cann and Marcus Fox. He presided over the 1990 leadership contest which saw the departure of Margaret Thatcher and the arrival of John Major.

A member of the secret service, MI6, before he became Conservative MP for Woking in 1964, he briefly held two ministerial offices, as Under-Secretary for Aerospace between 1972–74, and Minister of State at the Foreign Office from 1982–83. Particularly hostile to Labour's CND left, he once tagged MP Brian Sedgemore as 'a boil on the bottom of the Labour Party – painful to live with, better not mentioned and best kept out of sight'.

As a kinsman of the Earl of Onslow, representing a constituency containing the earl's seat, Onslow was one of the last Tory squires. Three Onslows had served as speakers of the Commons, the first from 1566. His replacement as chairman of the 1922 Committee by Fox, a self-made backstreet Thatcherite, seemed to mark the end of an era.

Born in Bexhill, Onslow was named after the earl, one of whose titles was Baron Cranley, because his ornithologist father wanted to maintain the family link. After Harrow and Sandhurst, he joined up in 1944, becoming a lieutenant in the Queen's Own Hussars. On leaving active service, he joined the Territorials – thus keeping up his marksmanship – and graduated in history from Oriel College, Oxford.

In 1951, he joined MI6 and its cover organisation, the Foreign Office, being posted to Burma in 1953 as third secretary. In 1955, he became consul in Maymyo, north Burma, near the communist Chinese border. Local communist insurgents once attempted to kidnap and ransom him, but by plying them with whisky, Onslow persuaded them to return to the jungle without him. He, in his turn, returned to London to marry Lady Jane Hay, daughter of the 14th Earl of Kinnoull, and to serve in the FO department that controls MI6.

Like other MI6 Tories, Onslow wanted to make his mark in politics. After resigning from the civil service in 1960, he was elected to Dartford Rural District Council the same year, and to Kent County Council in 1961. Two years later, he was selected as Harold Watkinson's successor for Woking. When elected, the Conservatives described him as director of an unnamed Indian-based news agency.

From his maiden speech in December 1964, Onslow proclaimed himself a classic right winger. He specialised in aviation, rising to chairman of the Tory MPs' aviation committee, a position he used to defend the British Aircraft Corporation, which had a plant in his constituency. He blamed Harold Wilson's cancellation of the BAC TSR2 warplane on Labour's CND supporters and wore a black and yellow tie, the black mourning the TSR2's demise and the yellow standing for the government's lack of courage in the decision.

Onslow supported hanging, attacked anti-Franco elements among Labour MPs, demanded reductions in third-world aid and tax cuts so the middle classes could send their children to fee-paying schools. He opposed televising the Commons. However, he showed a serious, nonpartisan interest in civil aviation when leading for the Tories in this field in 1968. After his party was returned to power, he held ministerial office under Michael Heseltine from 1972–74.

In the subsequent years of opposition, he introduced a bill to give the vote to servicemen and their wives, and again urged cuts in overseas aid. He became obsessed with the activities of Czechoslovak intelligence agents, seeking to link them with the 'disappearing' Labour postmaster-general John Stonehouse.

Mrs Thatcher made him Minister of State at the Foreign Office in 1982, replacing Richard Luce, who resigned with Lord Carrington over their failure to prevent the Argentine invasion of the Falklands. A year later, Onslow showed similar loyalty to his boss, Francis Pym, when Thatcher sacked him.

He found a new career in replacing Edward du Cann as chairman of the 1922 Committee in 1984. Here, he used tact in conveying the views of Tory backbenchers – including their 1988 decision that Leon Brittan should resign over his role in the Westland affair. But he did not hesitate to interrupt Thatcher's rants when she went over the top.

His abilities were put to the test in 1990, when Heseltine challenged her for the Tory leadership. As the custodian of backbench votes and views, it fell to Onslow to tell Thatcher, when she failed to win conclusively in the first round, that many MPs wanted a wider choice of candidates; the result was that she stood down and John Major emerged as Prime Minister. The Thatcherites fury led to Onslow's replacement in 1992 by Fox – though his consolation was a knighthood, and a peerage in 1997, when he stood down from Woking.

He is survived by his wife, three daughters and a son.

Andrew Roth

William Molloy

Lord Molloy of Ealing

born 26 October 1918, *died* 26 May 2001

It was surprising that the short, voluble, Welsh-Irish Lord ('Bill') Molloy should have allowed himself to die, even at 82, during an election campaign. His entry into national politics had been in 1964 as the victor of 'unwinnable' Ealing North. When, after many recounts, he won by 27 votes, confirming Harold Wilson's three-seat majority, he boasted typically, 'I am Labour's majority!'

Molloy's talent for dramatic oratory showed soon after his birth in Swansea. At St Thomas's elementary school, his effectiveness in declaiming Shakespeare won him the chance of a Royal Academy of Dramatic Art scholarship. He did not make it to RADA, but his florid Shakespearean speeches offered such gems as, 'It is, thank goodness, most unusual for British journalists to sojourn in the gutter of personal contumely.'

He was the son of a marine engineer from an Irish Catholic family that had migrated to Wales to dig coal. Molloy failed the 11–plus – which made him a lifelong opponent of selective education – but, as an extra-mural student, attended Swansea's University College.

Molloy served from 1938 to 1945 in the Royal Engineers, ending up in Germany. Demobbed, he became a Foreign Office civil servant, and, as its leading trade unionist, was chairman of the staff side of its Whitley Council and editor of the *Civil Service Review*.

In 1952, Molloy became secretary of the Association of Clothing Contractors and editor of its bimonthly. This job enabled him to join Labour and, in 1954, become a councillor in Fulham, where he became the party leader in 1959. His arduous campaigning in Fulham led to his selection in 1962 as Ealing North's candidate.

In 1964, Molloy was welcomed to the Labour benches as an eager left wing fundamentalist, deluging the Tories with oratory and outsmarting them with parliamentary devices. When they blocked the Labour MP Sidney Silverman's effort to ban capital punishment, he had their subsequent efforts counted out. His partisanship was not fine-tuned. He was one of the 'protect Maxwell group' that fought off 'unfair' criticisms of the then Labour MP. In 1965, Molloy came 27th in Labour's National Executive elections with 33,000 votes, meaning only 33 constituencies had voted for him. He joined the estimates committee in 1968 and, as part of his pro-Arab position, chaired the committee linking the Commons with Tunisia. He joined the Inter-Parliamentary Union and Commonwealth Parliamentary Association, whose members got free trips abroad. Some of his campaigns – such as protesting against keeping early-teenage girls in a police cell – were aimed at winning publicity in the *London Evening Standard* and *Evening News* to keep his constituents aware of him. But he called for improvements in the conditions of nurses long before he became a consultant to one of their unions, COHSE (later Unison), in 1974, and was one of the first, as chairman of the Parliamentary Labour Party's social services group in 1975, to raise the spectre of organised social services fraud.

Long a Wilson loyalist, he lacked empathy for his successor James Callaghan. He led a revolt against axing a child benefit scheme; Callaghan warned that the protest could lead to a general election.

In 1979, Margaret Thatcher's flood engulfed his seat. This was part of a triple blow. In 1980, his beloved wife of 30 years, Eva, died. Months afterwards, he married Doris, a divorcee; four years later they divorced, but continued to live in the same house since he refused, until threatened with imprisonment, to divulge his finances to secure the final decree.

Such turmoil made his Lords appearances infrequent and unpredictable. A brutal Tory commentator, Bruce Anderson, said he was one of the Lords' three champions at emptying the chamber.

He leaves a daughter by his first marriage.

Andrew Roth

Jimmy Knapp

born 29 September 1940, ***died*** 13 August 2001

The redoubtable Jimmy Knapp, who has died aged 60 of cancer, was a symbolic example of the deep, cultural, socio-political identity between the trade unions and the Labour Party. He was, for nearly 20 years, general secretary of Britain's largest railway workers' union, known until 1990 as the National Union of Railwaymen (NUR) and since re-christened as the National Union of Rail, Maritime and Transport Workers (RMT).

Knapp came to the leadership of the old NUR in 1983, in the midst of Margaret Thatcher's onslaught against organised labour. It was a difficult time for any trade union leader to inherit the hot seat of public sector trade unionism; still more so to take charge of an organisation so deeply threaded into the fabric of British labour history.

It was already clear when he took over from Sid Weighell that the Conservative Prime Minister held a special distaste for the nationalised railways, second only to her loathing for the miners. But Jimmy, 6ft 2in of Scottish socialist, was not in fear of the Iron Lady. He just didn't think much of her policies; and it didn't take long for her to discover that.

His first great challenge came when the National Union of Mineworkers' leader Arthur Scargill called his men out in 1984. The railways were a crucial element in the year-long miners' strike, and Knapp gave the miners every support that was feasible, short of joining them in the strike. More than any other union leader, he stayed loyal to Scargill, despite his private thoughts about the strategy of the miners' president; there was never a single word of criticism uttered in public.

Yet, although Knapp came to the NUR leadership with the reputation of being a 'wild lefty', as his predecessor called him, the practice of his power was substantially different. He believed in a cautious, sensible and rational approach to the terrible problems facing what was then still British Railways – especially the underinvestment – and often had to stand up to fierce criticism from within his 21–member executive, of which at least a third, to his left, demanded a much harder line.

But Knapp was determined not to follow in the footsteps of Scargill and the miners, despite temptations to challenge the Thatcher government policy towards the railways. To be sure, the disputes, actual and potential, were ever-present – among railway guards, train drivers, signalmen and London Underground workers. There was scarcely a moment during the 1980s when trouble did not lurk around the next bend in the track.

To cope with these problems, Knapp developed a policy of trying to build bridges with the main drivers' union, ASLEF. He established a firm relationship with the late Ray Buckton, the veteran, influential ASLEF leader, and, for a time, it seemed that a merger might take place between the two old rival unions. It didn't happen – though both Knapp and Buckton tried hard to achieve it.

Knapp also fought his own executive over its demand to defy the 1984 Trade Union Act. He argued vehemently that his union – unlike Scargill and the miners – must conduct ballots on strike action. He was always aware that railwaymen, more than most workers, had a direct, face-to-face relationship with the commuting public. He knew that any action by railwaymen, however morally just, needed the support of the passengers.

When he led a series of successful 24–hour wage strikes in 1989, he did so not only with the backing of his members' votes, but, to the government's amazement, with the support of many commuters, who agreed with the union case for more rail investment and an end to cutbacks. Knapp knew all about the decline of Britain's railways from the huge slippage in his own union's membership.

When he joined the NUR as a signalbox lad in 1955, the union had more than 500,000 members. By the time he became a full-time official in 1972 at the age of 31, it had fallen to 400,000; when he was elected general secretary in 1983, with a huge majority, it had crashed down to 142,675. Now, even after the merger that brought about the RMT union in 1990, the membership is down to 60,000.

Right to the end of his life, Knapp campaigned for an end to cuts in the railway system, for more investment, for a greater concentration – and spend – on safety, as well as modernisation under public ownership. Throughout the Conservative government's stampede to privatisation, he warned of the dangers and damage that would be done to the network if it was sold off and fragmented. But that was a time when government ears were closed to trade union appeals.

Jimmy Knapp was born in Hurlford, Ayrshire, a year after the beginning of the Second World War. His father, a working engineer, went into the army and young Jimmy had started school at Hurlford Primary before his father, also James, was demobbed.

He also learned his trade unionism early – at socialist Sunday school, the traditional cradle of so many labour leaders of the old brigade. On the bookshelves at home were the legendary socialist classics – Hewlett Johnson's *The Socialist Sixth Of The World*, Jack London's *The Iron Heel,* John Strachey's *The Theory And Practice Of Socialism*.

He went to Kilmarnock Academy and might have gone on to higher education, but, for the sons of Kilmarnock workers, a weekly wage packet was essential. So, at the age of 15, he went into the signal box in his own village of Hurlford, where his pay was £2 18s 4d a week, less his union subs.

Knapp once described to me his early work in that signal box, tough even for a well-built lad. 'We had to use all our body weight to release the signal lever from its locking frames.' 'Now, of course,' he reminded me more recently, 'in modern signal boxes it's all electronic, covering miles of track.'

He became a devoted railway signalman – which may explain why his most publicised industrial triumph was in 1994, when he led his signalmen members through the first big strike after rail privatisation, a 15–week dispute that won them substantial pay rises despite government opposition. That victory certainly helped when he was challenged for his job in 1999 by Greg Tucker, on the far left. Knapp won the contest by two to one, and was re-elected for another five years, his fourth term in office.

On his election as NUR general secretary in 1983, Knapp became a member of the TUC general council, and served on it for the rest of his life. He was TUC president in 1993–94. The only complaint from delegates was that his deep, gravelly voice sounded more like a train announcement at Glasgow Central station than a comment to a delegate over-running his or her speaking time. Even the Scottish delegates sometimes had difficulty translating that accent.

He also served on the executive board of the International Transport Workers Federation, and was a board member of the Unity Trust Bank, and its president from 1989. From 1986, he was the TUC representative on the governing council of Ruskin College, Oxford.

In his private life, Knapp surprised everyone when, in 1990, his 25-year marriage to Sylvia Yeomans split up. He went to live with a German divorcée, Eva Leigh, whom he had met at an international trade union conference. The whole incident, gleefully reported in the tabloids, created great acrimony, but Jimmy remained with his new partner, who survives him, as does Fiona, the daughter of his marriage.

Geoffrey Goodman

Sir Edward Gardner

born 10 May 1912, *died* 22 August 2001

Sir Edward Gardner, who has died at 89, was the last of the pre-war-style Conservative QC-MPs. The MP for Billericay (1959–66) and then for Fylde in his native northwest (1970–87), he was even more successful as a barrister, taking silk 13 years after he qualified for the Bar. His practice became so lucrative that it deterred him from taking lower-paid government legal posts, although in 1962 he was appointed PPS to Attorney General Sir John Hobson. Those who did not know the disparities in pay between law officers and a highly successful barrister might have thought he was scheduled for promotion. In fact, a less successful barrister, Ian Percival, became Solicitor General.

During Gardner's 25 years in the Commons, he became chairman of the Society of Conservative Lawyers, seeking to 'modernise' the criminal justice system to improve law and order. In his terms, this meant ending 'slopping out' but retaining capital punishment. He favoured short, sharp sentences for young thugs and extending life imprisonment to mean at least 25 years. He also campaigned against pornography and legalising homosexual sex. In 1979, he advised the incoming Conservative government on its reshaping of the nationality law, and on its plans to allow the building and running of prisons by private companies.

From the beginning, Gardner was, however, more liberal in international affairs. He was one of the first Tory right wingers to advocate recognising communist China, and to favour entry into the European Economic Community. Later, he was one of the first Tories to campaign for the incorporation of the European Convention on Human Rights into British law.

Born in Preston, the son of a jeweller, he was educated at Hutton Grammar School. After a four-year stint on the local paper, he joined the *Daily Mail* in London in 1937. This ended in 1939 when he enlisted in the Royal Navy as an ordinary seaman. He survived the sinking of HMS Fiji off Crete and of HMS Coventry off the coast of North Africa, winding up a commander and chief of naval information in the East Indies (Indonesia) when Lord Mountbatten took the Japanese surrender there.

After qualifying for the Bar at Gray's Inn in 1947, Gardner continued some surreptitious journalism until the law enabled him to earn his living. He never hid his political ambitions, contesting Erith and Crayford in May 1955. He was selected for Billericay in 1957, and won it in 1959. Considered one of the Tories' promising newcomers, he was selected to second the Loyal Address. In his magniloquent way, he found the increase in crime 'oppressive and startling'. He quickly established himself as a mildly reformist but harsh law-and-order man, voting against ending hanging in 1964.

Some Tories felt Gardner's pursuit of his lucrative practice led to his loss of Billericay in 1966, but that election was Labour's high tide, providing Prime Minister Harold Wilson with a 100 majority. Gardner quickly found a safer niche from 1970 in South Fylde, which in 1983 changed its boundaries and its name to Fylde.

His legal successes continued apace. Deputy chairman of the East Kent quarter sessions 1961–71, he became recorder of the Crown Court 1972–85. He was also chairman of Lancashire cable television.

He leaves a son and daughter from each of his two marriages. His second wife, Joan Belcher, who was his children's nanny in his first marriage, died in 1999.

Andrew Roth

Gordon Reece

born 28 September 1929, *died* 22 September 2001

A fugitive tape long floated around Broadcasting House, played to chums by senior news staff. Its male lead was the public relations man Gordon Reece, who has died aged 71. Its leading lady was Margaret Thatcher.

Thatcher, whose eye had been caught by Reece when he was advising Edward Heath's Conservative Party on its party political broadcasts, sought his help when she pitched against Heath for the Conservative leadership in 1975.

Thatcher was aware that she did not talk as a Conservative leader should. Pre-Reece, Thatcher had high notes dangerous to passing sparrows. But more worrying was her accent. Liable as a Lincolnshire girl to delightful words like 'frit', she had done a DIY job while an Oxford undergraduate on her vowels. The effect was a bad case of stage posh. Reece softened and lowered the voice, to a mournful contralto, and planed the accent to normality.

The tape shows him teaching from a simple text: 'The socialists must learn that enough is enough.' It shows Thatcher coming off her overkill stresses as in socialist, but struggling to get out of the duchessy 'enaff'. Reece hovers throughout the tape, kindly, encouraging, refusing to be beaten. His genial delight at the first approximation recalls Professor Higgins's 'She's got it, by George, she's got it.'

Reece stayed in the Thatcher camp through to the 1979 general election, and from 1978 to 1980 was head of publicity at Conservative Central Office. And he effected a transformation. We forget how widely Thatcher was derided, in opposition, for her voice, clothes and style. A suburban lady in a hat was the standard comment.

Reece threw out the hats – tight, bright, assertive petal-strewn little numbers, which sustained prejudice all round. He told her to stop acting, to be normal, or at any rate, work on normality. There would also be pictures, not all Reece's doing, such as Margaret washing up. But, in general, his soft focus efforts worked wonderfully well.

Reece was a Liverpudlian car salesman's son educated at the Roman Catholic Ratcliffe College in Leicestershire. After Royal Air Force national service, he read law at Downing College, Cambridge. He got his first credentials as a journalist on the *Staffordshire Sentinel*. The *Liverpool Daily Post* and the *Sunday Express* followed.

More pertinently, from 1960 to 1970 he was an ITV producer – his credits include the early medical soap opera *Emergency Ward 10* and shows with Bernard Braden and Dave Allen – and in 1970 he set up an EMI-backed video company with Cliff Michelmore. On top of this, he had kept his TV hand in with his work for the Heath-era Conservatives.

Unlike subsequent style merchants, Reece had no political ambitions at all. He was content to ply his trade in an expanding circle of business and political clients: Ronald Reagan, a natural for the Reece approach; the unappetising Bavarian politician Franz Josef Strauss altogether more improbably.

Reece had become a PR man late in life, and it showed. Although he would stay in that business, working for the oil magnate Armand Hammer, Mohammed Fayed and British Airways' Lord King, he never attracted the scorn and parody that fell on Tim Bell, Ian Greer, even Peter Mandelson. So much of what he did was mystique-free common sense, and, anyway, he was a lot nicer than most PR men. Neither a political meddler nor an eye-gouger in seeking trade, Reece achieved what few PR men enjoy, good PR for himself.

He got hired, did what he was good at – urging naturalness and relaxation on strenuous personalities – laughed a lot, told good jokes, took his fee and slipped away. In private, he was fun to be with, capable of saying to a bunch of young Thatcher aides after a speech-drafting session, 'Come on boys, let's raid her drinks cabinet', and producing the key, then pre-empting displeasure from an unexpectedly returning lady by gaily offering her her own whisky. In 1986, he was knighted.

There was a good deal of residual journalism in Reece – disrespect and hedonism. He liked cards and horses.

More gravely, though his marriage ultimately failed, and was dissolved in 1977, he remained an unostentatious but faithful Roman Catholic. He leaves three sons and three daughters.

Edward Pearce

Peter Shore

Lord Shore of Stepney

born 20 May 1924, *died* 24 September 2001

No political career could be sadder than that of a man who, having leap-frogged into the Cabinet over the ministers of state above him, is, 20 years later, voted, '12th most effective backbencher'. But that was the fate of Peter Shore, who has died aged 77.

To have been harassed towards the end of his time as a Labour MP – before he became Lord Shore of Stepney – with constituency insecurity at the hands of a local Asian machine playing the ethnic card was a cruel turn. But Shore's political life involved a long dwindling, without there ever having quite been a solid achievement to dwindle from.

No one ever doubted his integrity or devotion, but he was one of those politicians who fail to make final impact. In part, this stemmed from an eccentric standpoint – left wing, in a theoretical way, on the economy; for a while unilateralist; but most importantly, fiercely nationalistic in ways to which the Conservatives have lately returned. He was a Keynesian after it was useful, and a Eurosceptic before it became smart.

He might have had a reputation like Tam Dalyell for magnificent independence, but the melancholy truth was that undoubted courage, furious contradictions and some force as a speaker were never enough to make Shore interesting. He was a rebel with the flavour of a decent, dull ministerialist. As a rather tentative minister, his claim on history was not high, yet there was a time when he was thought of as a potential Labour leader, a thought which would diffuse into a final vote of less than 3%.

Shore was born in Great Yarmouth, the son of a commercial sea captain. He was educated at Quarrybank School, Liverpool, before King's College, Cambridge, where he took a second in history. From 1943–46, he was a flying officer in the RAF.

Politically, he rose inside the Labour Party machine at Transport House, where, from 1959–64, he was head of the research department. He was kept busy writing part of an admired tract, *Industry and Society* (1957), working on campaign tactics and the manifesto for the 1964 general election, having fought and narrowly lost at Halifax in 1959. He also drafted the 1966 Labour manifesto.

For a time, he was quite close to Hugh Gaitskell, whose high-mindedness and belief in economic intervention he shared. But in 1958, Shore became a convert to CND, which led to loss of rapport, though the relationship would be knitted up when Gaitskell made his Vimy Ridge speech against Europe in 1962.

A casual observer might have thought Shore opportunistic as he added to an anti-Europeanism then extensive in the Labour Party, the unilateralism which would become a ticket of security. But this judgment would be profoundly wrong. Shore was doggedly, even dull-mindedly, honest, and could no more fake an opinion than levitate. His honesty made him, at once, a unilateralist, a heavy-duty Keynesian and a Eurosceptic. In the hands of a skilled, disingenuous politician, such a combination of opinions should have guaranteed effortless ascent. But Shore was neither disingenuous nor skilled.

He was, however, drawn to Harold Wilson, someone who was both. A commentator in one of the political weeklies would describe him as 'the only known example of that rare species homo Wilsonicus'. Denis Healey, never florid in praise, called him 'Harold's lapdog'. The twists and shifts of a cynical, and increasingly unhappy, pragmatist briefly followed the same course as a principled idiosyncrat.

Shore, who had been elected to Parliament in 1964 for what was then Stepney, and had been joint-PPS to Wilson (1965–66), and then Parliamentary Under-Secretary at Technology under Tony Benn, and at the Department of Economic Affairs (DEA), was lifted, in 1967, into the Cabinet as Secretary of State for Economic Affairs. Entry to the Cabinet is normally made only from a number two job, as a Minister of State.

The DEA had, in fact, gone from exciting new challenge to dead end in three years, losing its struggle with the Treasury despite being right on devaluation. Michael Stewart, Shore's predecessor, was already care-taking, and was needed at the Foreign Office after the implosion of George Brown. Accordingly, Shore had the worst of worlds – maximum envious focus, minimum disposable power. In fact, he was so little regarded that, within 18 months, Wilson was giving serious thoughts to dropping him altogether, settling in 1969 for dissolving the department and shifting him to Minister without portfolio and deputy leader of the House. But Shore's failing was political, not ministerial.

Characteristically, he had joined the left and trade union loyalists to oppose Wilson and Barbara Castle's proposed union reform, *In Place Of Strife*. Characteristically, because this was his honest (and wrong) conviction, and because enjoying Prime Ministerial advancement, any halfway sensible politician would have tried to keep it. But Shore was not halfway sensible. Wilson's comment to Richard Crossman was the more deadly for lacking anger: 'I over-promoted him. He's no good.'

Drab attachment to the wrong idea would be a constant feature of Shore's political life. But it would also, periodically, give his career an uncalculated boost. In 1970, he launched himself as an inveterate anti-European, making thundering speeches and getting thunderous applause, notably at Labour's special conference in 1971.

There is a case for arguing that, despite the diminishing CND wrinkle, Shore, unlike Roy Jenkins and his friends, was the true Gaitskellite – statist and nationalist with some talent for the public platform. Yet he would be closely identified with Tony Benn. The term 'Benn and Shore' was widely used, and not challenged in the mid-1970s, but, as with the Wilson connection, it was a nautical error. Benn, setting a millennial impossibilist course, and seeing Europe as a capitalist ramp, covered a particular patch of water with Shore – Anglocentric, nationalist and a Fabian/Keynesian believer in virtuous interference.

However, once again, Shore's blameless pursuit of the things he believed in worked out accidentally as good career politics. The man who had been demoted in the real Cabinet in 1969, and had mustered only 39 votes for the shadow version in 1970, was, in 1971, elected to it with 105. He was placed for high office when Labour stumbled back into power in 1974. As Trade Secretary, he would be incorrigibly illiberal, refusing landing rights to Freddie Laker's Skytrain and being duly overruled by the High Court. Weirdly for a one-time unilateralist, he argued for purchase of Chevaline warheads to update Polaris.

In 1976, he became Environment Secretary. The useful things he believed in – like protection of inner city areas from degeneration – he proclaimed, but did little about. The recurring adjective used about him as a minister was 'indecisive'. Politically, he was keeping the company of the left, with a furious campaign against a 'Yes' vote in the Europe referendum and his support for Michael Foot in the 1976 leadership election.

But like another uncertain, but more comfortable politician, John Silkin, with whom he was associated at this time, Shore did not belong with the new rabidry which would soon suffuse the rank and file. A phrase of George Orwell's occurs here: 'a playing with fire by people who don't even know that it is hot'. In fact, Shore had left most of his unilateralist credentials behind, and the nationalist chauvinist strain was now the dominant one, something the real left understood.

Immediately after Labour's 1979 defeat, he was thought a serious leadership contender, as candidate of the left against Healey. In fact, as soon as Foot was nominated, that prospect went to nothing; he was eliminated on the first ballot. In 1983, he stood for the leadership again, and received less than 3 per cent of the aggregate vote.

The rest of Shore's life was spent in shoals and shallows. Ever more nationalistic, he applauded the Falklands War, and was supported by *The Times* as a sound man for the shadow defence post. Otherwise, he spent his time as shadow leader of the House, finally losing his Shadow Cabinet seat in 1987 before another 10 years on the backbenches.

There were occasional bursts of vivacity: the comment, when the Tory government economised on a booster station for the BBC World Service, that 'Nation shall murmur unto nation'; shrewd opposition to entry into the ERM 'at an unsustainable rate'; and an early warning to Nigel Lawson, in 1988, of the looming economic crisis.

He had now become a right wing figure, cluckingly approved of by Conservatives. Many of his prejudices were Margaret Thatcher's. He was devoted to Polaris and the absurdly expensive Trident; he denounced the European Social Chapter as 'a road to oblivion'. Indeed, after he had spoken of a 'Gadarene rush to European economic, monetary and political union,' the Iron Lady herself remarked that Shore was 'beginning to sound more and more like me'. He was made a life peer in 1997.

His career was less than the sum of his eloquent, serious-minded parts, but it contained, as between his nationalism and dirigisme, a contradiction which though honourable, came ultimately to look like a muddle.

Married in 1949 to Dr Elizabeth Wrong, Shore suffered a personal tragedy in the drug-related death of one of their two sons; they also had two daughters.

Edward Pearce

John Platts-Mills

born 1906, *died* 24 October 2001

John Platts-Mills QC, who has died aged 95, sat as Labour MP for Finsbury from 1945 to 1948, when he was expelled from the party for his pro-Communist sympathies. He continued to sit as an Independent in Parliament, until losing his seat in 1950, after which he devoted his energies to a successful career at the Bar.

His expulsion from the Labour Party was precipitated by his role in organising a telegram in 1948 to Pietro Nenni, the Italian Socialist, who was fighting a general election in alliance with the Communists. The telegram conveyed the 'hopes for your triumph' from a number of Labour MPs. The NEC supported a rival Italian Socialist Party and when, unlike most of his fellow signatories, Platts-Mills refused to retract and recant, the Party took the opportunity to expel him, thus ending a potentially brilliant political career, and re-launching a spectacular legal one.

John Faithful Fortescue Platts-Mills was born in Wellington, New Zealand, in 1906, the son of a wealthy businessman. He was a Rhodes Scholar who took a double first in Law at Oxford, where he was also an outstanding athlete. He was called to the Bar in 1933 at the Inner

Temple, leading a glittering social life and being patronised by Lady Astor, who saw him as a future Tory MP. But his revulsion over events in Abyssinia and then the Spanish Civil War drove him to the left and he joined the Labour Party where he campaigned for an anti-fascist Popular Front, with the Soviet Union. Like many intellectuals of his generation he revered the Communist achievements of the Soviet Union. In 1941, having been rejected for military service because of his Communist sympathies, he was introduced to Winston Churchill by Sir Stafford Cripps. Churchill gave him a job, saying, 'I have been teaching the British since 1918 that the Russians eat their young. For the sake of the war effort, take as much money as you need and change that public perception of them.' He tackled this task with gusto, speaking at rallies, ensuring that a new image of Russia was presented in schools, recruiting the Womens' Institute to collect warm clothing and knit balaclavas to be shipped to Murmansk, and establishing Soviet Friendship Committees in towns and villages, factories and universities, throughout the land. He succeeded remarkably. Russian war heroes toured British factories, balaclavas without number were knitted and Stalin was transformed into Uncle Joe. He also convinced himself, absolutely, that the Soviet Union could do no wrong. In 1944, his propaganda job complete, he volunteered to go down the mines and, at the ripe old age of 38, became a 'Bevin Boy', in Yorkshire.

In his brief period in Parliament after the 1945 landslide he was an active member of every Eastern European friendship organisation and a welcome guest in almost every country the other side of the Iron Curtain. His views generally echoed those of Phil Piratin and Willie Gallagher, the official Communists. His blind spot for the excesses of Uncle Joe remained huge. He attended Stalin's funeral in 1953 and even Khruschev's denunciation of Stalinism in 1956 hardly diminished his view of his late hero.

Following his brief stint as an MP, he returned to the Bar. His many well-publicised cases included the Kray twins and the Great Train Robbers. As a radical lawyer he also adopted unpopular causes, travelling the world to defend revolutionaries and civil rights activists. He was an outstanding figure at the criminal bar for over three decades.

In 1964 he unsuccessfully sought re-admission to the Labour Party. A second attempt failed in 1966, but in 1969, 21 years after his expulsion, he was re-admitted. He had hoped to aim again at Parliament, but this was not to be. He came back as a guest of Tony Blair and the Shadow Cabinet in 1995 to celebrate the fiftieth anniversary of the 1945 general election. He and the late Julius Silverman, a fellow new member in 1945, were the last to leave the party. These two old comrades, with a combined age of 180, were eventually helped by the secretary into a taxi to take them off to Platts-Mills' club, to continue the celebrations and to continue a very lively discussion about the rights and wrongs of the Nenni telegram and whether or not Stalin had been right at Yalta.

Alan Haworth

Maurice Miller

born 16 August 1920, *died* 30 October 2001

The former Scottish Labour MP Dr Maurice Miller, who has died aged 81, was the bright spark of the soft left in the battles of his 23 years in the Commons. From 1964–74 he sat for Glasgow Kelvingrove, and when that constituency was redistributed, moved to East Kilbride. His participation lapsed in 1987 only because he mistakenly relied on promises that he could continue fighting his causes in the Lords.

He fought for Scottish devolution, Catholic rights in Northern Ireland, the rights of immigrants in Britain, those of the black majority in Rhodesia/Zimbabwe, and the right of Israel to exist. These fights were characterised by his special mixture of humour and irascibility. The latter led him to denounce right wing Tory MP Tony Marlow as a 'fascist' because of Marlow's campaigns against immigration.

Miller was also the leading 'doctor in the house', organising medical care for fellow MPs, particularly the half-dozen 'walking wounded' crucially needed to keep Labour in power when its majority was wafer-thin. He secured the right to prescribe for fellow-MPs, which resulted in his prescribing for Labour MP John Stonehouse's anxiety and depression before the former postmaster general disappeared in a faked drowning in 1974.

His medicine was not partisan: on a delegation to India, he helped save the life of Tory Colonel Sir Malcolm Stoddard-Scott, by sewing back his scalp when it was ripped off by a tree branch in a car accident. Miller also set up a system of medical surveillance that detected at least one lung cancer requiring immediate surgery.

Born in Glasgow, the son of a company director, Maurice Miller attended Shawlands Academy before moving on to Glasgow University, where he completed his medical qualifications in 1944. Although he was not religious, his Jewish background made him ultra-sensitive to the rising threat of Nazism: in 1936 he made a month-long tour of Nazi Germany.

Having joined the Labour Party in 1947, in 1950 he was elected to Glasgow Corporation for Anderston ward, in which he had been practising medicine. Elected to the Commons for Kelvingrove in Labour's narrow win of October 1964, he devoted his maiden speech to deploring his constituency's slums. When MPs achieved pay rises, he gave his to local pensioners forced to wait months for their pension increases.

Miller's impatience with the pace of reform led to frequent clashes. Frustrated by the fuddy-duddy British Medical Association, he resigned from it in 1965 and denounced the outdated Scottish medical education system. Finding the negotiations with white Rhodesian rebel Ian Smith slow, he urged considering the use of military force to oust Smith's regime. A Zionist, he got into a fierce argument with pro-Arab fellow Tribune group MP Will Griffiths over the Arab-Israel war. In 1968, he stormed out of Athens in disgust at the 'bludgeoning' of the Greek colonels.

Above all, Miller hated discrimination. He urged a Royal Commission on Northern Ireland to end gerrymandering and discrimination there. He pressed for a ban on local authority grants to clubs that practised discrimination. He attacked the 'irrational and grossly exaggerated' anti-immigration diatribes of Enoch Powell, which he compared to those in 1902 against Jewish immigrants into the UK.

His peppery personality made him difficult to promote or retain. Named an assistant whip for Scotland by soft-left chief whip John Silkin in 1968, he resigned when right winger Bob Mellish took over as chief whip in 1969. He had to resign as PPS to Leader of the Commons Edward Short after voting against wage curbs in 1975. He resigned from the select committee on abortion because he feared the legalisation of abortion was being watered down. In 1979, he said he would go on fighting for Scottish home rule because 52 per cent of Scots had voted for it, although not enough under the terms of the referendum.

His only serious error was in believing a promise that, if he gave up his Commons seat, he would be elevated to the Lords, which he had decided would be more suitable for him. On this promise he announced in 1984 he would not stand again, but was repeatedly disappointed as Mrs Thatcher allowed only a small fraction of Labour nominees to be 'kicked upstairs'. His last decade was also disfigured by the gradual onset of Alzheimer's.

He leaves Renée, his wife of 67 years, two sons, Jerry and David, and two daughters, Andrea and Sonja.

Andrew Roth

William Whitlock

born 20 June 1918, *died* 2 November 2001

William Whitlock, who has died aged 83, was Labour MP for Nottingham North from 1959 to 1983, and gained a certain notoriety when, as Under-Secretary for Foreign and Commonwealth Affairs, he was chased off the eastern Caribbean island of Anguilla in 1969.

Two years earlier, the British Government had proposed linking the then colonies of St Kitts, Nevis and Anguilla. Hating the idea of playing second fiddle to St Kitts, the 6,000 Anguillans declared independence. Whitlock arrived on the island in March 1969 with a set of proposals aimed at solving the stalemate, including an amnesty for the rebels.

The visit, however, ended in disaster. Although welcomed by Anguillans singing 'God Save The Queen', he was forced to leave after armed men blocked the road to the house where he was lunching. Shots were fired and Whitlock had to beat a retreat.

Back in London, he lost his ministerial job. Some felt that he had been scapegoated and that Foreign Secretary Michael Stewart had offered him little support. Back in Anguilla, the threatened linkage with St Kitts was abandoned and colonial rule restored with the help of the Metropolitan Police. Today, Anguilla remains an overseas territory.

The episode overlooks the fact that Whitlock never received credit for his support for the right of Uganda Asians with British passports to enter Britain in 1968, a move opposed by Home Secretary James Callaghan and Richard Crossman, the leader of the House.

Although based in the East Midlands, Whitlock was born in Southampton, the son of a docker. He was educated at Itchen Grammar School and managed two years at Southampton University before his father's death forced him to go to work to help support the family.

During the Second World War, he spent six years in his father's regiment, the Hampshires. He served in Belgium in 1940, scrambling on to a boat on the last day of the Dunkirk evacuation. He then transferred to the airborne forces, narrowly avoiding capture after gliding in to land near Nijmegen in the disastrous Arnhem operation. He later served as president of the Nottinghamshire Parachute Association.

After the war, he became East Midlands area organiser for the shopworkers' union, USDAW. His organising skills enabled him to expand into regional union and political networks. He became president of Leicester Trades Council (1955–56), then of Leicester Labour Party. His soft-left outlook, and support for CND helped his selection for Nottingham North, which he won in the 1959 general election.

Making a typically quiet entry into the Commons, his organising skills, loyalism and persuasive manner again helped him into the Labour whips' office, where he moved steadily upwards from 1962 to become deputy chief whip in 1967.

Whitlock's parliamentary career ended in the 1983 election, when all three Nottingham seats fell to the Tories, although he lost by only 362 votes. Although he never complained publicly, he was angry that the then Labour leader Michael Foot refused to recommend him for a life peerage: this was partly because Foot loathed the Lords and partly, perhaps, because Whitlock was, by then, 65. He kept his counsel because he was the old sort of quiet loyalist.

He is survived by his wife, Jessie, whom he married in 1943, and five sons.

Andrew Roth

Sir Ray Powell

born 19 June 1928, **died** 7 December 2001

Sir Ray Powell, for 22 years the Labour MP for Ogmore, in south Glamorgan, has died from a suspected asthma attack at the age of 73. His knighthood, in 1996, was seen as his price for leaving the whips' office. The following year, he claimed Millbank offered him a peerage to make way for the Blairite former Tory minister Alan Howarth, but the controversial Powell, very much self-styled Old Labour, would not accede, warning that Peter Mandelson would be 'found in one of the gulleys' if he kept up the pressure.

Most confrontations with the stormy petrel Powell ended in purple language, not least in the cause of keeping stores closed on Sundays. He fiercely fought this battle on behalf of his sponsoring shopworkers' union, USDAW, rather than as a sabbatarian. His chief ally, the evangelical Christian Conservative MP, Michael Alison, described him as displaying 'doggedness, subtlety and ruthlessness'.

A strong supporter of Welsh devolution in the 1970s, Powell attacked the 'rabble-rousing, egotistical behaviour' of Neil Kinnock, Leo Abse and others who opposed it. He changed his mind in the 1990s, when devolution's main standard-bearer was Ron Davies, an enemy of long standing who had tried to have him removed from the whips' office. Powell defied what had become party policy by demanding a referendum on devolution, which was later conceded.

However, he never received credit for his good work from 1987, as chairman of the parliamentary new building committee. Had he not intervened to limit London Underground severely in building the Jubilee Line approach to the new Westminster station, Parliament Square would have been turned into a spoil heap for two years.

Born in Treorchy, Rhondda, the son of a miner, Powell attended his local Penerens Primary and Pentre Grammar Schools. He also benefited from courses provided by the National Council of Labour Colleges and at the London School of Economics.

He began work at 17 as a British Railways fireman for six years, and was then a shop manager until 1966, leaving to become secretary-agent to the Ogmore MP and USDAW president, Walter Padley. From 1969–79, he combined this as voluntary work alongside his job as an administrative officer with the Welsh Water Authority.

Elected to Ogwr Borough Council in 1973, he lost the seat three years later. Astonishingly, he became chairman of the Welsh Labour Party in 1977, but failed to be selected as parliamentary candidate for Rhondda, Monmouth, Aberdare or Caerphilly. Eventually, he was selected to succeed Padley after a much-disputed nine-hour selection conference, defeating Ann Clwyd, Ron Davies, William Edwards and

Gwynoro Jones. His huge majority of 16,000 in 1979 was a foregone conclusion.

Though short, Powell certainly made his voice heard. He called the Tory Welsh secretary Nicholas Edwards, 'Nick the Ripper, the industrial rapist of Wales'. During the Falklands War of 1982, he accused Mrs Thatcher of having 'blood on her hands'.

Showing some evenhandedness, he refused to appear on a platform with James Callaghan, claiming that he had 'ratted on Michael Foot' during the 1983 election by opposing unilateralism.

As a whip from 1983–95, Powell was credited with refusing Ken Livingstone a desk for a year after his arrival in the Commons in 1987. His behaviour was unpopular, but he managed to survive Ron Davies' attempt to oust him that year by seeking to have all whips elected.

Much later, he described the whips' office he had so long dominated as 'the Gestapo', when it put him on a hit list of rebels who repeatedly voted against lowering the age of male homosexual consent to 16.

His longest series of campaigns, starting in 1984, was to keep shops shut on Sundays. This wound up with his 1992–93 Shops Bill, scuppered by Tory MP Angela Rumbold's 99 amendments. After that, he defied his own frontbench by tabling wrecking amendments to the Tory government's Sunday Trading Bill.

On the eve of the 1997 general election, Powell alleged various attempts by Peter Mandelson and Ron Davies to prise him out of his seat to make way for Alan Howarth. After he chalked up an enlarged majority of 24,000, he became increasingly counter-devolutionary. He voted 'no' in the Welsh referendum that September, and threatened to resign and stand as an Independent if his views were not tolerated.

The Howarth drama was re-enacted before last June's general election, this time with Tory defector Shaun Woodward. By then, Sir Ray, already ailing, had been narrowly reselected, and held on, perhaps hoping to pass the seat to his daughter, Janice Gregory, Labour Welsh Assembly member for Ogmore.

She survives him, as do his son Haydn and his wife Marion, whom he married in 1949.

Andrew Roth

Sir Humphrey Appleby

born 5 April 1929, *died* 26 December 2001

Sir Humphrey Appleby, who died last Thursday at St Dympna's Hospital for the Elderly Deranged, was perhaps the most outstanding civil servant of this generation. The principles he formulated, the practices he instituted and the probity he exemplified have become the model for his successors right up to the present day.

After a classical scholarship to Winchester and a first in Greats at Balliol College, Oxford, followed by two years' National Service in the Army Education Corps, he entered the civil service as an Assistant Principal in the Scottish Office. His administrative gifts were soon recognised, and when the Department of Administrative Affairs was set up in 1964, he was brought into it as Assistant Secretary. He quickly established himself as a sound official with a safe pair of hands and rose inexorably to the top, becoming Permanent Secretary at a surprisingly young age – in fact he was not yet fifty. The civil service is often compared to salad dressing, on the grounds that in both of them the oil rises to the top and the vinegar stays at the bottom, but while Sir Humphrey was certainly not vinegary it would be unjust to ascribe his smooth manner to oiliness. He was indeed in all respects a model of deferential propriety in his dealings with politicians, but underneath his suave and diplomatic exterior there was a firmness of will and a clarity of purpose that many ministers came to value.

His qualities were perhaps seen at their best when James Hacker arrived as minister after many years on the opposition benches. The political skills Hacker had developed there were not, one might say, wholly adequate for the task of running a department of some 20,000 people, with the result that his dependence on the support of his permanent officials was very nearly total. Fortunately Sir Humphrey was more than up to the task of steering him through the ministerial mine-fields. All he asked in return was freedom to run the department in his own way, without the distractions of political interference.

Recently released documents have shown that in the early days, Hacker did try to persuade him to implement some of the government's manifesto commitments, but Sir Humphrey was always able to demon-strate that they were inconsistent with the orderly and organised administration of government affairs for which he was so justly renowned throughout Whitehall. He was sometimes characterised as a traditionalist of the old school, and even blamed for Britain's failure to adapt to the second half of the twentieth century. It would be fairer to say that he was acutely aware of the dangers of tinkering with a machine that was running smoothly, even if the vehicle it drove was not at the moment winning the race. He was privately scornful of the endless new initiatives proposed by ministers and although change did take place while he was at his post, he cannot be accused of conniving at it in any way.

When the post of Cabinet Secretary fell vacant on Sir Arnold Robinson's retirement, his appointment to it came as no surprise to anyone. No other candidate came within miles of him. What did come as a surprise, however, was the arrival of Hacker in 10 Downing Street only a few weeks later. As a complete outsider in the premiership stakes, he had received no sort of preparation or grooming for his new role, nor for the complex issues of defence, security and foreign affairs that had been well beyond the remit of his previous ministerial portfolio. Once again, a heavy responsibility fell upon Sir Humphrey's shoulders, and once again they proved more than adequate for the burden.

Critics of Hacker's administration have complained that almost nothing was actually achieved during his comparatively brief tenure of office.

Others have pointed out that at least there were no disasters. For this latter fact, the credit must go to Sir Humphrey. Hacker frequently lamented that the delays at Number 10 seemed interminable, but his Cabinet Secretary knew that speed was the enemy of good administration. He had in his career spent too many hours clearing up after snap decisions and panic legislation to be willing to short-circuit established procedures and traditional practices. He was wonderfully meticulous in consulting every interested party about any new proposals, and also about circulating not only the revisions but also the revisions of the revisions for further comment. One of his favourite quotations was Bacon's 'Counsels to which Time hath not been called, Time will not ratify'. He also used to say that, in legislation as in medicine, diarrhoea was a much more offensive and dangerous condition than constipation. He showed a commendable caution in his approach to innovation, having found time and time again that words like 'novel', 'bold' and 'imaginative' were heralds of disaster outside the world of literature and the arts (and often there as well). He believed in precedent, in the tried and tested, and in the wisdom of the ages rather than the fashionable idea of the moment.

His minutes, papers and memoranda (many of which are still treasured to this day by their recipients) were models of literary eloquence. He eschewed the temptations of easy brevity and deceptive simplicity, giving every subject extensive evaluation and applying the fullest possible consideration to every contributing fact and conflicting argument. If he was accused of leaving the reader unsure of what conclusion he had finally reached, he would reply that if they wanted the cheap certainties of tabloid journalism, they could go and read the *Sun* or the *News Of The World*.

His retirement not only deprived the nation of one of its most distinguished public servants; it also marked the end of an era. His successors lacked his skill and determination in resisting pressure for change, and the new breed of politicians were distressingly assertive. To him the steady improvement in Britain's economic performance and standing in the world which followed his departure was a small recompense for the diminution of power and influence of the institution he had so loyally and industriously served for all his career. He was especially pained by the reduction in size of the civil service; he knew that good administration could not be had on the cheap and took pride in the steady increase in the number of civil servants over the years when he was head of the service.

It would be unfair to say that he despised politicians, though there were none he spoke of with reverence and few with respect. He believed their role to be important in its way, even if subservient to his own. He recognised his inability to whip up popular support for the government's policies, and to defend them to the press and parliament, and was happy to leave that job to them. He also accepted that they were necessary to extract from the Treasury the budget that good government demanded. His wrath was reserved for those who tried to use their temporary eminence to change the practices that had served the country so well for so many centuries. He was not implacably opposed to reform; he saw some good in Thomas Cromwell's changes under Henry VIII and he did not condemn out of hand the Northcote-Trevelyan reforms of 1854, though he believed it to be too early to pass a final judgement on them. But he had no time for what he saw as the half-baked ideas of jumped-up polytechnic lecturers who had never even run a whelk stall, owing to lack of the necessary qualifications. This not to say that he was undemocratic, though his idea of democracy was not so much executing the will of the people as securing their consent to the policies advocated by those qualified to decide on their behalf.

It is unfortunate that he has left no diaries or memoirs, though not surprising since his discretion was legendary. The less respectful of his younger colleagues used to say that he would not tell you the time until he had checked the level of your security clearance. Perhaps he now appears as a figure from a bygone age. The days may have passed when public men were admired most for their loyalty, discretion, integrity and ability to quote Plato, but we are not necessarily the richer for their passing.

Antony Jay and Jonathan Lynn

Anthony Royle

Lord Fanshawe of Richmond

born 27 March 1927, *died* 28 December 2001

Lord Fanshawe of Richmond, who has died aged 74, was better known as Sir Anthony Royle while Conservative MP for Richmond (1959–83), Under Secretary of State for Foreign and Commonwealth affairs (1970–74) and vice chairman of the Conservative Party (1979–84). His pro-European stance, both during the entry of the United Kingdom into the European Community in 1973 and in later Conservative relationships with Europe, was perhaps the most significant aspect of his political career.

He was among the last of the 'kissing' ring. This did not refer to his wealth or his black-browed good looks. Rather, the 'kissing ring' was a phrase of the sixties and seventies used to deride those in the inner circle of the Tory establishment because they had known each other since attending snobbish preparatory schools, particularly Royle's own, St Peter's Court in Broadstairs.

Tony Royle owed all his advantages to his father, Sir Lancelot Royle, an Olympic athlete who became a wealthy businessman: chairman of Home and Colonial Stores, two Lipton tea firms, deputy chairman of Liebigs Extract of Meat. Young Tony had followed his father to Harrow, then diverged from his father's path to attend the Royal Military Academy at Sandhurst, instead of Woolwich. Young Tony was commissioned into the Life Guards in 1945, serving in Germany, Egypt and in the Palestine troubles of 1946–47. After the war, he joined, as a Territorial trooper, the 231st Special Air Service Regiment, training as a parachutist. In 1950, he was commissioned in the independent squadron of the SAS and shipped out to Korea. En route, he contracted poliomyelitis; he had to be offloaded in Malaya, and fought for his life in an iron lung. He survived, with a permanent limp.

On his return to London, his father provided £75,000 to enable him to become a member of Lloyd's. He had already started, in 1948, his career as an insurance broker at Sedgwick Collins. These were undemanding ways of earning his living while trying to become a politician.

He started at the bottom, by fighting a St Pancras LCC ward in 1953, then a ward in North Paddington, again unsuccessfully. He then fought but failed in the constituency of St Pancras North in 1955 and, in 1958, at the by-election for Tory-held Torrington. He was tagged 'Runaway Royle' when he abandoned Torrington to discreetly chase both Richmond upon Thames and Folkestone. When Richmond came through first, his Folkestone backers, peeved at losing a rich candidate with a beautiful wife, thought his secretive behaviour 'outrageous'.

In the Commons he soon became an acolyte of, then PPS (1960–64) to, Julian Amery, the advocate of 'Euro-imperialism': the linking of the British and French empires to stave off the Americans. It was this which inspired Amery, when Minister of Aviation, to rivet Britain into the Anglo-French Concorde project. Royle, whose election address had stressed the Commonwealth as 'the world's strongest bulwark against communism', became an Amery-style pro-European. With Amery, whose brother had been hanged as a traitor, he voted against capital punishment in 1964.

As a constituency MP he was a persistent critic of the noise of Heathrow overflights, but preferred to spend weekends with his wife and two daughters at their Cotswold home. He was an assiduous visitor to Asia and Africa, and even enjoyed an interview with Fidel Castro. When Labour returned to power in 1964, he became secretary of the Tory MPs' foreign affairs committee.

His pro-Europeanism endeared him to Edward Heath, who asked him to prepare a plan for Hong Kong, even before making him Under Secretary for Foreign Affairs after the June 1970 Tory victory. Royle announced the Tories would keep troops in south east Asia after 1971, instead of withdrawing them, as Labour had intended. In 1972, he paid the first official visit to communist China since its 1949 recognition by

Britain. That same year, the Foreign Secretary, Sir Alec Douglas-Home, extended his responsibilities to Europe as well as Asia.

Suddenly, in January 1974, Tony Royle threw in his hand, but not for any political reason. His 76–year-old father wanted to retire and hand over his parcel of boardroom seats on the British Match Corporation, Brooke-Bond-Liebig and Wilkinson Sword. Heath, grateful for someone else who was both pro-EEC and pro-Beijing, made him a knight in his dissolution honours list.

Long before Margaret Thatcher was elected Prime Minister in 1979, Royle had been preparing a list of the 'great and good' Tory businessmen to replace Labour's trade unionists on government quangos. On election, she named him vice-chairman of the Conservative Party, initially for international affairs but then for candidate selection as well. This was a brutal class snub to his predecessor, Marcus Fox, who had chosen self-made men.

In 1980, he announced he would not be standing again. This may have been a recognition that the Liberals were gaining ground in his constituency. Or that his pro-Europeanism was setting him on a collision course with Mrs Thatcher. This came to a head in the crisis over Westland, of which he became a director in 1985. In 1986 he was one of those, like Michael Heseltine, who favoured linking the helicopter firm with a European consortium, rather than with American Sikorsky. By then he had become a life peer (1983).

He leaves his wife Shirley, a former Vogue model whom he married in 1957, and two daughters, Susannah and Lucinda.

Andrew Roth

Ian Grist

born 5 December 1938, *died* 2 January 2002

The independent-minded Tory MP Ian Grist, who has died after a stroke at 63, was always sensible in private, but partisan in his marginal constituencies: Cardiff North from 1974–83, then Cardiff Central from 1983–92. He unexpectedly became Parliamentary Under Secretary for Wales from 1987–90.

Grist acutely described himself as 'hard-headed but soft-hearted'. He was 'dry' on economics and loyal to the Anglo-American alliance. 'We should all remember with gratitude what we owe the US,' he said.

Grist was a pro-European who backed the 1990 candidacy of Michael Heseltine. Ahead of fellow Tories on social matters, he opposed bringing back the death penalty and corporal punishment in schools. One of the first to urge banning cigarette advertising, he also opposed curbs on abortion and became a pillar of the Planned Parenthood Federation. He backed low-cost essential drugs for the Third World. Unlike most Tory MPs, his children were educated at local comprehensives.

Tall, jovial and widely popular, Grist was born in Southampton, the son of a land agent who became a garage owner. From Hildersham House Preparatory School in Broadstairs, he was sent to Repton. An open history scholarship took him to Jesus College, Oxford, where he became secretary of the Conservative Association.

Grist first aspired to the colonial civil service, starting in 1960 as a colonial office plebiscite officer in the South Cameroons. He then became a sales manager in Nigeria for the United Africa Company, before deciding against a career as a Colonel Blimp.

Although a quarter Welsh (the rest being Scots, Irish, English and Jewish), he identified with Wales when he became the Tories' Welsh information officer for nine years from 1963. This whetted his political appetite, which was not dented by losing hopeless Aberavon in 1970. Selected for marginal Cardiff North in 1972, he won it in 1974.

In opposition, Grist seemed very partisan, attacking 'neo-Marxist' Neil Kinnock, Welsh devolution, pop festivals, alternative social 'creeps and freebooters', soccer hooligans, union pickets and intolerant students.

When the Tories returned in 1979, he became Parliamentary Private Secretary to their new Welsh Secretary, Nicholas Edwards, but resigned after two years. He used his freedom to attack water privatisation and Mrs Thatcher's poll tax as 'regressive by nature' and a 'legal nightmare'. He also opposed cuts in mortgage payments for the unemployed.

It was a pleasant surprise, therefore, when Mrs Thatcher named him Parliamentary Under Secretary for Wales in 1987, and a disappointment when he was sacked by John Major three years later. As a pro-European he had supported Michael Heseltine, as had Welsh Secretary David Hunt and his deputy Wyn Roberts. 'I was the most sackable of the three leaves on the tree,' he said philosophically.

He was not surprised when he lost Cardiff Central in 1992, part of the Tories' electoral shrivelling in Wales. He spent the next four years as the cheerful chairman of the South Glamorgan Health Authority.

He leaves his wife Wendy and two sons, Julian and Toby.

Andrew Roth

Neville Sandelson

born 27 November 1923, *died* 12 January 2002

The historic 'achievement' of Neville Sandelson, who has died aged 78, and was MP for Hayes and Harlington from 1971–83, was to organise, in 1981, seven right wing Labour MPs – all planning to defect to the new Social Democratic Party – into voting for Michael Foot instead of Denis

Healey in the Labour leadership elections. This was in the hope of making Labour unelectable. Six years later, when he left the SDP for the Conservatives, he dismissed the Social Democrats as a misguided 'middle-class elite'.

Sandelson himself was a middle-class hedonist, who had inherited a fortune from his corporate lawyer father, which initially enabled him to live a pleasure-loving lifestyle, if not quite on the level of his millionaire cousin, Harold Lever. The loss of that early fortune pushed him to devote too much time to the Bar, which later led to clashes with Hayes and Harlington's left wingers. He missed giving his maiden speech on school milk – 'I got detained at the Old Bailey' – but made up for it by a later one attacking Heathrow noise pollution.

Yet for 21 years he had pursued a parliamentary seat with unparalleled zeal. Starting at hopeless Ashford, which he lost to William (now Lord) Deedes in 1950, 1951 and 1955, he went on to the 1957 Beckenham by-election, then to marginal Rushcliffe in 1959. His articulate feistyness brought him close to a winnable seat in 1966, when the Labour candidate for marginal Heston and Isleworth pulled out at the last moment, but he lost by 926 votes.

Worse still, in 1967 he lost the Leicester South West by-election after the former Labour chief whip, Bert Bowden, deserted it to become Lord Aylestone and chairman of the Independent Television Authority. Sandelson seemed such a Jonah that in the 1970 general election he could only fight hopeless Chichester. It was finally the death of Arthur Skeffington that gave Sandelson his Hayes and Harlington seat in a 1971 by-election.

In the initial tussle over entry into the European Community, he was one of the 69 Labour pro-Europeans who sided with Conservative Prime Minister Edward Heath. This, plus resentment of his Epsom stock-broker-belt lifestyle, began his clashes with the left.

Sandelson was born into a prosperous Leeds Jewish family and educated at Westminster School – where he claimed to have bloodied the nose of young Tony Benn – and Trinity College, Cambridge, where he read law and chaired the university Labour club. He was called to the Bar at Inner Temple in 1946.

His one unchallenged parliamentary achievement was legal. In 1972 he got onto the statute book his private member's bill, the Matrimonial Proceedings (Polygamous Marriages) Act. This enabled those who had contracted polygamous marriages overseas to have the same rights, such as divorce, as those in monogamous marriages in Britain.

The death of his father at the age of 51 had left Sandelson with a fifth of the fortune. He invested it in the North London Observer Group and Putnam's the publishers, roughly breaking even. What really hit him hard was his investment in oil shares, which plummeted in the wake of the 1956 closing of the Suez Canal.

He had to go back to the Bar, and also try to earn money in TV documentaries. He never gave up his effort to regain a comfortable middle-class living style, not possible on the £4,500 salary on which he started as an MP. This helped set him at odds with his constituency activists, many of them Irish Catholics working at Heathrow.

Sandelson had no sympathy for the left-moving trade unionists who strengthened their hold on the Labour Party in the 1970s. He became one of the founder-members of the SDP in 1981. By 1987 Sandelson had also deserted the SDP for the Conservatives, and became president of the Radical Society, whose most prominent member was Lord (Norman) Tebbit.

After he lost Hayes and Harlington in 1983 to the right wing working-class philistine Tory, Terry Dicks, Sandelson spent much of his non-legal time as deputy chairman of Westminster and Overseas Trade Services and as a director of Profundis Ltd.

He leaves his French-born wife, Nana (Karlinski), a son and two daughters.

Andrew Roth

Moss Evans

born 13 July 1925, *died* 12 January 2002

Perhaps the most difficult problem in the career of Moss Evans, who has died aged 76, was his inheritance. He succeeded to the general secretary-ship of the Transport and General Workers Union (TGWU), the most politically influential union in Britain, following four names engraved in labour history, Ernest Bevin, Arthur Deakin, Frank Cousins and Jack Jones.

Evans refused to be intimidated but it was a rough passage. He was at the pivotal point of resistance during the 1978–79 'winter of discontent' which led to the collapse of James Callaghan's Labour Government.

Some members of the Callaghan cabinet still attribute much of the responsibility for that Labour disaster to the chubby, loquacious Welshman. The most outspoken criticisms come in the memoirs of Lords Healey and Callaghan – especially from Denis Healey in his *Time of My Life* (1990) in which he denounces Evans as 'a very inadequate substitute for Jack Jones'.

It was the time of the social contract; the government would offer concessions to the unions in return for moves to contain wage inflation. Jack Jones was one of the architects of that policy, but Evans succeeded Jones at the very moment when employers and shop-floor workers were in revolt against wage restraint.

The Callaghan Government and the TUC had placed too much weight on a policy that simply couldn't take the strain. Even if Evans had been an Ernest Bevin he would not have been able to hold the ring. His critics are unfair, but they may be on firmer ground in criticising his leadership style. At a crucial TUC meeting on November 14 1978, when the government was negotiating with union leaders on the social contract, he was on holiday. Healey marks that moment as the critical point of departure and 'a triumph for Mrs Thatcher'. Certainly, once back, Evans was at the forefront of most of the pay demands which led to the winter of discontent.

The strain of that period took a severe toll and Evans fell ill not long afterwards. For most of 1981 his deputy, Alex Kitson, was acting general secretary, presiding at the Labour Party conference at which Tony Benn came within a fraction of defeating Healey for party deputy leadership. The TGWU voted for the late John Silkin, which some observers, described as 'Moss's revenge' – even in his absence – on Healey.

Evans was a miner's son, born in the Welsh mining village of Cefn Coed near Merthyr Tydfil. His mother, originally widowed during the First World War, married Moss's father and bore 12 children. During the depression, his father was only occasionally employed so his mother took a job in a local brickyard.

For much of Evans's childhood the family remained on parish relief: the children slept four to a bed and often begged for bread from the posh houses across the valley. When Evans was 12, the family joined the 1930s Welsh migration and moved to Smallheath in Birmingham where his father found work. 'My experience during my formative years was of living in a society which, quite frankly, believed in the law of the jungle,' Evans recalled. He was a bright pupil and sat for hours absorbing classics such as Robert Tressell's *The Ragged Trousered Philanthropists* and Jack London's *The Call of the Wild*. At 14 he moved to a Joseph Lucas factory where he joined the Amalgamated Engineering Union. Bombed out during the Second World War, the family moved back to south Wales where Moss made machine-gun breech blocks for BSA. He began to take an active part in trade unionism. He was later recruited to work in Berkshire on the D-Day Mulberry Harbours – and met his wife Laura.

Back in the Midlands, in 1950 he took a job at the Bakelite company in Tyseley, joined the TGWU, became a shop steward, took day-release (unpaid) courses at Birmingham University and planned to go to Ruskin College, Oxford. But in 1956 he was accepted as a TGWU full-timer and appointed Birmingham east area official for the engineering and chemical industries, and in 1960 midlands region trade group secretary.

His mentor was Jack Jones, then regional secretary for the TGWU's powerful Midlands area. When Jones became number three to Frank Cousins he brought Evans with him as national officer for the TGWU's engineering section.

The making of Evans as a negotiator and industrial peacemaker was his work as chairman of the Ford national joint negotiating committee. It was also where his lifelong friendship was established with his successor as general secretary, Ron Todd.

Ford was plagued with unofficial strikes – in 1970 and 1971 there were two serious official stoppages, followed by unofficial action. Evans resolved these disputes and secured peace after a number of unofficial strikes at Ford's Merseyside and south Wales plants. In 1973 Jones appointed Evans as TGWU national organiser following his negotiations on a shorter working week for Ford's 50,000 workforce.

Already he was seen as a successor for Jones, but his problem was that the outstanding candidate was Harry Urwin, Jones' deputy and a brilliant leader who had been close to Jones for 30 years. But he was only two years younger than Jones and refused to run – arguing that he would have only two years in the job before he was forced to retire – unless Jones proposed a rule change. Jones wouldn't, which cleared the way for Evans.

So in April 1977, Evans won a majority of more than 200,000 over his nearest rival on a 40 per cent poll of the union's two million members and took over at the end of March 1978, aged 52, with the prospect of serving for 13 years – but he only remained for seven years. Illness had weakened him, and in 1984 Todd succeeded him, although the two men worked in harness until July 1985, when Evans finally retired on his 60th birthday.

Evans was still smarting from the criticism of his role during the winter of discontent. He was particularly wounded by the frequent speculation about what might have happened in 1979 if Urwin, and not he, had succeeded Jones. Remarkably, in Jones's 1986 autobiography there is no mention of Evans, despite the latter having tried to continue with Jones's general policies.

Evans was a member of the TUC General Council (1977–1985) and on the National Economic Development Council (1978–1984). He described himself as a 'man of the shop floor', he was a staunch socialist but not an ideological theorist, a man who regarded trade unionism as the cornerstone of representative democracy for working people. That was why, when the social contract was collapsing under rank and file pressures, Evans's allegiance was to shop-floor influences rather than the government's holy grail. The Callaghan cabinet never forgave him.

After his retirement, the Evanses left Hemel Hempstead for Norfolk. He became a King's Lynn Labour councillor and mayor of King's Lynn and West Norfolk in 1996. He also became a trustee of the 3R Centre, a charity he helped set up for abandoned racehorses.

The death of a son in an accident soon after his own illness profoundly affected him. He leaves his wife Laura, two sons, three daughters and 10 grandchildren.

Geoffrey Goodman

Sir Frank Cooper

born 2 December 1922, *died* 26 January 2002

It is a measure of Frank Cooper's remarkable capabilities that he was one of two obvious contenders to become head of the Civil Service when Sir Douglas Allen retired in 1977 and the favoured candidate to head the Prime Minister's Department had Margaret Thatcher gone ahead with it in 1983. The qualities that attracted her attention were perhaps those that had led to the choice of the other candidate six years earlier, but it was to the immense benefit of the Ministry of Defence that he remained as its permanent head from 1976 until 1982.

The son of an area manager for Terry's chocolate, Cooper was born in Manchester in 1922 and educated at Manchester Grammar School, and read history at Pembroke College, Oxford. His education was interrupted by the Second World War, which saw him flying Spitfires in Italy. Shot down over enemy territory, he evaded capture and made his way back to the Allied lines. Emerging from the RAF in 1946, he completed his degree and took up employment with a firm of chartered accountants.

That he found far too dull and joined the Air Ministry in 1948. Within a year he was in private office, initially with two successive junior ministers, then from 1951 to 1953 with the Permanent Secretary, Sir James Barnes, and finally with the Chief of Air Staff, Sir John Slessor, a central figure in developing Britain's nuclear capability. As an assistant secretary he headed the Air Staff secretariat, but his most memorable achievement was his work alongside Julian Amery in securing Britain's sovereign bases in Cyprus. Cooper recalled no less than 109 meetings with the wily Archbishop Makarios before a settlement was reached.

Nor was his upward path checked by the amalgamation of the three service ministries into the Ministry of Defence in 1964. The incoming Labour Secretary of State, Denis Healey, recalls him as a major support: he was relaxed where his great rival in the department, Patrick Nairne, was intense; and his memoranda were brief and pungent.

In 1968 he was promoted to be Deputy Under-Secretary of State for Defence. After a spell as deputy to William Armstrong in the newly formed Civil Service Department, Cooper took over the Northern Ireland Office, where his great administrative skill was taxed to the full by the generation of the Constitution Act and the Assembly elections. The then Secretary of State, William Whitelaw, confessed himself 'frankly amazed' by the amount that had been achieved in short measure. Cooper played a key role in the negotiations between the Northern Irish parties which followed and which led to the doomed Sunningdale Agreement.

When, after the 1974 election, a new Secretary of State arrived on the scene, the SDLP's Paddy Devlin memorably observed that the newcomer had been Frank Cooper's fitter during the war and the relationship was still the same. It was not true. Merlyn Rees had served with Cooper in Italy, but as an operations officer on the base from which Cooper operated. The latter cherished the greeting that Rees gave him on his return from baling out in enemy territory: 'Where the hell have you been?' The two men got on well and, as Rees recalls, 'did not always play in public the usual 'Yes Minister' game'. They were equally a team in private and Rees describes him as 'swift and incisive in thought and action, keenly aware of what was happening in the province'. He was very sorry to see him go.

It was Cooper's delicate negotiations with the IRA to secure a ceasefire in 1975 that first brought him into the public eye. Asked whether he had talked himself with Sinn Fein, he said 'No', but he had 'organised the people who talked . . . The object was to get rid of internment and bring back the rule of law.' He denied he was changing British policy, simply 'clarifying it'.

The unexpected death of Sir Michael Cary in 1976 precipitated Cooper's return to Defence and, as Healey remarked, the ministry 'benefited greatly from having an expert on defence in the engine room'. An inveterate Whitehall watcher, Peter Hennessy, reckons that a new generation of top civil servants emerged between 1974 and 1976, men for whom everything was possible, and the most powerful axis that developed amongst them was that between the Cabinet Secretary, Sir John Hunt, and Cooper. They were tough, no-nonsense fixers and great friends. Their ability was at a premium at a time when it was fashionable to write of a crisis in governance.

At Defence, Cooper reckoned that three-quarters of his job was management and he thought the department overmanned. By the time he left it in December 1982, 55,000 others had gone before him. Another achievement, as befitted a former Director of Accounts, was to shift the pattern of defence spending in such a way that he freed up 10 per cent extra spending on equipment. But he was convinced that, if he were allowed to roll over money from one year to another and to take a longer-term look at the defence spend, even greater effectiveness could be achieved; and he waged a ferocious and ultimately successful battle with the Treasury to gain his point.

But he could be brutally frank about mistakes made by or forced on his department, admitting, for example, that the Chevaline project to modernise Polaris was 'a classic case of reinventing the wheel'; and he was subsequently strongly in favour of purchasing Trident from the United States. It was, he said, 'the safe option: you were not going to get into a situation where the money graph went right off the corner'.

He had established the Financial Management and Planning Group in 1977 and it came to rank with the Chiefs of Staff Committee and the Equipment Policy Committee as a major centre of power. Fed up with inter-service bickering and horse trading, he created a working party to see how defence programmes could be managed as a whole. The result was the Defence Programme Steering Group, which worked directly to FMPG. He was in favour of the strengthening of the powers of the Chief of Defence Staff in 1981 and welcomed the further reorganisation that took place under Michael Heseltine in 1985.

Implementing the 1974/75 defence review had been amongst Cooper's first tasks, but he came to the conclusion that no government had yet matched Britain's commitments to the resources the country could afford. As a result, everything was spread too thin. Sceptical though he was of the exaggerated nature of threat assessments in general, he welcomed the advent of the Conservative government in 1979, not for party reasons, but because it would ensure continued development of the nuclear deterrent.

Defence White Papers became franker about the continued Soviet threat. Though Cooper backed Francis Pym's fight against defence cuts in 1980, he welcomed his more Thatcherite successor, John Nott, because of his determination to review Britain's defence posture and concentrate her efforts on the areas that mattered. Ironically, what wrecked that effort was the Royal Navy's success in the Falklands crisis.

Again Cooper came into the public gaze, this time attacked for not telling the truth to the press. While he would tell no lies, he had no intention of revealing all. If that misled them, so be it. Lives were not there to be risked for the sake of a good story. He vigorously defended that attitude when the House of Commons investigated the Defence Ministry's handling of the press. Few who served would think him wrong. In general, however, he thought governments too secretive and was much more open than most. The journalist Ivan Rowan in a valedictory piece described Cooper as 'Whitehall's frankest mandarin' and in retirement he was always ready to co-operate with young academics. From 1986 to 1992 he presided over the activities of the Institute for Contemporary British History.

Although he enjoyed playing the tycoon, his career in industry was marred by controversy over his association with defence-related companies, not least the troubled helicopter company Westland. 'What the bloody hell am I supposed to do?' he asked with characteristic pugnacity. 'Put on my carpet slippers?' But, after three years as chairman of United Scientific Holdings, the post that had generated most of the attacks, he resigned in 1989.

Cooper was the most unstuffy of men. His talk had nothing of Whitehallese about it and was memorable for its vivid phraseology. He conveyed always an enormous sense of fun. He was sometimes unpopular with subordinates, but invariably they had fallen short of the expectations he had of them and resented the way in which he made no secret of his feelings. Generally he was more relaxed, but behind the breeziness lay an immensely sharp mind and an ability to get to the point.

When profiling him in 1981, Hennessy was told that Cooper 'gets away with it because he is more of a politician than the politicians themselves' and they did not know how to handle that. Cooper always thought of himself as a Manchester radical, but in truth he was the supreme pragmatist, always aware of the art of the possible, even if frequently he chafed at the results.

John Barnes

Lord Gibson-Watt

born 11 September 1918, *died* 7 February 2002

Minister of State in the Welsh Office from 1970 to 1974, and Tory MP for Hereford from 1956 to 1974, Lord (David) Gibson-Watt, who has died at 83, was the tallest, bravest – and squarest man – in the House of Commons. Gibson-Watt's disregard for political safety echoed his wartime Welsh Guards service. He earned his first Military Cross in Tunisia in 1943, the second in the fighting for Monte Cassino in 1944, and the third a couple of months later in the crossing of the Po.

In the Commons he exposed himself to the withering fire of Labour's Kevin Hughes, his mirror-image. Hughes was a sharp-witted Welshman representing a Scottish seat, Gibson-Watt was a slow-thinking traditionalist, a descendant of James Watt, born in the house his ancestor had founded near Llandrindod Wells 150 years before and the heir to its 30,000 acres.

Gibson-Watt, the consummate countryman, clearly preferred spending his time in the Wye Valley with his herd of Welsh black cattle to the Lords, to which he was elevated in 1979. One of his rare contributions, in 1988, was in defence of private forestry owners like himself. And, a self-confessed square, he opposed any violation of Sunday, even by skilled cricketers like himself. His family had been rooted in Wales for 150 years, but he never learned Welsh and opposed extending the language beyond those families who already spoke it, for fear of deterring needed English incomers. He derided even modest steps toward Welsh self-rule as 'separatism'. Another of his rare Lords speeches was in 1998, opposing the establishment of the Welsh Assembly.

He was captain of house at Eton – and a contemporary of Julian Amery – and read history at Trinity College, Cambridge. Then came the Welsh Guards. He left the army in 1946 a major, taking up farming and politics like his father before him. He found a seat on Radnorshire County Council in 1946, but failed in 1950 and 1951 to unseat Tudor

Watkins, the Labour MP for Brecon and Radnor. His chance came in Hereford in 1956, when Gibson-Watt won a by-election with a reduced majority in a Tory seat, increasing his majority in 1959 against the Liberal broadcaster Robin Day, who ridiculed him as a 'walking robot' who had hardly ever spoken in the Commons.

It had taken him five months to make his maiden speech, but he had done better with a private member's bill to erase the stigma of illegitimacy from children born to a couple who later married. He became an assistant whip in 1957, a full whip in 1959. His greatest kudos came from his aggregate – 166 in four innings – for the Lords and Commons cricket team. He resigned as a whip against his government's decision to import Charollais cattle. As a breeder of Welsh blacks and chairman of the livestock export group, he objected to this 'contamination'.

Then in 1966, the new Tory leader, Edward Heath, named him Welsh spokesman. But when the Tories won in 1970, he was disappointed to be named only Minister of State. He stood down unexpectedly as an MP after Welsh Secretary Peter Thomas refused to establish a Cambrian mountains national park, which would have included the Gibson-Watt estate.

He was a forestry commissioner (1976–86) and, at Timber Growers UK (1976–98), he was chairman and then president. His wife, the former Diana Hambro, died in 2000. He leaves two sons and two daughters, one son having predeceased him.

Andrew Roth

Margaret Wingfield

born 19 January 1912, *died* 6 April 2002

Fame came to Margaret Wingfield, who has died aged 90, during the denouement of the Jeremy Thorpe affair in 1976. She was the Liberal Party president at the time of the special assembly in Manchester that June, when the Party resolved to involve the membership in the election of its leader.

With her style and voice, Wingfield looked and sounded like a Conservative, but she was one of those rare, natural Liberals who accepted the burden of the Liberal millstone in pursuit of their cause. At the time, Thorpe, the then Liberal leader, had largely lost the confidence of his parliamentary party, following the sometime male model Norman Scott's claim – denied by Thorpe – that the pair had had a sexual relationship 15 years earlier.

The Liberals had polled badly in the Coventry North-West by-election of March 1976; party activists across the country were reporting embarrassing responses on the doorstep. Thorpe realised that the leadership election rules were about to change, and proposed to Wingfield that he should offer himself for re-election under the new rules, thereby circumventing the wrath of Liberal MPs. Neither Wingfield nor Thorpe thought to mention this tactic to the chief whip, Cyril Smith, who was rightly outraged.

Chaos reigned until Richard Wainwright, MP for Colne Valley, on a local radio broadcast on 8 May, effectively urged Thorpe to sue the newspapers for libel, or resign. Two days later, Thorpe quit. The former leader Jo Grimond was prevailed upon to return as caretaker leader, and Wingfield presided over the leadership election that produced David Steel. She travelled widely to reassure local Liberal associations that she was in control, and that they could have confidence in the future.

Wingfield came from a political family – an uncle, Charles McCurdy, had been Liberal MP for Northampton, and Lloyd George's coalition chief whip in 1921 – and was educated at the University of Freiburg and the London School of Economics. Her experience as a care committee organiser for the London County Council, including wartime experience helping bombed-out families, focused her political determination.

Such were the constraints on women politicians that she was unable to find a seat to contest until 1961, when she fought the LCC election in Putney. Thereafter, she contested the 1964 and 1966 general elections in

Wokingham, and the 1970 election in Chippenham. All were disappointing, particularly Chippenham, which had been regarded as winnable, although, in the event, the Liberal vote fell by 10 per cent.

Her best result was at the Walthamstow West by-election in September 1967. The constituency had been Clement Attlee's seat, but the by-election was highly marginal, with the Conservatives eventually gaining the seat from Labour. None the less, Wingfield more than doubled the Liberal vote to 23 per cent and, that year too, she joined the Party executive.

She campaigned successfully for the National Liberal Club to open its doors to women members and, in 1978, became the first woman on its general committee. A Justice of the Peace, she also served on the Lord Chancellor's advisory committee that recommends magistrates for inner London.

Wingfield's experience led her to be a lifelong internationalist, maintaining her active involvement in the Liberal International until shortly before her death. She was awarded the CBE in recognition of her long service to politics. A practical politician, who could be relied upon to turn up at every by-election campaign, she retained the affection of party activists up to the end.

She was well supported by her husband Guy, a civil engineer, whom she married in 1940 and who was invariably at her side. He survives her, as do her two sons and two daughters and seven grandchildren.

Michael Meadowcroft

Jeremy Bray

born 29 June 1930, *died* 31 May 2002

Dr Jeremy Bray, who has died aged 71, was not everyone's pin-up. Baroness Falkender, who as Marcia Williams was Harold Wilson's secretary, conceded that he was brilliant, but dismissed him as akin to 'every mad professor of comic fiction'. Perhaps she had forgotten that he won back Middlesbrough West from the Tories in 1962, in Labour's first by-election victory of the 1959–64 parliament. And in his Motherwell seat, from 1974, he had increased his majorities by fighting to save the Ravenscraig steelworks.

What she was remembering was that he was not a fan of Harold Wilson, and had resigned from his government in 1969 when refused permission to publish his *Decision In Government*, which mildly satirised Wilson's 'white heat' of scientific revolution.

Bray was to the right of Wilson on defence, but to the left of him on such issues as the unilateral declaration of independence in Rhodesia (now Zimbabwe) by Ian Smith's white minority regime.

With a mathematics double first from Jesus College, Cambridge, Bray had difficulty in communicating with lesser minds. He became an econometrician, or mathematical economist, obsessed with the Treasury's computer model of the British economy and increasingly impatient with those who did not understand his conviction that the model was out of date.

Despite such pitfalls he was an excellent constituency MP, and an expert battler for the steelworks in both his constituencies. He was among the first in 1980 to attack the 'farcical misjudgement' of naming Ian MacGregor to chair the British Steel Corporation.

He was a pioneer of the need to transfer scientific discoveries into industrial products. He pushed these proposals as a member of the nationalised industries select committee (1962–64) and while chairing the parliamentary Labour Party science and technology group (1964–66).

His religious convictions as a Methodist lay preacher gave him hesitations about divorce, abortion and genetic engineering of human embryos. In his last years as an MP, he developed an enthusiasm for improving mental health. He also became a fervent supporter of allowing Hong Kong residents with British colonial passports to migrate to Britain.

He himself had been born in Hong Kong, the son of a Methodist missionary. Educated in Eastnor Village School in Herefordshire, Ardwyn Grammar School, Kingswood School, Bath and Cambridge, he was a Choate Fellow at Harvard (1955–56) after his Cambridge PhD.

He worked from 1956 to 1962 in ICI's Wilton works on planning and computerised automatic control, followed by two years at Elliott-Automation and further years at RTZ and Imperial Smelting. He was a director of Mullard Ltd (1970–73).

At Cambridge he had been in the Labour club as well as president of the student Christian movement, and had joined the Labour party at 26. In 1959 he contested the hopeless Thirsk and Malton seat and in 1962 ran in the Middlesbrough West by-election, seeking to overturn a 8,710 Conservative majority. Despite a campaign in which his Liberal opponent, George Scott, described him as 'remote and withdrawn', Bray won by 2,270 votes.

That autumn his hero, the Labour leader Hugh Gaitskell, unexpectedly unveiled himself as an opponent of the European Economic Community, of which Bray was a supporter. When choosing Gaitskell's successor a few months later, Bray voted for George Brown.

When Labour came back to power under Harold Wilson in 1964, Bray became Brown's Parliamentary Private Secretary, but could only stand for a few months Brown's drunkenness and the job's imposed loyalism. He was roundly booed when he told students: 'There are very few parliamentary members of the Labour Party who want to see the Americans withdraw from Vietnam.'

He launched a Fabian pamphlet, *The New Economy,* which proposed planning based on local firms' decisions. He urged modernisation of Commons' procedures and reform of British industrial methods. He also demanded tighter controls on oil being smuggled, against sanctions, into Rhodesia. When he later visited the rebel colony, he was manhandled by half-drunk Rhodesia-firsters.

After he achieved the highest Labour vote ever in his constituency in the 1966 election, Wilson named him Parliamentary Secretary at the

Ministry of Power. The next year he became Parliamentary Secretary at the Ministry of Technology. His boss, Tony Benn, found him a 'non-political' technocrat.

Having resigned his post in 1969 over Wilson's refusal to let him publish his book, Bray then lost his seat in the 1970 general election. In October 1974, he was returned for the safe Scottish seat of Motherwell and Wishaw, which became Motherwell South from 1983. He also served as a visiting professor at Strathclyde University and as deputy chairman of Christian Aid.

In 1981 he drafted a select committee report on monetary policy and made his comeback as Labour's spokesman on science and technology (1983–92) for Neil Kinnock. He did not speak often on the subject, partly because his tendency to lecture at people could empty the Commons. Instead he wrote the Party's policies.

Even if Labour had won the 1992 election, it was not likely that Kinnock would have named him the planned science minister because in 1991 he underwent major heart surgery. In 1994 he announced that he would not stand again. This eliminated him from consideration by Tony Blair, whom he supported.

He is survived by his wife, Elizabeth, and four daughters.

Andrew Roth

Madron Seligman

born 10 November 1918, *died* 9 July 2002

Madron Seligman, who has died aged 83, was an hereditary industrialist and a very pro-European MEP for West Sussex (1979–1984), but his main contribution to Conservative politics was as a friend to Edward Heath. He provided the former Prime Minister with a warm and alternative family.

Heath became a caring godfather to Lincoln, Seligman's eldest son. Seligman also made Heath more acceptable to the Conservative middle classes by teaching him dinghy-sailing, helping him to become a champion yachtsman.

The two had met at Balliol College, Oxford, and the friendship was sealed by a foolhardy 1939 hiking trip through Germany and, in the weeks before Hitler's troops marched in, Poland. This trip was particularly dangerous for Seligman because his passport bore his unmistakable German-Jewish surname. At the British Embassy in Warsaw, they were told to get out fast; on the way back, via Leipzig, Heath complained because Seligman kept playing inappropriate songs like Colonel Bogey on his penny-whistle.

On his father's side, Seligman came from a German Jewish banking family that emigrated to London in the nineteenth century. Seligman, born in Leatherhead, was the son of Richard Seligman, a metallurgist who abandoned the City to become the founder and president of the successful Crawley-based equipment manufacturers for the food and drink industries, APV.

He was educated at Rokeby School, Wimbledon, Harrow, and Balliol where he read politics, philosophy and economics. An outstanding sportsman, he played cricket for Harrow, and rugby and tennis at Oxford, representing the university at skiiing. He became president of the Oxford Union. At the time of the Spanish civil war, with other Balliol undergraduates, he backed Heath, who was anti-Franco, for chairman of the Oxford Union Conservative Association, unexpectedly defeating the favourite, pro-Franco future Conservative MP John Stokes.

In the Second World War, Madron served in the 6th Armoured Divisional Signals in North Africa and Italy, including Monte Cassino, ending as a major. He then joined APV, emerging as its group managing director. He also became chairman of Incinerator Company, and a director of Westfalia Separator, Fluor (GB) and Fluor (Europe) Ltd.

He was elected the MEP for West Sussex in 1979, with the country's largest majority, just as Margaret Thatcher, Heath's nemesis, became

Prime Minister. He remained a fervent pro-European, a very good and conscientious MEP, and became the Tory MEPs' energy spokesman.

His friendship with Heath never flagged. On the day when Mrs Thatcher was ousted in 1990, he was among the first phoned by Heath with the message 'Rejoice! Rejoice!' He continued to fight the pro-European fight. In 1999 he and eight other former MEPs and MPs attacked William Hague's sharpening euroscepticism, hinting they might support the breakaway pro-European Tories fighting the looming Euro-elections.

He is survived by his wife, Nancy-Joan, three sons and a daughter.

Andrew Roth

Ron Brown

born 7 September 1921, *died* 29 July 2002

Ron Brown, who has died aged 80, was, for 19 years, the Labour, then SDP, MP for Hackney and Shoreditch in east London, and a man with three shadows lowering over his political career. One was his older brother George, Harold Wilson's volatile Foreign Secretary from 1966 to 1968; the second was his namesake, the MP for Leith, whose left wing views he detested; the third was the challenge by the Militant Tendency in the 1980s to right wing MPs like himself.

Ron adored George, though he did not share his worst faults of egomania and paranoia. Having been a senior lecturer in electrical engineering at the Borough Polytechnic in south London, where he was educated, his judgements were more judicious. His more principled approach occasionally differed on policy too: partly because he was linked to the low-paid furniture workers' union, he opposed his brother's prices and incomes policy. However, he was utterly loyal, and hoped George would become Prime Minister after Wilson.

The sons of a Bermondsey docker and TGWU organiser, and right wingers rooted in the unions and working-class communities, the brothers shared an anti-communist, pro-NATO, pro-European ideology – and a loathing for Harold Wilson and Marxist infiltrators into the Labour Party. Ron was proud of having served in the wartime 156 (Pathfinder) Squadron.

Ron's second shadow was the appearance in the Commons of the manic Scottish Marxist with an almost identical name: Ronald H Brown instead of Ronald W. Brown – their mail and telephone calls were frequently confused. Ron H's extreme left wing views, including his defence of the Soviet-backed regime in Afghanistan, were bad enough, but what really hurt Ron W was the reaction of his friends. 'I'm hurt and wounded that people who have known my political beliefs for 20 years can even begin to think that I have said such [left wing] things.'

The most compelling shadow, however, was the challenge of the Militant Tendency, which Brown thought was insufficiently resisted by Labour's new leader, Michael Foot. Foot's ineptitude was symbolised by the adoption of the gay Australian Peter Tatchell as candidate for Bermondsey, the seat being given up by Bob Mellish, like Ron's father, a former TGWU organiser. The penetration of Labour seats by the 'vicious extremism' of the hard left was his breaking point, and, in December 1981, he became the 25th sitting MP to join the SDP. Unhappily however, when the SDP joined the Liberals, and a shareout of seats became necessary, Ron's was one of the few in which the Liberal refused to stand down, and he was easily defeated by Labour's Brian Sedgemore.

It was a sad burial for someone who had assiduously built up a political base among working-class communities in London's slum areas. Earlier, he had been leader of both Camberwell and Southwark Borough Councils, and, as an MP, had fought hard for improvements to local housing. In 1984, he became director of industrial relations for the Federation of Master Builders, and, from 1987 until 1991, was its deputy director general.

He is survived by his wife, Mary, a son and two daughters.

Andrew Roth

Richard Wood

Lord Holderness of Bishop Wilton

born 5 October 1920, *died* 11 August 2002

Lord Holderness, known until 1979 as Richard Wood, was perhaps the most popular of the paternalistic patricians of his generation. He has died aged 81 after a lifetime in politics, business and aid for the war-disabled.

A disarming modesty was his strong suit. When people tried to make him out a war hero because he lost both legs in the north African campaign, he insisted his military career had been 'undistinguished'. He took pleasure in pointing out that he had survived the unexploded bomb which destroyed his legs because it had been misassembled by anti-Nazi Czech munition workers.

This same modesty was displayed when his name surfaced as a possible Conservative Party leader after Edward Heath lost his third election in October 1974. He quipped: 'Some of my friends have ideas above my station.'

Holderness was also subtle about disassociating himself from his father, the Earl of Halifax, who had been Viceroy of India (1926–31) before becoming Neville Chamberlain's Foreign Secretary, and the man the long-dominant appeasement section of the British Establishment wanted to succeed Chamberlain rather than the 'warmonger' Winston Churchill. Holderness wrote a biography of his mother rather than his father, and, when he retired as Tory MP for Bridlington after 29 years, he took his title from a section of his Yorkshire constituency and an extinct title of his wife's ancestors, the aristocratic earls of Holderness.

However sympathetic in other aspects, he was very dry as a churchy moralist. He was totally against easier divorce, helping to defeat the initial divorce reform proposals of Eirene White, though he failed against Leo Abse's later effort, which became law in 1969. He was also a fierce opponent of women's ordination; it was the 1993 defeat of his negative Lords amendment that opened the way for Anglican women priests.

In contrast, he was one of the rare Tory wets on voting reform, and a vice president, with Roy Jenkins, of the constitutional reform centre. Perhaps because of Labour's absolute domination of Yorkshire's big cities, in 1981 he said that the single transferable vote made sense in local government elections.

Born a third, and youngest, son in London, in his youth Holderness was overshadowed by his father's high profile, which explained his rough handling by schoolmates at Eton. In 1940, he spent a few frenzied months as an honorary attaché at the British embassy in Rome, leaving only days before Italy entered the war.

After enlisting as a private in the local King's Own Yorkshire Light Infantry, he was sent to Sandhurst and commissioned in the King's Royal Rifle Corps, before being dispatched to north Africa from 1941 to 1943. As soon as he could manage his artificial limbs, he toured the United States encouraging other wounded servicemen.

Back in Britain in 1945, Holderness resumed his studies at New College, Oxford, where he read politics, philosophy and economics, and ran the junior common room with Tony Benn. On leaving, he became a director of the Yorkshire Conservative Newspaper Company Ltd, publishers of the ultra-Tory *Yorkshire Post*.

By February 1950, he was in the Commons, and, with his intelligence, man-management skills and family background, rose steadily: he was Parliamentary Private Secretary at the Ministry of Pensions (1951–53), the Board of Trade (1953–54), and the Ministry of Agriculture (1954–55); joint Parliamentary Secretary in Pensions (1955–58); Minister of Labour (1958–59), of Power (1959–63), and of Pensions (1963–64); and finally, on the Tories' return to government, Minister of Overseas Development (1970–74).

Holderness did not seek publicity in these jobs, but did make a difference because of his ability to pour the oil of his modest charm on troubled waters. In 1960, he made the Labour MP Alf Robens chairman of the National Coal Board, temporarily minimising coalfield conflict. The only blot on his escutcheon was in 1972, when, at overseas development, he suppressed the critical Stevenson committee report into misbehaviour in the Crown Agents – though, by 1977, and in opposition, he urged a public inquiry.

His 1979 retirement from the Commons, and emergence as a life peer, represented partly a shift into local industry, as a director of the Hargreaves Group (1974–86), and of the regional board of Lloyds Bank (1981–90). He also served as chairman of the disablement services authority (1987–91).

Holderness's maiden speech in the Lords in 1980 prophesied that the Russian invasion of Afghanistan might 'backfire', and, after that, his soft, but authoritative, voice was heard most often on church and disablement matters. He spoke movingly on the need to help the disabled war-wounded in former Yugoslavia.

He leaves his wife Diana, a son and a daughter.

Andrew Roth

Janet Young

Baroness Young of Farnworth

born 23 October 1926, *died* 6 September 2002

Baroness Young, the former Leader of the House of Lords who has died aged 75, was the only other woman ever to serve as a member of Margaret Thatcher's Cabinet. Her greatest public notoriety was achieved much later, however, when she emerged in her last years as a fervent political advocate of the moral crusade for traditional family values.

After the election of the present government in 1997, Baroness Young led the successful campaign in the House of Lords against the repeal of Section 28 of the Local Government Act in England and Wales, a measure introduced by the Conservatives in 1988 to forbid the promotion of homosexuality in schools.

She was also at the forefront of the opposition to moves to lower the age of consent for gay men and to prevent adoption by any unmarried couples. In January last year she unsuccessfully tried to prevent the sale of 'over the counter' emergency contraception to women. She staunchly rejected John Major' attempt to introduce no-fault divorce law reform. One of her last campaigns was for 'abstinence education', to try to persuade young people to abstain from sex before marriage.

The wellspring of her moral activism was her belief in Christian marriage and family life, her concern for children's welfare and her belief that as a Conservative she should stand up against what she saw as the slide towards an entirely secular society. She repeatedly insisted that she believed in tolerance, that she did not wish to see homosexuality crimi-nalised once again and that she did not presume to dictate what adults did in private. She was criticised for being judgemental, she once complained, but everyone was judgemental – the difference was that some judgements were politically correct, and some, such as stressing the importance of marriage, were not.

'What we have lost are the great ideals,' she said in an interview at the height of her campaign against Section 28. 'One needs ideals. None of us live up to them. I fail. Everyone fails. But at least we should know what we are aiming for. What is dreadful is to have no ideals.'

There were plenty of ideals in her childhood. Janet Baker was the daughter of John and Phyllis Baker. Her father, on whom she doted, was an Oxford don, although he had initially wanted to follow his father in becoming a vicar.

It has been suggested that John Baker disapproved of his ambitious daughter's political career, believing that a woman's place was in the home, and that she therefore embarked on her campaigns as an attempt at defending the traditional way of life in justification of her independence. But this is probably much too complicated: Janet Young had a sentimental attachment to the world in which she was raised.

She went to the Dragon School, in Oxford, where she played rugby and was a good cricket player, and then to Headington School. She had a spell at school in New Haven, Connecticut, before returning to read politics, philosophy and economics at St Anne's, Oxford, where she met her future husband. She married Geoffrey Young, an academic chemist, in 1950 and they had three daughters.

She was already interested in politics, and juggled the early years of motherhood with membership of Oxford City Council. She sat first as a councillor, then as an alderman for 15 years, and for the last five years, until 1972, was leader of the Conservative group.

It was as a result of her stalwart service in local government that in 1971 Edward Heath rewarded her with a life peerage and the following year appointed her to her first government post as a whip in the House of Lords, and subsequently as a junior environment minister. Although she was known, somewhat disparagingly in the schoolboy parlance of the upper House, as 'Old Tin Knickers' she was also admired there as a competent minister and a 'bloody tough operator'.

It was when Margaret Thatcher became Prime Minister though that Lady Young's political career took off. She was made a Minister of State in the Department of Education and then in 1981 was appointed Chancellor of the Duchy of Lancaster and the leader of the Lords. It was a post that she was to only hold for two years.

In 1983 she was asked to stand down by Mrs Thatcher to make way for Viscount Whitelaw, who had been moved to the Lords after the election of that year. Mrs Thatcher wrote in her memoirs that Janet Young 'had turned out not to have the presence to lead the Lords effectively and she was perhaps too consistent an advocate of caution on all occasions.'

Privately, other cabinet ministers suggested at the time that Mrs Thatcher found that Baroness Young spoke too often and at too much length in meetings. It is also worth noting, however, that in Hugo

Young's account of the Thatcher years, *One Of Us*, published some time before the Prime Minister's own memoirs, Janet Young opined that Mrs Thatcher was somewhat cautious, notably during the Falklands campaign, because of her feminine anxiety about the effects of action in human terms.

Baroness Young admitted to being disappointed by her demotion, but she recognised the inevitability of political life and was compensated by being made deputy Foreign Secretary to Sir Geoffrey Howe and a Minister of State in the Foreign Office. She travelled widely during her four years in the post and then resumed a business career outside politics. She used to claim that she had no interest in the doctrine of feminist politics, yet she was the first woman to join the boards of Mark's & Spencer and the Natwest Bank. She also took up a number of public posts in education and public service.

She adored her family and although she worked throughout her married life, she insisted it was right that women could choose how they spent their lives without any sense of guilt, whatever they decided.

Julia Langdon

Sir Frederic Bennett

born 2 December 1918, *died* 14 September 2002

Frederic Bennett was an unabashed, not to say pugnacious, right wing Conservative, who sat in the House of Commons for nearly 35 years. Not always popular with his own side, he was even more infuriating to the opposition, as he branded organisations such as CND as fronts funded with laundered money from the KGB and serving the purposes of the Soviet Union. He was acutely aware of the threat of Soviet expansionism, and the part that might be played by 'ideological fifth columns' in weakening the resolve of the West and preparing countries for Communist takeovers. As détente became fashionable, he warned of the danger of making concessions to the Soviet Union and hailed its break-up as full justification of the nuclear deterrent and the peace-through-strength policy that he had always advocated.

Frederic Mackarness Bennett was the son of Sir Ernest Bennett, who had sat as a Liberal MP in the 1906–10 Parliament, joined the Labour Party during the First World War and was elected as the Labour MP for Cardiff Central in 1929. Bennett backed Ramsay MacDonald in 1931 and continued to sit as a National Labour MP until 1945, serving as Assistant Postmaster General in 1932–35.

His son, educated at Westminster School, was articled to a solicitor, but joined the Middlesex Yeomanry in 1939 and was commissioned into the Royal Artillery in 1940. He was seriously injured conducting weapons research in 1941 and commended for gallantry and initiative. From 1942 until 1946 he served as a military experimental officer in the Petroleum Warfare Department and ended the Second World War a brevet Lieutenant Colonel. During the immediate post-war period he led a technical intelligence mission in Germany.

His first effort to get into the Commons as National Liberal candidate for the Burslem division of Stoke-on-Trent in 1945 failed. On demobilisation therefore he read for the Bar at Lincoln's Inn and qualified in November 1946. He was subsequently called to the Southern Rhodesian Bar in 1947, but practised mainly on the Midland circuit. But he also visited Greece twice as a guest of the Greek government to study the operations conducted against Communist insurgents. In the 1950 election he was the unsuccessful Conservative candidate for Birmingham Ladywood and until 1952 operated as the diplomatic correspondent of the *Birmingham Post*.

However, in October 1951, at the age of 33, he was elected for Reading North and clearly found favour with the whips: in 1953 he was appointed PPS to Sir Hugh Lucas-Tooth, the junior minister at the Home Office. Boundary changes briefly checked his parliamentary career. Reading became a single seat and he went down to defeat in May 1955 by just 258 votes.

Almost immediately Bennett re-entered the House as the successful Conservative candidate in the Torquay by-election at the end of 1955 and continued to command a comfortable majority until 1974, when his seat shorn of its South Hams wards was renamed Torbay. He retained this seat until 1987, despite a series of strong Liberal challenges. His successor finally lost the seat to the Liberals 10 years later.

Although he loyally served Reggie Maudling as PPS in a whole series of ministerial posts between 1955 and 1961 and was one of the organisers of his leadership campaign in both 1963 and 1965, the only time Bennett was considered for office was in 1962 when the Chief Whip suggested him to Duncan Sandys as a possible junior minister at the Commonwealth Relations Office. Sandys was persuaded by his Parliamentary Under-Secretary, Nigel Fisher, that Bennett was too committed to his own line on Africa and the job went elsewhere.

As a leading member of the Party's Commonwealth Affairs Committee (successively its secretary and vice-chairman) Bennett had been openly critical of Iain Macleod's handling of African policy and had resigned as PPS when Maudling took his place as Colonial Secretary in June 1961. He wished to remain free to comment on affairs in Central Africa. Later he became one of Sir Roy Welensky's staunchest supporters. After voting in 1976 for the 11th time against the renewal of sanctions against the Smith regime in Southern Rhodesia, Bennett pointedly remarked that almost every African country which had achieved democracy on the basis of one man, one vote, had held a single election and had then relapsed into authoritarian rule.

Although correctly regarded as a bitter critic of his government's policies in Africa, Bennett was by his own lights a realist. He had been ready to contemplate the break-up of the Federation in 1960 so long as Southern Rhodesia gained its independence and as an executive member of the demi-official Joint East and Central Africa Board had not objected to Jomo Kenyatta's release. Subsequently, at the second Kenyan

Constitutional Conference, he acted as adviser to the minority tribal party, KADU. He was knighted in 1964.

Bennett remained an active backbencher until his retirement, specialising mainly in foreign affairs, although he served on the Public Accounts Committee from 1974 to 1979. He had been appointed to the British delegation to the Council of Europe and Western European Union in 1974 and in 1979 was appointed its leader. He also led the European Democrat Group on the Council and chaired the Assemblies before standing down in 1987. Margaret Thatcher appointed him to the Privy Council in 1985.

In 1981 Bennett won a libel action against the *Sunday Express*: they had cited from a supposed poll of MPs the finding that he was 'universally and deservedly disliked by his parliamentary colleagues'. That may explain why he was far less influential in his later years in Parliament than he had been over Africa. But he was also subject to distrust engendered by his receipt of honours from some very questionable regimes. Nevertheless he had his successes, notably with the preamble to Gibraltar's constitution in 1969 and the admission of Turkey into the Council of Europe. He continued to believe that Gibraltar should be integrated into the UK. Another of his campaigns was directed against British participation in the 1980 Olympics. To further this he had a gold medal struck to be worn by those athletes who did not take part.

He wrote a pamphlet in 1960 that lived up to its title, *Speaking Frankly*, and published *Détente and Security in Europe* (1976) and on the bearing that first *China* (1978) and then the *Near East* (1979) had on these questions. But his most typical publication was *Reds under the Bed,* or the *Enemy at the Gate – and Within*, first published in 1979, which went through three editions by 1982.

After leaving politics Bennett concentrated on his business interests. He was a director of several financial institutions, among them Kleinwort Benson Europe and Commercial Union Assurance, and of other companies, including Harlech Television. He was a long-standing Lloyd's underwriter. While representing Torquay, he lived at Kingswear

Castle, but he also owned land in Wales and delighted in being Lord of the Manor of Mawddwy. Yachting, shooting and fishing were his principal means of recreation.

Inevitably a man of such strong and often unfashionable convictions aroused dislike, but Bennett did not care. As he studied the state of the world in the closing years of his life, he could see much to justify the views that he had held with such tenacity.

John Barnes

Sir George Gardiner

born 3 March 1935, *died* 16 November 2002

George Gardiner was a combative right wing Thatcher loyalist, although curiously not one that Margaret Thatcher was at all keen to promote.

The journalist Frank Johnson once described him as a 'brilliant demagogue who knows how to play on the passions of the dispossessed suburbanites', but he was more articulate on the leader pages of the *Daily Express* than in the Commons. He was an instinctive plotter, who exercised far more influence than he would have done as a minister as the mastermind behind the right wing's campaign to break the hold that the more moderate Lollards group had exercised over the election of officers for Conservative backbench committees.

He was specifically recruited to Sir Patrick Wall's 92 Group in 1979 to carry out that operation and as its chairman from 1984 until he stood down in 1996 remained the principal organiser of the 'Sound Slate' that secured key chairmanships for members of the group or those it favoured.

Although sensible enough to strike deals to ensure that the Tory 'wets' had a fair share of the joint vice-chairmanships, he relished his role in testing out the ideological soundness of new recruits to the Commons and dragging them into his cabals. At one stage, he boasted, every chair was held by a member of his group and, when the Whips Office sought to replace him as Chairman of the 92 with Tony Durant, his skills were equal to the challenge. However, he was unable to prevent his defeat in the elections for the executive of the 1922 Committee, to the unconcealed delight of No 10. John Major described him as 'so convoluted he could have featured in a book of knots'; others were even less complimentary. Certainly he thrived on rebellion and was very good at organising it.

Ironically, although he claimed to be the most principled of the 'bastards' excoriated by John Major (he was deselected for his Reigate constituency because of his Eurosceptic views in 1997 and contested the seat unsuccessfully as a candidate for the Referendum Party), he had been a founder member of the Conservative Group for Europe and had argued in *A Europe for the Regions* (1971) that they would benefit from entry into the EEC. Like many others, he would claim that he was consistent in his advocacy of a 'Europe of Nation States' and that it was the belated recognition that the integrationists had a different political agenda that led him to oppose European Monetary Union and the Maastricht Treaty.

In the early months of 1994 it was reported that he had promised Michael Portillo the support of the 92 Group 'when the time came' and his last-minute vote for John Redwood in 1995 was cast explicitly to bring about a second ballot in which Portillo would feel free to run. But, while that was true, his final break with Major came surprisingly late and undoubtedly owed much to the whips' efforts to displace him from the chairmanship of the 92 and the executive committee of the 1922, compounded with a carefully staged put-down that was leaked to the press to the great glee of those who disliked him in the Commons.

George Arthur Gardiner was born in 1935, the son of the manager of three village gasworks in East Sussex, but after his parents' marriage broke up towards the end of the Second World War, his mother moved to Hythe and Gardiner obtained a place at the Harvey Grammar School in Folkestone. It was during the Attlee government that he developed an abiding dislike of socialism and at the age of 15 he joined the Young Conservatives.

Typically when confronted by a Keynesian economics teacher in the sixth form, he argued for Imperial Preference, an odd stance for a future free marketeer. Somewhat to the surprise of his teachers he won a place at Balliol to read PPE and gained a State Scholarship. Before going up, he completed National Service in the RASC, where he became a sergeant tester of entrants and was posted to the Pioneer Corps.

His Oxford career was mainly notable for his organisation of a massive petition in support of Anthony Eden's Suez policy and for his effort to defeat Tony Newton for the Presidency of OUCA, in which he used forged ballot papers. He was probably lucky not to get sent down, but an enforced sabbatical from politics left him sufficient time to achieve a first.

He had already obtained a graduate apprenticeship with the *Bristol Evening Post* and a successful journalistic career followed. After a spell as political correspondent for the *Western Daily Press* in 1961–64, he became deputy political correspondent of the *Sunday Times*, 1964–70, and chief political correspondent of the *Thompson Regional Papers*, a job which he held until 1974.

John Gummer drew him back into politics as his press officer in the Greenwich constituency and a successful application for the candidates list brought him the chance to fight Coventry South in the 1970 election. His deep hatred of union power developed from his experiences of the motor industry in Coventry, but he also built a relationship with the immigrant community that led him to distance himself from Enoch Powell. However, it was in his capacity as Jimmy Margach's deputy on the *Sunday Times* that he was able to alert Edward Heath to the 'rivers of blood' speech in 1968 and to forecast correctly, in the light of Heath's reaction, that Powell would face the sack.

Gardiner's search for a safe seat to fight was rewarded with his adoption for the new Reigate seat in 1973 and his election in February 1974 began a long and happy association with the seat that ended in bitter recrimination when he became a Maastricht rebel. From 1972 until 1979, however, he edited the official *Conservative News*.

Initially a Heath loyalist, he rapidly lost confidence in his leader and, when Margaret Thatcher decided to stand against him, he offered his services and was drafted on to her leadership team. He was subsequently asked to write her biography and his *Margaret Thatcher: From Childhood to Leadership* (1975), while superseded by later accounts, remains a readable account of her early career with some value as a source.

Although he was an active member of her briefing team for Prime Minister's Questions, wrongly identified as the 'Gang of Four' dragging the Tory party to the right, he was not included in her government. He had perhaps made himself too obnoxious to the Chief Whip by his efforts in organising the Union Flag group campaigning against devolution and still more by the major rebellion that he masterminded against the renewal of economic sanctions on Rhodesia. When the Conservative government came into office he was equally vigorous in his efforts to force the pace on trade union legislation.

In all these efforts, it should be added, he was not without encouragement from on high. In return he was quick to expose any efforts, most notably those by Peter Walker, to undermine the economic policies being pursued by the government. From the mid-1980s he was advocating the privatisation of coal, electricity, the post office and the railways and he was an early and dedicated supporter of the Community Charge. His energy seemed not a whit diminished by the heart-bypass operation that he had in 1982, and the knighthood he received in Margaret Thatcher's resignation honours was some reward for the dedicated support that he gave her.

Other campaigns had varied success. He was unable to secure the return of the death penalty or prevent Jim Prior's plans for a Northern Ireland Assembly from being passed. Nor could he do much to the settlement with Robert Mugabe in Rhodesia. Throughout the eighties he remained a bitter critic of the ANC and an opponent of economic sanctions on South Africa, and he became identified with Bophuthatswana as the 'ideal non-apartheid state'. He waged a successful campaign as an executive member of the Monday Club to remove the repatriation of immigrants from its objectives, although in general taking a tough line on immigration.

Most successful of all were his efforts to prevent the closure of the Tadworth Court children's hospital. Eventually it was agreed that it would be run as a charitable trust outside the NHS, but with government support for three years. Although he valued his Thatcherite campaigns, it was perhaps the achievement that he treasured most.

He had become secretary of the Conservative backbench European Affairs Committee in 1976 as a known opponent of withdrawal from the Community, but after a year as vice-chairman he felt bound to run against the man he described as its 'Eurofanatic' chairman, Hugh Dykes, in 1980 and he won. He was avowedly a supporter of the Single European Market, but he wanted it to become 'a genuine common market and a full internal market'. But he was equally determined that the British approach to Europe should be 'Gaullist' and it was inevitable perhaps that he should become a critic of the Maastricht Treaty.

However, the intense bitterness that he felt about it sprang from his inability to prevent Margaret Thatcher's fall and still more the thought that he had been deceived about the nature of the proposals that emerged from Maastricht. For this he blamed John Major, whom he felt had misled his supporters at the time of his election as leader and who had obtained his vote for the second reading of the Bill under false pretences.

When the Danes rejected the treaty in June 1992, he signed the 'Fresh Start' early day motion and supported the formation of the group that coalesced around that cry. But, to his ultimate regret, when, in defiance of his pleas, Major made the next vote on Maastricht a matter of confidence, Gardiner gave him his support, fearing that Major might resign and Kenneth Clarke succeed him.

Although he was one of the rebels who fought against the Maastricht Bill throughout the committee stage and, in spite of Major's personal blandishments, voted against the third reading, he remained a supporter of the Prime Minister, hard though it was for Major to believe it. After the party's shattering defeat in the European elections and the loss of the Eastleigh by-election, it was rumoured incorrectly that he was seeking the 34 signatures to trigger a leadership election in the autumn. However, he was undoubtedly privy to the efforts that others were making and may well have held back because his own calculations suggested that they would not succeed.

Gardiner had become increasingly impatient with the way Major managed the party by balancing the factions rather than giving a Eurosceptic lead. Although the Upstairs Club, which he formed to influence policy, was explicitly not seeking a change, Gardiner finally concluded shortly before Major put his leadership to the test in 1995 that a new leader was essential. He was one of those who encouraged Redwood to run, although he made it clear that his eventual support would go to Portillo.

His first reaction to Major's victory was to renew his support and that of the 92 for Major, but as battle lines in the party hardened over Europe, with sizeable revolts on Iain Duncan Smith's Bill to limit the powers of the European Court and proposals for a referendum, Gardiner became a key figure in the Eurosceptic IGC monitoring group and eventually, together with John Townend, sought with considerable success in the autumn of 1996 to engineer a commitment from all Conservative candidates against the single currency. When, in December, Major let the *Daily Telegraph* know that he too was in favour of retaining the pound and then denied it, Gardiner was outraged.

He had beaten off a challenge to his continued membership of the House of Commons the previous June, but he now let fly in the *Sunday Express* with the charge that Clarke was now effectively Prime Minister and Major his puppet. It cost him his seat. His constituency association carried a motion of no confidence in him followed by another deselecting him and his legal challenge to the moves was turned down by the courts. Instead he ran as a Referendum candidate and lost heavily, taking only 7 per cent of the vote.

When William Hague became leader, Gardiner rejoined the Conservative Party, but he knew his political career was at an end. He wrote his political memoirs, *A Bastard's Tale* (1999), and it gave him some satisfaction that his own stance was now the policy of his party and that a referendum would act as a road block to further British integration in Europe.

Dismaying though the result of the 2001 election was, he retained the hope that the government's inevitable defeat over the single currency would pave the way to a renegotiation of Britain's position in Europe. It was a forlorn hope, but all he had to cling to.

John Barnes

Frank Allaun

born 27 February 1913, *died* 26 November 2002

Frank Allaun, who has died aged 89, was a veteran of left wing causes, especially the Campaign for Nuclear Disarmament, of which he was vice president from 1983, and disarmament in general. He and Stan Orme, his fellow MP for the two-seat city of Salford (Frank for Salford East; Stan for Salford West), were, for years, steady presences at Labour conferences' biggest sideshow, the Tribune meeting, and signatories of letters protesting at the same things, in the same way and same company – honourable leftists, and part of the geography.

But there was a distinction: Stan – kindly, union-connected, slightly oppressed by fellow left wingers – was apt for office. As for Frank, few MPs have been less career-minded. Unquestionably abler – and less amenable – he still inspired, quite wrongly, the sort of paranoia about 'fellow-travellers' and 'pinkos' which obtained with some of the Labour right. His very mildness inspired the absurd description 'sinister', though the chairman of the Labour Peace Fellowship, and author of *Stop The H-Bomb Race?* (1959) and *The Wasted 30 Billions* (1975), could hardly expect sophistication from the spooks.

His *Who's Who* tally of office read: 'Appointed parliamentary private secretary to secretary of state for the colonies October 1964–March 1965, resigned'.

Naive or optimistic, or just unappreciative of war culture, Allaun was a straight up-and-down idealist. His style was intensely gentle, the voice never raised, but the questions – chiefly on peace and housing – insistent. The beautiful manners and the soft Lancashire voice must have got on ministerial nerves. But then, as one of the organisers of the first Aldermaston march, he helped launch a movement whose appeal in the late 1950s and 1960s did more than get on nerves.

However annoyingly, he also served the Labour Party busily and anxiously. Elected, in 1967, to the National Executive Committee, he was there for 16 years, and was chairman in the grim year of 1978–79.

At the beginning, Allaun won a scholarship to Manchester Grammar School, though he took his BCom degree at night school before qualifying as a chartered accountant. He joined the *Manchester Evening News*, covering the City Council before becoming industrial correspondent, and then joined the *Daily Herald*.

After unsuccessfully contesting the old Moss Side division in 1951, Allaun was elected for Salford East in 1955. At Westminster, he would sit, until retirement in 1983, alongside Dennis Skinner, Ian Mikardo and Emrys Hughes – permanent oppositionists, troublemakers, left wingers, a plague on Labour in government and opposition. Some were soured resenters, others, like Allaun, were genuine people of principle, unequipped for compromise. And it showed.

Ministerial diaries contain many entries like this from Barbara Castle on 21 February 1967: 'I had to leave the NEC early, missing Frank Allaun's resolution on the economy cuts in order to have an office meeting about transport bill amendments.' Governments which cut things in those days spent half their time in anxious propitiation of the NEC.

The same minister would complain next year, when a liaison committee was set up to link government and NEC, that she was 'a bit tired of being treated as an untouchable because I am a minister'. Allaun and Mikardo had joined the miners' leader, Joe Gormley, in objecting to any NEC representative being, like Castle, also ministers. But with the squabbling went better things. It was Allaun, who, when Labour was selling arms to the central government during the Nigerian war, sought a Commons debate on the treatment of seceding Biafra – and provoked a major argument in Cabinet.

Outside the peace movement, his preoccupation was with public housing, and the vastly increased expenditure he urged should be paid for by cuts, equally massive, in defence. Defence cuts would, of course, come, but, despite Allaun's life work, Britain remained a nuclear power. His other books included *Spreading The News: A Guide To Media Reform* (1989) and *The Struggle For Peace* (1992). His recreations were walking and swimming.

His first wife, Lilian, whom he married in 1941, died in 1986. He is survived by his second wife, Millie, and the son and daughter of his first marriage.

Edward Pearce

Sir Paul Hawkins

born 7 August 1912, *died* 29 December 2002

The former MP Sir Paul Hawkins, who has died aged 90, just won South-West Norfolk for the Conservatives against the 1964 Labour tide. When he stood down from Parliament after 23 years, he had a majority of almost 15,000.

In rural Norfolk, Hawkins had the advantage of being a hereditary livestock auctioneer and estate agent, part of the family firm founded by his grandfather. This meant that, from boyhood, he was in touch with the area's stockmen and farmers, whose interests conditioned his outlook. He was an early pro-European, because he was sure the Common Market would benefit local cattle farmers. He campaigned against outside pension funds buying tracts of land in Norfolk and farming it themselves, instead of letting it out to locals.

Although it may merely have reflected local prejudices, Hawkins was also a fervent campaigner against immigration, and worried about 'bogus' marriages if rules on Asian fiancés were eased. This immigrant-bashing seemed out of character from a Heathite centrist, who had quietly backed sanctions against white-supremacist Rhodesia in 1966. This quiet self-effacement was as characteristic of him as his plastered-down hair and waist-expanding girth.

Yet, in 1945, Hawkins had returned to Britain from five years as a prisoner-of-war weighing just 6st. He had been born at Downham Market, and, after Cheltenham College, qualified as a surveyor before joining the family firm. This work was interrupted by war service as a captain in the Royal Norfolk Regiment, and capture at St Valéry in 1940.

After the war, he joined the Conservatives, qualified as a chartered auctioneer, rejoined the family firm and won a seat on Norfolk county council in 1949. His networking resulted in his replacing Elaine Kellett (later the Conservative MP Elaine Kellett-Bowman) as the candidate to stand against Albert Hilton, the local farmworkers' leader and Labour MP for South-West Norfolk. When he took the seat in 1964 by 123 votes, Hawkins was the only Tory to have won a seat from Labour.

He launched himself at Westminster by calling for higher pay for farmworkers. He went into the whips' office when Edward Heath became Prime Minister in 1970, and was knighted in 1982.

Although already past 70, Hawkins resisted suggestions that he step down before the 1983 election, and was selected from a shortlist of four for the redrawn South West Norfolk. He won by 14,910 in a seat thought marginal, but, when it came to 1987, he decided to retire.

He is survived by his second wife, Tina, a childhood sweetheart he married after the death of his first wife, Joan, in 1984, and by two sons and a daughter of the first marriage.

Andrew Roth

Sir William Shelton

born 30 October 1929, *died* 2 January 2003

In 1974–75 Sir William Shelton, who has died at 73 from Alzheimer's disease, was Margaret Thatcher's unofficial 'chief whip' in her Conservative leadership campaign against Edward Heath. He then agreed to become one of her Parliamentary Private Secretaries, but resigned after six months, having learned that bag-carrying for her was a full-time occupation.

Thus did Sir William gain a reputation, with his then fellow Conservative MP Airey Neave, as having been largely responsible for replacing Heath with Thatcher. Yet he had been a mild Heath supporter until his monetarist views led to a parting of the ways in 1973.

Sir William was a competent advertising man who became a very able constituency MP, first for Clapham (1970–74) and then for Streatham (1974–92) in south London, with a special interest in education. He was a man of mature judgement, who suffered from the polarisation within his party – and opposed Thatcher's poll tax.

The son of an army officer from Guernsey, he was born in Plymouth, and educated at Radley College, in Oxfordshire, until he was evacuated in 1940, to Tabor Academy in Marion, Massachusetts. He graduated from Worcester College, Oxford, and then briefly lectured in economics at the University of Texas.

From the age of 23, he was a professional adman, initially for Colman, Prentice and Varley, which then had the Conservative Party account. Sent by the firm to Venezuela, he met and married Anne Warder, daughter of the president of Shell Oil there. He then became managing director of CPV's Colombian subsidiary. He was appointed CPV (International) director in 1964, managing director in 1967 and MD of Grosvenor Advertising in 1969. Further executive posts followed.

In 1964 he also became president of the Wandsworth Young

Conservatives He was elected to the Greater London Council for Wandsworth and in 1968 became the Inner London Education Authority Conservative chief whip during the three-year period when the Tories dominated it. Then in 1970 – without playing the race card – he won Clapham against Labour's West Indian-born Dr David (later Lord) Pitt.

By 1973 his ambivalence towards the EEC had turned into antipathy. And in a letter to the *Daily Telegraph* he denounced what he saw as the stoking up of inflation. It was Thatcher's tight money policy which won her his backing.

Anxious to find a new role for comprehensive schools in big city areas, in 1981 he became Under Secretary for Education. He introduced computer training into primary schools and strengthened vocational training for the over-17s, but was dropped by Thatcher in 1983.

Subsequently he seemed to lose his moderate pragmatic way. He lost his seat to Labour's Keith Hill in 1992.

His last decade was not a happy one, with losses at Lloyd's, in the property slump, and the collapse of a free-legal-advice firm, which led to his being barred as a company director.

He is survived by his wife and his adopted son and daughter.

Andrew Roth

Richard Wainwright

18 April 1918, *died* **16 January 2003**

The role of Richard Wainwright, who has died aged 84, was pivotal in the post-war revival of the Liberal Party. His particular skill and emphasis was in taking on the broad brush. Sometimes, particularly in the case of Jo Grimond, leader from 1956 to 1967, he took the high-flown generalities about the party and its organisation, and translated them into the detail of workable structures that the somewhat anarchic party activists would accept and operate.

A key aspect of such practicality was his role in the five-strong organising committee, chaired by Frank Byers, which, in the early 1960s, largely sidetracked the party's cumbersome committee structure with its all-embracing remit to do whatever was necessary 'to strengthen the impact of Liberalism upon the electorate'.

Similarly, following the 1974 general election, when the party urgently needed to transform its financial affairs, it was to Wainwright that it turned; his report was significant in the subsequent growth of special sections of the party, with their own direct funds. In this approach, he was influenced by the example of the successful local government department at Liberal headquarters, which he had inaugurated – and funded personally – from 1961.

Wainwright had a shrewd instinct for reading the mood of his party, and almost invariably topped the poll for any office voted for by the membership at large. He camouflaged his shyness with the image of the bluff Yorkshireman, which enhanced a natural openness and an ability to talk on equal terms with those at every level of the party. He enjoyed his popularity with the grassroots, and fostered it by taking on a heavy load of speaking and campaigning engagements.

The small group of party officers and executives – including Gruffydd Evans, Pratap Chitnis, Tim Beaumont and this writer – who wanted to prevent Jeremy Thorpe following Grimond as party leader in 1967 attempted a 'draft Wainwright' initiative. But, without any support from the man himself, and with his having only been in Parliament for one year, it had no chance of success.

It was significant that Wainwright risked his relationship with the party by finally causing Thorpe's resignation in 1976, when he called publicly on the leader to sue Norman Scott over the homosexual allegations that eventually figured in Thorpe's trial. At the time, so little could be said openly by party officers about Thorpe's autocratic style – and of the potential danger to the party of his personal affairs – that delegates to the following Liberal Party assembly in Southport, unaware of the true situation, gave Wainwright the only rough ride of his career.

Wainwright's political views and motivation were a consequence of being deeply affected by the social conditions of Britain in the 1930s. His long association with the Methodist church, particularly on difficult housing estates in east Leeds, pointed him more towards liberalism than socialism, and he joined the Liberal Party while at Cambridge University, where he took a history degree in 1939 – he had earlier attended Shrewsbury school.

A conscientious objector during the Second World War, he served with the Friends Ambulance Unit, and missed being involved in the 1945 general election because he remained in Europe for the first phase of post-war reconstruction.

Wainwright followed his father into the Leeds accountancy firm of Beevers and Adgie, becoming a partner in 1950. He was very much a Leeds person, as was his wife Joyce, who has been a formidable campaigner in her own right. He held directorships in a number of Leeds-based companies, including Charles F. Thackray (surgical instruments) and Jowett and Sowry (office equipment).

He contested Pudsey in the 1950 general election, and again in 1955, but for the 1959 contest moved to the Colne Valley seat, which spanned the West Riding between Huddersfield and the outskirts of Oldham. He assiduously cultivated the towns and villages of this widespread constituency, and was elected in 1966, losing the seat in 1970 but then winning the following four general elections before his retirement in 1987.

Wainwright and his wife were devastated when their son Andrew committed suicide in the middle of the February 1974 campaign. Later, they set up a non-charitable trust in Andrew's name, which has quietly supported a number of projects to extend democracy in Britain and abroad. After his retirement, Richard chided those who hinted that he might go to the Lords for even suggesting that he 'would go to the crematorium'.

His policy specialism remained employment, trade and public finance. He was a member of the Commons Treasury select committee from its inception in 1979 until his retirement, and was Liberal Party spokesman, first on trade and industry, working with Eric Varley during the Lib-Lab pact of 1977–78, and, later, employment.

Curiously, despite being much involved in policy formation, Wainwright only produced one publication in his own name, the 1958 booklet *Own As You Earn*, preferring otherwise to foster and prompt others to write, through, for instance the unservile state group, of which he was a founder in 1953.

His aptitude for understanding the practicalities of putting together projects and campaigns was also seen in his membership, from 1959 to 1984, of the Joseph Rowntree Social Service Trust (now the Joseph Rowntree Reform Trust). During my time on the trust staff, I recall fellow trustee Jo Grimond making typically devastating critiques of applications for funding. Following a Jo performance, there would usually be a short silence before Richard would gently ask, 'So what do we do with this idea?' Bit by bit, with Richard's prompting, a workable project would then often emerge.

Wainwright did a great deal to foster the careers of those he saw as promising young Liberals (as I recall with affection). In the wider context, his dependability over more than 50 years gave stability to a party not overly enamoured of that virtue.

He is survived by his wife Joyce, his son Martin and daughters Tessa and Hilary. Martin is northern editor of the *Guardian*; Hilary edits the radical magazine, *Red Pepper*.

Michael Meadowcroft

Renée Short

born April 1916, *died* January 18 2003

Renée Short, who has died aged 86, was one of the first women MPs to make a fuss about the hours of the House of Commons and to warn – more than a quarter of a century ago – that it would be impossible for most women to undertake a political career until parliament recognised the need for change.

Although it is 15 years since she retired as the first-ever Labour MP for Wolverhampton North-East, the new daily timetable introduced this month at Westminster would have been an enormous source of satisfaction to her. Short regarded the lack of women MPs in the Commons as 'scandalous', and took every opportunity to assert her views; she was one of those backbenchers who was always described as 'outspoken' because she had firmly held convictions on a wide range of social and political issues. While she would have welcomed the increase in the number of women elected in recent years, she would have been appalled by how cowed so many of them have proved.

Her readiness to state her mind – and her refusal to cut her conscience to fashion – were two reasons why she failed to secure office as a minister. She was first elected in 1964, and was obviously then too inexperienced. By the time Harold Wilson became Prime Minister again in 1974, she had marked her own card as a left winger, but still hoped for a government job. When Wilson did not oblige, Short denounced some of his appointments as 'downright offensive'.

She was best known within the Labour party as a long-standing member of the national executive committee (NEC), at a time when that body was a repository of much of the party's political power. Elected in 1970, she served until 1988, with a break of two years during the Labour civil wars in 1981–83.

She was a representative of the women's section on the NEC, but was not afraid to stand up to feminist militancy if she disagreed with it; she was even given a slow handclap at the 1985 Labour conference when she opposed the idea that women NEC members should be elected only on the votes of women members. Labour's internal strife had the effect of redefining Short's position on the NEC. Sponsored by the transport workers' union, she had always been an active member of the left, but, in the early 1980s, she shifted to what was then termed the soft left, joining Neil Kinnock, Joan Lestor and Judith Hart in supporting Michael Foot against the aggressive stance of Tony Benn.

She was always her own woman, as the various political diaries of her colleagues confirm: she stood her ground. For those two years, it cost her the NEC seat, and then, in effect, her seat in the Commons.

She announced her intention to retire in the summer of 1985, just before facing a tough reselection battle; in 1981, she had been reselected by only three votes, and the likelihood was that she would not have been chosen again. It was, in many ways, an ungrateful response from a party she had loyally served with a profound commitment to the simple socialist belief of the need to improve the lot of the greatest possible number of people.

After the establishment of parliamentary select committees in 1979, Short was the first person to chair the social services committee, a position she held until she retired. She espoused a wide range of campaigning issues, including medical research, abortion, Aids, prison conditions, cancer control and – most notably – nursery education, to which she was devoted throughout her life. She was also interested in the theatre, and in relations with eastern Europe.

The daughter of an engineer, the redheaded Renée was born in Leamington Spa, Warwickshire, and educated at Nottingham county grammar school and Manchester University. She worked as a freelance journalist and then as a theatrical costumier, running her own stage design business. She also bred standard poodles and showed at Cruft's, managing to combine all this with a career in local and national politics, and raising two daughters. 'I couldn't have done it without the best possible husband,' she said once in tribute to her spouse, Andrew.

Her political career started with election to Watford rural district council (1952–64) and to Hertfordshire county council (1952–67). She became thoroughly immersed in local education and health issues – 'I was never a conventional housewife' – and stood unsuccessfully for parliament at St Albans in 1955, and Watford in 1959, before winning her Wolverhampton seat.

Her husband predeceased her; her daughters survive her.

Julia Langdon

George Younger

Viscount Younger of Leckie

born 22 September 1931, **died** 26 January 2003

As George Younger, Viscount Younger of Leckie, who has died aged 71, was a popular politician. He served in Margaret Thatcher's administrations, first as Secretary of State for Scotland (1979–86) and then as Defence Secretary (1986–89). Then he resigned to become the much better paid chairman of the Royal Bank of Scotland, where he remained until 2001.

More a descendant of the Scottish beerage than its peerage, his easy manners gave him the nickname of 'Gentleman George'. His emollience made it all the more surprising when, in 1994, he was accused by his normally restrained former colleagues, Douglas Hurd and Geoffrey Howe, of bearing the main responsibility for the Pergau Dam scandal in which Malaysia had promised to buy £1bn in arms from Britain in exchange for £200m in aid for the controversial dam. The ratio had been set by Younger as Defence Secretary. Younger's department was also accused of having connived at the illegal diversion of shells nominally headed for Saudi Arabia to forbidden Iran.

His wealth sprung from Younger's Ale, which was first produced from the family brewery in the 1740s. His great grandfather had been a Conservative MP and chief whip to Lloyd George's coalition government. He had shattered that coalition by leading the 1922 Carlton Club Tory walkout. For this he was rewarded by Lloyd George's successor, Bonar Law, with a viscountcy and the Conservative chairmanship.

George was born in Stirling, the eldest son of the third Viscount Younger of Leckie, where the family's estate is located. After Cargilfield School, Edinburgh, he attended Winchester (like his equally well-mannered uncle, Kenneth Younger, who became a Labour MP). As a teenager, he had lost two fingers on his left hand in a shooting accident, but at 19 he became an Argyll and Sutherland Highlanders national serviceman and was posted to Korea. Having survived as a platoon leader, he emerged as a lieutenant and served as an Argyll territorial until 1965. After studying modern history at New College, Oxford, he joined the brewery and became a director by his mid-20s. He then became sales director in the wine and spirits division of Tennant Caledonian, which acquired Younger's in 1960.

After contesting North Lanarkshire for the Conservatives in 1959, in 1963 he became Kinross and West Perthshire's candidate but stood down in favour of Sir Alec Douglas-Home, who needed a Commons seat to become Harold Macmillan's chosen successor as Prime Minister. Younger was rewarded with the more marginal seat of Ayr, which he won in 1964. In 1965 he was made Scottish whip by chief whip, William Whitelaw, thereafter his mentor. He survived, by 484 votes, Labour's 1966 general election victory.

By 1968 he was spearheading a 1m signatory 'Save the Argylls' regimental campaign, and when Edward Heath's Conservatives returned to power, in 1970, he became a quietly effective Under-Secretary for Development in the Scottish Office. He was promoted Minister of State in defence in January 1974, a month before the Tories were ousted.

In opposition, he became chairman of the Scottish Conservatives in June 1974 while serving in the Commons as deputy spokesman on defence. When Margaret Thatcher took over in 1975, she promoted him to principal defence spokesman before replacing him with Sir Ian Gilmour eight months later, to Younger's dismay.

Younger was a pragmatic paternalist: a pro-European, he also supported proportional representation for a proposed Scottish assembly. By the end of 1976, he was enough of a devolutionist that whips expected him to abstain on Labour's proposed devolution bill for Scotland. When Alick Buchanan-Smith and Malcolm Rifkind resigned from the front bench because of Mrs Thatcher's hardline attitude against home rule, she named Younger a junior spokesman for Scotland in January 1977.

Thatcher had planned to name Teddy Taylor as her Scottish secretary. But Taylor lost his seat, so Younger, the ablest and most experienced of the 22 remaining Scottish Tory MPs, ran Scotland for nearly seven years. The 'king of Scotland' boasted that decisions on Scotland were made in Edinburgh, not London. In an unwritten compact with Thatcher, he was allowed to resist most Scottish industrial closures in contrast to England. He fought to retain nuclear repairs at Rosyth and in 1984 threatened to resign if Ravenscraig rolling mills were scrapped. He pleaded that uncaring Conservatism would destroy what was left of the Scottish party and managed to wheedle money out of chancellors. 'He's a classic old-time Tory paternalist,' insisted a colleague, 'with noblesse oblige to the poor.' His greatest error was to underestimate the impact of rating revaluation which resulted in Scotland getting the poll tax early. When he had outlasted all previous continuous holders of his post, his cabinet colleagues gave him a silver-gilt miniature replica of a bed of nails.

Then again, it was someone else's disaster which gave him a boost. When Secretary of State for Defence Michael Heseltine stormed out of the Cabinet over Westland in 1986, Younger took over a job for which he had hungered. As a mainstreamer, he had few ideological hang-ups. But when US defence secretary Caspar Weinberger, asked to use a US airbase in Britain to launch the 1986 attack on Libya, Younger had doubts, as did Thatcher and Foreign Secretary Sir Geoffrey Howe. But none of them thought it possible to refuse.

Younger tried to curb his new department's expensive tastes. But as a relatively modest purchaser of expensive new equipment, it was in his interest for these prices to be brought down by their simultaneous sale to other friendly states. He was therefore more supportive than the Foreign Office of offering dam aid in exchange for arms sales to Malaysia.

He was also at risk from those involved in international 'dirty tricks', although he insisted he had had no personal knowledge of such projects. It was thought useful, for example, for the Iran-Iraq war of the 1980s to be encouraged by the sale of forbidden British arms. In such a way would two unpleasant regimes be weakened.

Double-dealing was not attractive to so open and straightforward a man as Younger. We cannot be sure what role this aversion played in his 1989 decision to quit the Cabinet.

Younger was made a Royal Bank of Scotland director in 1989; the next year he was made deputy chairman and then chairman. He did not baulk at cutting 3500 jobs – but he also expanded jobs.

In 1997, Younger, who had been made a life peer in 1992, became a hereditary peer following the death of his father. He is survived by his wife Diana Rhona, whom he married in 1954, a daughter, and three sons.

Andrew Roth

Thomas Boardman

Lord Boardman of Welford

born 12 January 1919, *died* 10 March 2003

Lord Boardman, who has died aged 84, was the last and most successful of his generation of political squires. Although best known as chairman of the National Westminster Bank (1983–89), a Minister for Industry (1972–74), Chief Secretary to the Treasury (1974) and treasurer of the Conservative Party (1981–82), he described himself as a Northamptonshire squire, having 'lived and hunted in the Pytchley country for over 60 years'.

A behind-the-scenes approach to politics helped to conceal his position on the right of mainstream conservatism. As a local MP, he was as resistant to the influx of Commonwealth immigrants into Leicester as was Enoch Powell in Wolverhampton. But instead of making inflammatory speeches, Boardman confined himself to guarded warnings about 'intolerable strains in the community' if more Uganda Asians were allowed to settle.

Likewise, he was as hostile to unchecked union power as was Norman Tebbit, but hid this in euphemisms, only revealing his antipathy at Natwest, when he defended support of the Economic League, which provided companies with lists of union activists. He was among the last to insist that homosexuals be removed from the armed forces.

The son of a Northamptonshire farmer, whose land he also cultivated, Boardman was educated at Bromsgrove, the Worcestershire public school. When the war broke out, he joined the Northants Yeomanry as a trooper, rising to lieutenant-colonel and winning a Military Cross in Normandy. When the yeomanry became territorials, he commanded them.

After the war, he qualified as a solicitor, and practised for 20 years, until promotion to company boards in the local leather companies, and then the giant Allied Breweries, crowded out legal work.

In 1964, the Tories of Leicester South-West saw Boardman as their best chance to oust Bert Bowden, the local MP and Labour chief whip. Boardman put up good fights that year, and in 1966, but was only able to win against Neville Sandelson in the 1967 by-election when Bowden stood down.

In the Commons, he made his maiden speech on the need for the 14 factories of which he was a director to enjoy flexibility in transport, including private carriers. Though modest and publicity-shy, he impressed fellow Tories as an informed and combative colleague, particularly when he attacked Tony Benn's top-heavy Beagle aircraft company and spoke up for the brewers. Within two years, he was on the back-benchers' 1922 committee.

When Prime Minister Ted Heath felt it necessary to nationalise Rolls-Royce, in order to preserve it, Boardman tried to insist on a firm target for its return to private hands. By 1972, he was Minister for Industry, taking credit for the generous petrol tax regime which encouraged the development of the North Sea oil fields. A month before the Tories lost the February 1974 election, he joined the Cabinet as Chief Secretary to the Treasury. In that year's second election, in October, he lost his renamed Leicester South seat to Labour.

For Boardman, political defeat meant a return to business. Back on the board of Allied Breweries, the Steetly company and MEPC, he also did a stint as president of the Association of British Chambers of Commerce (1977–80).

He re-emerged in 1980 as a life peer and, in 1981, as joint treasurer of the Conservative Party, charged with raising more money from industry. He managed to buy the Tory central office site at Smith Square from Westminster Council for £1.32m – enabling it to be sold for three times the amount only two years later.

Boardman was elected to the board of the National Westminster Bank in 1979, becoming chairman in 1983. In his decade with what was then the biggest high street bank, he helped make it the country's most profitable and dynamic. Unhappily though, some of his subordinates cut corners, notably at County Natwest, whose handling of the Blue Arrow takeover of Manpower was savaged by inspectors at the Department of Trade and Industry – to Boardman's fury. Three top executives resigned, and Boardman stepped down three months early.

Although by then past 70, he became even more active in the Lords, repeatedly attacking any plan to give the Bank of England more freedom to set interest rates, long before Gordon Brown did precisely that. He resisted the Tories' attempts at divorce reform, became increasingly Eurosceptic, and, after 1997, fiercely resisted the removal of hereditary peers from the Lords. On that other contentious issue, fox-hunting, he observed: 'I have never seen anything which I can condemn as cruelty in any shape or form.'

He leaves his wife Deirdre, whom he married in 1948, two sons and a daughter.

Andrew Roth

Aubrey Jones

born 20 November 1911, *died* 10 April 2003

The death of the former Conservative minister Aubrey Jones, at the age of 91, brings back echoes of an age of incomes policies, economic planning and government intervention on what now seems a vast scale; a period when consensus politics seemed quite normal, and the public sector was still a dominant force within the British economy. A period chanting phrases like 'the white heat of technology', and all that.

In that era, Jones was MP for Birmingham Hall Green (1950–1965) and a Minister (first of Fuel and Power, and then of Supply) in the governments of Anthony Eden (1955–57) and Harold Macmillan (1957–63).

He was almost a classic expression of a post-war Conservative party coming to terms with the social and economic revolution ushered in by the Second World War and Clement Attlee's 1945 Labour government. He believed in political bridge-building, and, to the end of his life, remained convinced that much of that agenda was still valid for any political catalogue based on rationality.

Of course, he was an improbable Conservative to begin with. He was born the son of a south Wales miner from Penydarren, Merthyr. He went to the local Cyfarthfa Castle Secondary School, Merthyr Tydfil – a breeding ground for trade union leaders, socialist politicians and all the clamour of Welsh radicalism.

He later recalled that his father was promoted to a pit deputy – a social status to be sure – but then contracted pneumoconiosis and had to take a job away from the pits. Jones senior became a labourer in the Dowlais steel works, and was one of the men dismantling the blast furnaces when Edward VIII made his famous visit to south Wales to declare that 'something must be done'.

Jones said of his father: 'I believe he died of frustration.' Frustration is contagious, not least in families from working-class backgrounds.

For all his early allegiance to Conservatives – first as a failed candidate in 1945, and then as an MP – he was to confess in later years that his happiest moments were his five years as chairman of the national prices and incomes board (PIB), which Harold Wilson's Labour government set up in 1965 and Edward Heath's Conservative government demolished in 1970.

In that heady period of the Wilsonian honeymoon, with George Brown at the equally pioneering Department of Economic Affairs, Jones drifted well away from the Conservative Party, and probably from conservatism as such. He became involved in economic planning concepts in terms of wages and prices, and in the whole character of economic interventionism. He was a convert to the role of the public sector in helping to shape social and economic priorities.

In 1973, his book *The New Inflation; The Politics Of Prices And Incomes* showed just how far he had removed himself from Heath's thinking. His later book, *Britain's Economy* (1985), had little good to say about Mrs Thatcher's ideas – 'I could not be a member of that government,' he declared.

Yet in a curious way, Jones also shared some of Margaret Thatcher's distaste for elements of Tory traditionalism. He resented the old-school-tie network, which was the embodiment of pre-Thatcher Toryism; he couldn't stand the casual superiority of the Old Etonians. He once observed: 'My Welsh heritage has given me an independence of spirit –

unlike most of my old Etonian cabinet colleagues, I had my own ideas.'

Macmillan sacked him after the 1959 election, when the Ministry of Supply was wound up – a surprising move, although it was clear that Macmillan simply could not understand him.

Jones was, in reality, a natural [Hugh] Gaitskellite member of the Labour Party, although he would have resisted such a suggestion. Instead, when he was already 70, he joined the Liberal Alliance, much influenced by that old Gaitskellite, Roy Jenkins. In the 1983 election, he actually stood as a Liberal Alliance candidate. He came a poor second to Norman Fowler in Sutton Coldfield; the Tories polled 65.4 per cent and Jones only 26.3 per cent. After that he setled down to writing, and the occasional lecture.

After schooling in Merthyr, Jones won a scholarship to the London School of Economics. That was in the 1930s, the period of professors like Harold Laski, when the LSE was in its prime as an academy training future socialist leaders for the world. Yet Jones somehow slipped away from that net to become a first-class graduate with the Gladstone memorial prize as his award.

From there, he took a job with the League of Nations in Geneva, where he decided he wanted to be a journalist. In 1937, he joined *The Times* as a sub-editor on the foreign desk; one of his colleagues was Kim Philby. Jones prospered and moved to the Paris office, and then to Berlin at the peak of Hitler's power – he left the Berlin office just three days before the outbreak of war.

He then joined the army and, after serving in the War Office, moved into military intelligence, which took him to north Africa and Sicily. After the war, he returned to *The Times,* but he had already become fascinated with politics and – no doubt because of his wartime connections and influences – with the Tory party.

Before he entered Parliament, he also joined the British Iron and Steel Federation – that old, high-Tory steelmasters' trade union – where he gained first-hand experience of the inner workings of big business and industry. It was a sphere he returned to in 1970 after the destruction of his beloved PIB.

Jones was a meticulous, careful, polished executant of power, yet, ever the paradox, he never seemed comfortable with power. He possessed great breadth of vision – long ago, he was predicting that technology would transform our thinking about the nation state, industry and the economy; he was a man with a vintage crop of ideas, yet his boldness of vision often seemed ineffectual in the execution. Like his father, he became frustrated,

Oft-times he appeared to lack the sheer energy and vitality to match an ambitious soul. He was very much a loner; someone in search of that Holy Grail which might, perchance, contain some eternal truth about the path toward a more rational human order. Harold Wilson and George Brown spotted that quality; they saw it as the perfect specification for the chairmanship of their innovative PIB. They helped Jones to discover himself – at least for five fascinating years.

He is survived by his wife Joan, whom he married in 1948, and their two sons.

Geoffrey Goodman

Robert Dunn

born 14 July 1946, *died* 24 April 2003

Bob Dunn, who has died of cancer aged 56, saw himself as the Tory mirror image of Labour's Dennis Skinner. He was an uncomplicated Lancastrian, working-class, right wing fundamentalist, in the same mould as Dr Rhodes Boyson, whom he succeeded as Under-Secretary for Education in 1983.

He was against unions and progressive educators, and in favour of private schools, educational vouchers and caning. He was an enthusiastic member of all the right wing groupings that were anathema to left wing teachers: No Turning Back, Conservative Way Forward, the 92 Group and the Selsdon Group.

His father Robert had been a Salford manual worker. Bob was educated initially at St Peter's Church of England School, Swinton. Having failed his 11–plus, he attended Cromwell Road Secondary Modern School. He received a BA in politics from Manchester Polytechnic, then a management diploma from Brighton Polytechnic. From 1973, he was a management trainee and then a buyer for Sainsbury's.

He was elected chairman of the Eccles Young Conservatives and contested Eccles's parliamentary seat in February and October 1974.

The south smiled more warmly on his views, and he was elected to Southwark Borough Council in May 1974, and selected as the candidate for Labour-held Dartford in 1975, which he won narrowly in 1979. He soon established himself as a firm Thatcherite by urging curbs on strikes and closed shops, and the extension of privatisation.

He became Under Secretary for Education in 1983, a post he initially fumbled at the dispatch box. Even fellow right winger Alan Clark said he 'made the most frightful hash of his question time, fumbling, stumbling and sitting down halfway through the answers until a Labour member cruelly suggested that he may consider taking a course in articulacy.'

Only his doctrinal purity saved him as he battled to introduce private contractors into schools, pushed the assisted places scheme and urged daily religious services. He decried 'the trendy, so-called progressive 60s and 70s which were so damaging to education' and called for the reintroduction of direct grant schools.

Chris Patten was promoted over his head to become deputy to the Education Secretary, Sir Keith Joseph. Reports of Bob's imminent sacking proliferated, allegedly pushed by the chief whip John Wakeham, but blocked by Mrs Thatcher. He lost her protection in 1988, when he clashed with Nicholas Ridley over the latter's refusal to allow building on semi-derelict land bordering the Thames in his own Dartford constituency.

On the backbenches he urged wholesale privatisation, was elected to the 1922 Committee and joined Cecil Parkinson's Thatcherite

Conservative Way Forward. He fought against the 'damaging' route of the Channel Tunnel rail link bisecting his constituency. The 1992 election reduced his majority, and it was narrowly wiped out in Labour's 1997 landslide by the local GP Dr Howard Stoate. Elected to Dartford Borough Council in 1999, in 2001 he was one of 19 Conservative candidates to try to recapture their seats, only two of whom succeeded. When I last saw him in the Commons lobby shortly before he died, he was still hopeful of retaking his seat.

He is survived by his wife, Elizabeth, a former deputy headmistress, and two sons, Alexander and Oliver.

Andrew Roth

James Stodart

Lord Stodart of Leiston

born 6 June 1916, *died* 31 May 2003

Lord Stodart of Leaston, who has died aged 86, was an informed and commonsensical Scottish Conservative politician and farmer who served 15 years as the MP for Edinburgh West (1959–74) and 22 years in the House of Lords from 1981. He was a pro-devolution Under-Secretary in the Scottish Office under Prime Minister Sir Alec Douglas-Home (1963–64) and was involved in the failed 1973 fishing negotiations with Iceland, after being promoted to the role of Minister of State for Agriculture, before the Conservatives lost office in 1974. His most lasting monument lay in his 1981 report, enhancing the power of self-government for four Scottish cities.

Stodart seldom secured the credit he deserved because he never overstated his case, believing that no politician could know it all. His humour was pawkish, suited to both chambers but seldom reported outside. In the Commons he scored when he likened a committee's housing discussions to Gilbert and Sullivan's Iolanthe, admitting that he had played the Fairy Queen in that opera 25 years before. In the Lords, he attracted outside attention when he inquired into the well-being of pelicans in St James's Park, recalling how they had formed 'an extremely appreciative audience' when he had rehearsed on them his maiden speech for the House of Commons at 4am on a summer's morning 30 years before.

His father, Colonel Thomas Stodart, was in the Indian Medical Service and the young Stodart's political inclinations made themselves felt early. He had left Wellington School to take over the family's North Berwick farm, to which his father had retired just before his death. Stodart was asked to propose a vote of thanks to a visiting Conservative MP, a supporter of the then Conservative Prime Minister Stanley Baldwin, Neville Chamberlain's predecessor, and another appeaser of Hitler.

A supporter of the anti-Nazi Winston Churchill, then in the Tory doghouse, Stodart ridiculed the idea of praising do-nothing Baldwin. Ostracised by local Tories as a result, he joined the Liberals, becoming vice-chairman of the Scottish Liberals in 1949, and fighting Berwick and East Lothian for them in 1950.

Unsuccessful there, and in Midlothian in 1951 and 1955, after he had rejoined the Tories, his reputation grew as a successful farmer and stockbreeder on his inherited 800–acre farm, and as a writer and speaker on Scottish agricultural problems. He became president of the Edinburgh University Agriculture Society and won Edinburgh West in 1959 with a majority of 11,932.

In the Commons his Tory colleagues found his good humour and strict views on crime and punishment acceptable, electing him vice-chairman of their agriculture committee and secretary of the Scottish unionist committee. When Sir Alec Douglas-Home replaced Harold Macmillan in 1963, Stodart became his Under-Secretary for Scotland for the year before Labour's narrow 1964 victory. When the Heath government took office (1970–74), he served it with diligent good sense as Parliamentary

Secretary and then Minister of State in the Ministry of Agriculture. His arguments were always more plausible because informed by his own experience, rather than civil service advice. He managed to survive the Tories' February 1974 defeat but lost his seat that October.

He then became chairman of the Agriculture Credit Corporation for a dozen years. He was rewarded for serving as chairman of the committee of inquiry into Scottish local government by being made a life peer in 1981. There his dry humour re-emerged: he complimented a fellow peer who had not spoken for a decade by comparing him to a Scotch whisky which had matured for 10 years.

His wife, Hazel, predeceased him in 1995, after 55 years of marriage.

Andrew Roth

Sir John Stokes

born 23 July 1917, *died* 27 June 2003

Sir John Stokes, who has died at 85, was the self-parodying, reactionary Conservative MP for 22 years whom Andrew Rawnsley, in the *Guardian*, called 'Parliament's last surviving link with the middle ages'. He had a more contemporary impact, giving Edward Heath an inadvertent early leg-up to his political career, and was one of the first four signatories for Margaret Thatcher in her 1975 Tory leadership campaign.

His backhanded help to Heath occurred in 1937, when university campuses were riven over the Spanish civil war. Stokes, already president of the Oxford University monarchist society, was expected to walk it in the contest to become president of the university Conservative association. But his support for General Franco incensed anti-fascists at Oxford, who nominated against him the little-known Heath, who had confirmed his sympathies by a visit to republican Spain – and went on to beat

Stokes by seven votes. This presidency, together with his war record, enabled Heath to overcome the deep, upper-class Tory discrimination against the son of a carpenter and a housemaid in post-war Britain.

By the time Stokes reached the Commons, for Oldbury and Halesowen in 1970, he hated everything the new Prime Minister stood for. A social snob, who believed Britain should be ruled by its landed aristocrats and public-school-educated gentry, he condescended to 'solid, reliable, decent and loyal' workers untouched by unions, whose leaders should be shot when too left wing.

Heath was pro-Europe; Stokes was pro-empire. Heath wanted a better deal for blacks in southern Africa; Stokes sympathised with Rhodesian and South African whites – his first praise for Heath was when he sold maritime arms to South Africa. He hated black and brown immigration, and was disgusted by homosexuality.

It was possibly Stokes's early religiosity, which he attributed to his 'Christian public-school education' at Haileybury, that explained why this stockjobber's son, born in Sandy, Bedfordshire, was such a political throwback. An Anglo-Catholic, he was always willing to link up with evangelicals against liberals in the Church of England. While serving on the General Synod, he was credited with having helped George Carey become Archbishop of Canterbury.

He was certainly a fully-fledged young fogey by the time he reached Queen's College, Oxford, after Temple Grove and Haileybury. Apart from Franco, he enthused for appeasement of the Nazi-fascist axis. In 1939, he joined the Royal Fusiliers, landing in Dakar in 1940, being wounded in north Africa in 1943, and serving in the Lebanon from 1944 to 1946 as aide-de-camp to Sir Edward Spears. He emerged a major with a DSO and DSC.

For Stokes, the post war world as a personnel manager at ICI, British Celanese and Courtlands was dull, despite Tory candidacies for Gloucester in 1964 and Hitchin in 1966. He only got into his stride when he ousted former fire brigades union leader John Horner from Oldbury and Halesowen after 25 years of Labour control.

His outrageous views, delivered in a self-parodying style from beneath a cocked eyebrow and bristling moustache, made Stokes an almost instant Commons hit. After he urged 'a complete halt to any further immigration and a humane and generous scheme of repatriation for all those immigrants who want it', it was little wonder that the *Daily Telegraph*'s Frank Johnson referred to him as a 'blunderbuss of a Tory right winger'.

During the 1974 fuel crisis, he objected to the 'vulgar' suggestion that couples should share their bath water. When he asked Mrs Thatcher in 1988 whether there was still room in the Party for 'nobility and gentry', she twinkled coquettishly 'if only there were more like him'.

Stokes's first two wives predeceased him, and his third marriage was dissolved. He is survived by his fourth wife, and a son and two daughters from his first marriage.

Andrew Roth

Sir Denis Thatcher

born 10 May 1915, *died* 25 June 2003

Even in an obituary, Denis Thatcher must be remembered in a genial light. Ordering a gin and tonic from an air stewardess he provoked from his spouse the mild comment, 'Oh, Denis, isn't 11 a.m. rather early?', responding immortally 'It's never too early for a G&T'.

His sounds like Dear Bill in *Private Eye*, but was real life. One friend said that the caricature was very close to the man,. Not that drink was ever a problem. He simply enjoyed it, always remaining sharp, lucid and in command. Through a lifetime's appreciation of snifters, tinctures and what William Whitelaw called 'Christian refreshments', he brought the convivial style of the Surrey road house into good humoured repute.

The consorts of Prime Ministers have generally sought the shade, and not always found it. Margot Asquith was an exception, a volcanic, witty, often wrong headed and rude Downing Street wife. Mary Wilson was thoroughly unhappy and with good reason. She became, in addition the butt of a running *Private Eye* commentary which snobbishly delighted in showing her as a northern suburban dowd so unlike us. Elizabeth Douglas Home and Norma Major lived shrewd, helpful lives, never giving the satirists much purchase. Thatcher did not seek publicity. He tried hard to avoid it and to fit helpfully into the background.

But there was no escape. He became a national figure in almost strip cartoon fashion, largely through the pen of the late John Wells. He was Denis the golfer, Denis the man at the 19th hole, Denis ruefully ducking the furies waiting in the ideological sweatshop called Downing Street.

But having had celebrity and its accompanying derision thrust upon him, he triumphed. His great victory was to have lived through a media-obsessive time, married to a Prime Minister very much disliked by the colour writers, and, despite being a Tory businessman with a slightly snappish style, to have emerged likeable and liked. 'Anyone who dislikes Denis', said a (non-Tory friend) 'is a fool'.

He absorbed the joke, manfully attending a dramatisation of Anyone for Denis, John Well's dramatisation of the Eye column, not actually much amused, but gritting teeth like the wartime artillery major he had been, and finally riding on the back of the joke, while Well's fortnightly wit grew indulgent and collaborative towards its victim. It was a two way process, An MP, joining him in a Commons lift, was told self-satirically, 'Well, the rain's done for golf, so I might as well get myself a tincture'.

He had the advantage when the futilities of celebrity arrived, of having proved himself in life. His friend, Bill Deedes, has observed that he was the sort of businessman who judged both circumstances and men extremely well. 'Someone who could read a balance sheet upside down and tell you what was wrong with which directors.'

Unencumbered by university, but with an education from one of the less grand, more utilitarian public schools, Mill Hill, and then at 23, joining the Royal Artillery ahead of the way through which he would serve, he was discharged in 1946. He proved his business abilities through Atlas Preservations before later becoming in 1963 a director of Castrol. Keith Joseph's judgment of Thatcher, the businessman, was that he got things right more by intuition than minute calculation, but that for him it had proved a sure route. He showed his strength and stature when Castrol was taken over by Burmah Oil in 1969. Some directors of absorbed companies are paid off, others jog along. Denis Thatcher became a dominant force in the boss firm. Another businessman with a fine record elsewhere, who had served in the Thatcher family business as chief executive, described him 'as the best chairman I ever worked for.'

The personality was milder than the caricature. Despite the brisk manner, he was not a harsh man, for example quietly disagreeing with his wife about the death penalty. Best described as an old fashioned business Tort, he always had money, was good at making more in solid, reputable ways rooted in industry rather than finance. As honest as he was capable, Denis Thatcher had many of the qualities of a nicer sort of Mr Worldy Wiseman. Calm, grown-up, unflashy, he was also blessed with immaculate courtesy. Interestingly Labour politicians saw much of it, leaving him well spoken of in surprising quarters. The Manichean quality of 1980s Toryism owed nothing to him.

He made a vital contribution to the Downing Street ménage of 1979–90. Although he was immensely loyal to his wife, he could sometimes pull her back from emotional mood swings. There is a story on good authority that he saved the career of the young John Major when that rising whip had told the Prime Minister valiantly, but inopportunely, of a degree of backbench unhappiness over one of her policies. This was something which she did not want to hear. Major received a long cold blast and told his wife that he reckoned he was done for. A quiet husbandly word afterwards was reckoned to have diverted the storm. It would also be a mistake to see him as any sort of subordinate. One Tory candidate watched with admiration when visiting Margaret who had gone to thank staff after a constituency lunch and had lingered rather, was hauled out by a husband saying very crisply that she was behind schedule and should step on it.

The comment of a long term Tory Minister of State was succinct. 'Denis has no business being made a baronet. With all he's had to do, it should have been a dukedom.'

Marriage to Margaret Roberts, chemistry graduate and barrister, followed his own first marriage and according to legend, her rebound after attachment to an aspirant Conservative politician and future back-bencher. Denis Thatcher was ten years older, a rich man able to provide for everything and underwrite the struggles of a political career – also a wise one, never showing a flicker of the Svengali instinct.

Edward Pearce

Hartley Shawcross

Lord Shawcross of Friston

born 4 February 1902, *died* 10 July 2003

Sir Hartley Shawcross is often remembered, thanks to a clever invention by Bernard Levin in the 1950s, as 'Sir Shortly Floorcross' because of his tenuous moorings in the Labour Party. He never actually physically crossed the floor of the House of Commons, but he became alienated from the Labour Party during the latter half of his long and productive life.

Hartley William Shawcross was born on 4 February 1902 in Giessen, Germany, where his father John Shawcross was in post as Professor of English Literature. Hartley was among the first individual members of the Labour Party. He canvassed in Wandsworth during the 1918 general election and served as ward secretary while at Dulwich College and as election agent for Lewis Silkin in 1922. He acted as interpreter for the British delegation to the first post-war meeting of the Socialist International in Geneva, and was persuaded by Herbert Morrison to start a legal career to facilitate his political ambitions. His first career was as a barrister; he trained at Gray's Inn and was called to the Bar in 1925, and appeared in celebrated cases such as the Gresford Colliery disaster inquiry in 1934 and several murder cases, taking Silk in 1939. He married Alberta Shyvers in 1924, although their life together was blighted by her ill health. She died in 1943. He married his second wife, Joan Mather, in 1944, and they had three children, including the journalist William Shawcross.

Hartley was Regional Commissioner for the North West in 1942–45, was knighted in 1945, and was approached by both Labour and the Conservatives to stand in the post-war election. He accepted the Labour nomination for the safe seat of St Helens, Lancashire – Labour in every election since 1918 except 1931 – which he duly won in July 1945 and represented until his resignation in 1958. His brother Christopher won Widnes.

Shawcross's Labour career was a singular product of the hope and idealism that surrounded the victory of 1945; he was angered by the gap between wealth and poverty and impatient at the inefficiency and even corruption he encountered in private business, and had faith that Labour could do something about it. His legal expertise made him the obvious choice for Attorney General when the Attlee government was formed. Among his responsibilities was acting as the British prosecuting counsel at the Nuremberg War Crimes Tribunal, which was the most notable episode of his legal career. He has retained an interest in international and human rights law, which he played an important part in developing at Nuremberg.

As a front-bench speaker in the Commons, Shawcross spoke in the forceful style of the law courts, which occasionally got him into trouble. He is much quoted as having boasted in 1946 that 'We are the Masters now', when introducing the bill repealing the 1927 Trade Union Act, but like many such oft-cited remarks it is recorded inaccurately: he actually said that 'We are the masters at the moment', in response to a challenge from Churchill.

Shawcross occasionally prosecuted criminal cases as Attorney General, including William 'Lord Haw-Haw' Joyce and Haigh, the acid bath murderer, but his role in the Lynskey Tribunal of 1948 into allegations of corruption at the Board of Trade was most notable. His questioning of the accused minister, John Belcher, was brutal, although he made little headway with the confidence trickster Sidney Stanley. Shawcross, with Attlee very much behind him, enforced the puritanical standards of conduct expected in the Labour government of 1945–51.

After the resignation of Nye Bevan, Shawcross enjoyed a brief period in the Cabinet, as President of the Board of Trade from 24 April 1951. He had hoped to be appointed Foreign Secretary after Bevin, but Morrison took on the post instead to the detriment of his historical reputation. He started work on ending Resale Price Maintenance but left the Board of Trade before it could be accomplished.

Hartley Shawcross was one of the stars of Labour's very first Party Election Broadcast on which he appeared with Christopher Mayhew. The broadcast presented two articulate, upper-middle-class Labour MPs talking about their commitment to Labour's values. Mayhew addressed the camera: 'You may, for instance, be wondering how somebody so obviously well-off, well-educated, well-dressed as Sir Hartley Shawcross comes to be in the Labour Party. What is your answer to that, Hartley?' Shawcross replied: 'My answer to Christopher Mayhew is 'Why on earth not?' It may be surprising to have a working man amongst the Tories. But in the Labour movement there are tens of thousands like me.'

The broadcast was something of a triumph, but it did not bring the middle class flocking back to Labour despite the well-educated, well-dressed advocacy of Sir Hartley. In the party civil wars of the 1950s Shawcross was a partisan of the right wing, and was regarded by some commentators as a potential leader, but he was increasingly discontented with party politics and although a regular speaker at Labour weekend meetings he was an irregular attender in the House of Commons. On returning to opposition Shawcross resumed practising, prolifically, as a barrister, but in 1957–58 he stepped down both from the Bar and from Parliament to concentrate on family life and a steadily expanding set of commercial interests. Among his many directorships were Shell, EMI, Morgan Guaranty, the *Observer* and Upjohn & Co; he also served on bodies such as the British Hotel and Restaurant Association and the Press Council. He was appointed Baron Shawcross of Friston in the second set of life peerages in 1959 and took up a position on the cross-benches in the House of Lords; he allowed his Labour Party membership to lapse.

Shawcross did not particularly approve of the social changes of the 1960s, condemning the prurience and sexual content of the press during the Profumo affair and the 'malaise' of society and popular culture: 'The new morality … is too often the old immorality condoned.'

Never an admirer of Harold Wilson, Shawcross became highly critical of the record of the Labour government in 1964–70 and was reported as calling for Wilson's resignation in January 1968. When the parlour game of forming a potential 'national' or 'non-party' coalition was played in the late 1960s and early 1970s, Shawcross always seemed to be in play. He became close to Cecil King, the deposed head of the Mirror Group and an inveterate anti-Wilson plotter, and considered a joint statement during the 1970 election that a Labour victory would be an economic disaster. During the early 1970s he was a sought-after source for *Private Eye* and others about Wilson's career.

Shawcross suffered a cruel loss in January 1974, when his wife was killed in a riding accident. After 1974 he continued City and commercial activities on a modest level, including being Chairman of Thames Television and running the City panel which investigated takeovers. He intervened occasionally in the Lords, including helping to impede the passage of the War Crimes Act in 1991. In 1995 he published his memoirs, *Life Sentence* (London: Constable). Although an important minister in the Labour government of 1945–51, the political career of Sir Hartley Shawcross was rather an interlude between the Bar and business.

Lewis Baston

The Marquess of Salisbury

born 24 October 1916, *died* 11 July 2003

The sixth Marquess of Salisbury, who has died aged 86, strikingly lacked the gene of political manipulation that has marked out the Cecils for over four centuries. Though he sat as Conservative MP for Bournemouth West from 1950 to 1954, he resigned on grounds of ill health.

He was thus utterly unlike his father 'Bobbety', the fifth marquess and kingmaker of immediate post-war Tory politics, who saved hereditary peers from extinction under Clement Attlee by proclaiming the Salisbury doctrine. In exchange, the Tory majority in the House of Lords accepted Attlee's reforms, provided they were contained in Labour's 1945 election manifesto.

Salisbury was equally unlike his own son, tagged Viscount Cranborne until his father's death, who arrogated to himself the right to make a deal with Tony Blair and Lord Irvine to cull nine-tenths of the hereditaries, without bothering to consult the then Tory leader William Hague.

It was not as though the sixth marquess did not have his own right wing attitudes. He voted against the ordination of women; he was president of the Monday Club, and backed the right wing Salisbury Group and its publication, *Salisbury Review*.

Earlier, as president of the Anglo-Rhodesian Society, he had been an enthusiastic supporter of white supremacy in Rhodesia, whose capital was named after the third marquess, three times Prime Minister, and where his family co-owned 80,000 acres of farmland. He felt African self-rule would only help Soviet ambitions.

Worth an estimated £120m, and having studied farming and estate management, the marquess ran holdings of 8,500 acres around Hatfield House, Hertfordshire, and 1,300 acres at Cranborne Manor, Dorset. Considerable property around Leicester and Leicester Square, London, was held by the family's Gascoyne Holdings. Their art treasures were valued at £20m in 1994.

Somewhat shy, the marquess prized his privacy, and thus was not suited to the hurly-burly of political life. In 1946, he was fined for an assault on a press photographer. He hated telephones, admitting 'I always take the phone off the hook when I'm alone.'

Educated at Eton and commissioned into the Grenadier Guards, in 1942 he was wounded by friendly fire by an out-of-control Hurricane, but recovered enough to take part in the 1944 Normandy invasion. He then served as military assistant to Harold Macmillan, resident minister at General Eisenhower's side in north Africa.

In 1945, he failed to win Ince, in Cheshire, for the Conservatives, but succeeded in Bournemouth at the next general election. He left the Commons after repeated bouts of an illness he picked up on a parliamentary visit to Yugoslavia. On succeeding to his father's seat in the Lords in 1972, his most frequent interventions were on Rhodesia/Zimbabwe.

He is survived by his wife Mollie, four sons and a daughter. His son Richard was killed in Rhodesia in 1978.

Andrew Roth

Sir Gerard Vaughan

born 11 June 1923, *died* 29 July 2003

Sir Gerard Vaughan, the former Conservative MP for Reading for 27 years 1970–97 and Health Minister for three, was a psychiatrist who could not control his occasional explosions.

Although his political bedside manner was genial to the point of unctuousness, one of his occasional explosions ended his ministerial career. When he discovered that the then head of CND, Joan Ruddock, was the head of his local Citizen's Advice Bureau, he threatened, as Consumer Affairs Minister, to halve the government's contribution to CABs nationally. The backlash from this announcement ended his ministerial career in 1983.

His unpredictable behaviour owed a lot to the clash between his medical training and his far-Right political ideology. His medical training resulted in wonderful work for children afflicted by thalidomide. He sounded loud warnings about the threat of AIDS, including a proposal for posting health warnings on NHS personnel so affected.

His right wing ideology led him to privatising actions within the NHS while in charge, together with much more drastic planning for wholesale privatisation in secret party enclaves.

In 1986 he warned against 'horrendous prospects' unless people entering the UK from AIDS-infected areas of Africa were screened. This was intriguing because he himself had been born in 1923 in Portuguese East Africa, the son of a sugar planter who was later killed in wartime as an RAF flyer.

By then young Gerard, who had been educated privately in East Africa, was winning his BS at London University and went on to secure his MB from Guy's Hospital and his DPM, or psychiatrist's qualifications, from Maudsley's.

He worked as a consultant at Guy's Hospital in charge of its Bloomfield Clinic 1958–79 and wrote medical tomes for Allen and Unwin and Heinemann. He showed his enthusiasm for Conservative politics early by contesting hopeless Poplar in 1955, resulting in his being co-opted to the London County Council, being elected to it in 1961.

His parliamentary ambitions were realised when he narrowly won Reading from Labour left winger John Lee in 1970, thus helping Ted Heath become Prime Minister. In his maiden speech he supported prescription charges and the end of free school milk.

He somewhat redressed this by co-sponsoring Sir Gerald Nabarro's Bill to place danger warnings on cigarette packages. Intent on politics rather than psychiatry, he served his time as a Whip and a PPS to Francis Pym, the Northern Ireland Secretary.

After winning the safer seat of Reading South in February 1974, which saw the return of a Wilson government, he made clear his intention to privatise the NHS with his proposal for basing it on 'total insurance cover'. To back his efforts, he formed the Conservative Medical Society, becoming its president.

The 1975 replacement of Ted Heath by Margaret Thatcher resulted in his becoming her health spokesman. He complained that British doctors were emigrating, being replaced by 'low standard' Commonwealth doctors. He chaired a party working group which proposed tax relief for private health insurance, later extended to users of private medicine.

The Tories' 1979 victory resulted in his becoming Health Minister. Although he showed slight administrative talents, his ideological drive was undiminished. He promised to end £30m in NHS waste, partly by ending its abuse by foreigners. He urged reluctant regional authorities to contract out more of their work to private clinics. He pushed to replace the NHS's tax income with insurance income, along US or Continental lines. But when his boss, Patrick Jenkin, investigated the California health service, he found a third of personal bankrupcies were due to health bills, despite its health insurance schemes.

Despite Cabinet meanness, he tried to improve Britain's supply of safe blood products. Although hostile to abortions, he backed the use of the Pill for under-16s, under exceptional circumstances.

After Denis Thatcher told him that sport would be hit by tough action against tobacco companies, Vaughan's fanatically anti-smoking junior minister, Sir George Young, was transferred out. After clashes with his new boss, Norman Fowler, in 1982 he was reshuffled to become Consumer Affairs Minister in Sally Oppenheim's wake.

After a good start like banning exclusive outlets for car parts, he destroyed his ministerial career after he followed his threat to halve CAB grants with a Commons speech of magnificent ineptitude. After being sacked he continued his parliamentary career on the select committees on education and science and technology, until he retired in 1997.

He leaves his wife, Thurle, a son and a daughter.

Andrew Roth